Credit Default Swap Markets in the Global Economy

This book provides a comprehensive overview for various segments of the global credit default swap (CDS) markets, touching upon how they were affected by the recent financial turmoil. The book uses empirical analysis on credit default swap markets, applying advanced econometric methodologies to the time series data. It covers not only well-studied sovereign credit default swap markets but also sector credit default swap indices (i.e., CDS index for the banking sector) and corporate credit default swap indices (i.e., Markit iTraxx Japan CDS index), which have not been fully examined by the previous literature. The book also investigates causality and co-movement among several credit default swap markets, or between CDS and other financial markets.

Go Tamakoshi is Research Fellow at the Department of Economics of Kobe University, Japan. He received his PhD in Economics from Kobe University and an MBA from MIT Sloan School of Management. He has published many papers in refereed journals. He is the co-author of *The European Sovereign Debt Crisis and Its Impacts on Financial Markets* (Routledge, 2015).

Shigeyuki Hamori is a Professor of Economics at Kobe University, Japan. He received his PhD from Duke University and has published many papers in refereed journals. His titles include *Introduction of the Euro and the Monetary Policy of the European Central Bank* (World Scientific, 2009), *The European Sovereign Debt Crisis and Its Impacts on Financial Markets* (Routledge, 2015), and *Financial Globalization and Regionalism in East Asia* (Routledge, 2014).

Routledge Studies in the Modern World Economy

For a full list of titles in this series, please visit www.routledge.com/series/SE0432

166 **Human Evolution, Economic Progress and Evolutionary Failure**
Bhanoji Rao

167 **Achieving Food Security in China**
The Challenges Ahead
Zhang-Yue Zhou

168 **Inequality in Capitalist Societies**
Surender S. Jodhka, Boike Rehbein and Jessé Souza

169 **Financial Reform in China**
The Way from Extraction to Inclusion
Changwen Zhao and Hongming Zhu

170 **Economic Integration and Regional Development**
The ASEAN Economic Community
Edited by Kiyoshi Kobayashi, Khairuddin Abdul Rashid, Masahiko Furuichi and William P. Anderson

171 **Brazil's Economy**
An Institutional and Sectoral Approach
Edited by Werner Baer, Jerry Dávila, André de Melo Modenesi, Maria da Graça Derengowski Fonseca and Jaques Kerstenetzky

172 **Indian Agriculture after the Green Revolution**
Changes and Challenges
Edited by Binoy Goswami, Madhurjya Prasad Bezbaruah and Raju Mandal

173 **Credit Default Swap Markets in the Global Economy**
An Empirical Analysis
Go Tamakoshi and Shigeyuki Hamori

Credit Default Swap Markets in the Global Economy

An Empirical Analysis

Go Tamakoshi and
Shigeyuki Hamori

Routledge
Taylor & Francis Group
LONDON AND NEW YORK

First published 2018
by Routledge
2 Park Square, Milton Park, Abingdon, Oxon OX14 4RN

and by Routledge
605 Third Avenue, New York, NY 10017

First issued in paperback 2020

Routledge is an imprint of the Taylor & Francis Group, an informa business

British Library Cataloguing-in-Publication Data
A catalogue record for this book is available from the British Library

Library of Congress Cataloging-in-Publication Data
Names: Tamakoshi, Go, author. | Hamori, Shigeyuki, 1959– author.
Title: Credit default swap markets in the global economy : an empirical analysis / by Go Tamakoshi and Shigeyuki Hamori.
Description: Abingdon, Oxon ; New York, NY : Routledge, 2018. | Series: Routledge studies in the modern world economy ; 173 | Includes bibliographical references and index.
Identifiers: LCCN 2017047542 | ISBN 9781138244726 (hardback) | ISBN 9781315276663 (ebook)
Subjects: LCSH: Swaps (Finance) | Default (Finance) | Capital market.
Classification: LCC HG6024.A3 T324 2018 | DDC 332.64/57—dc23
LC record available at https://lccn.loc.gov/2017047542

ISBN 13: 978-0-367-50421-2 (pbk)
ISBN 13: 978-1-138-24472-6 (hbk)

Typeset in Galliard
by Apex CoVantage, LLC

Contents

Figures

Tables

Introduction

1. What is a CDS?

In this chapter, we explain a credit default swap (CDS), its basic structure, and its role in the Lehman collapse of the fall of 2008 and the European financial crisis.

Rather than trading in financial products such as stocks and bonds, traders may enter contracts to buy and sell the claims derived from them. These contracts are called "derivative products" or "derivatives." A CDS is a derivative that acts as insurance against a trading partner's bankruptcy. Although conventional derivatives involve trading market risk, CDSs are credit derivatives; that is, they involve trading credit risk. Here, credit risk refers to the risk that the borrowers and issuers of corporate bonds will default on their obligations.

Next, we will briefly explain their basic mechanism. Suppose that company A has a credit exposure in the form of a corporate bond or loan with its trading partner, company B. Company A enters a CDS contract with bank C, and each year, pays a premium to the bank in lieu of guaranteed compensation in case company B goes bankrupt. If company B does go bankrupt, bank C compensates company A for its losses. In this way, company A does not suffer a loss, even if company B goes bankrupt, while bank C, as the party providing the guarantee, can collect regular premiums for its role as guarantor. In other words, a CDS is a type of insurance contract a creditor purchases to obtain compensation in the event that a debtor cannot redeem its corporate bond or loan obligation during the contract period. Conversely, in return for collecting the premium, the CDS seller pays CDS buyer the amount it would lose in the unlikely event of a default. In this type of transaction, the buyer's right to receive an amount equivalent to the loss resulting from a default is called "protection." (Please see Figure 0.1.)

The guarantor is the "seller" of the protection (the guarantee), while "buyer" receives the guarantee of the protection. The buyer receives a guarantee that the seller will pay the amount that the debtor or "target" company owes in exchange for paying premiums in case of a "credit event," such as a bankruptcy or payment default. Counterparty risk is the risk that the counterparty (the seller) that is supposed to provide the guarantee defaults on its compensation payment. In such case, the buyer needs to conclude a separate contract with a different guarantee provider and incurs an additional cost to obtain additional protection.

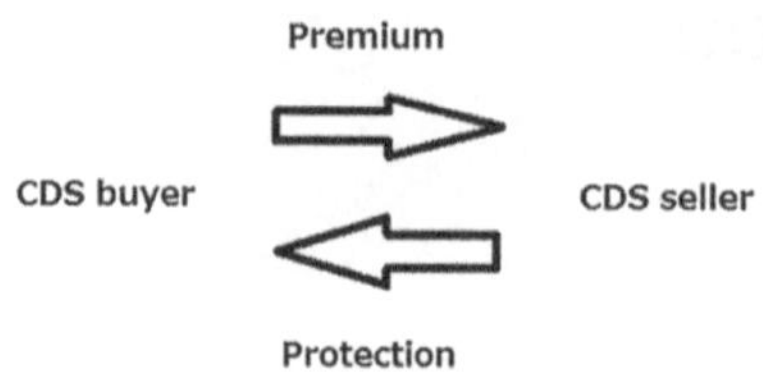

Figure 0.1 The CDS mechanism

In general, a CDS is a swap of a premium payment for protection, and the premium will fluctuate depending on the credit level (the risk) of the company targeted by the premium. Normally, the buyer is a party such as a financial institution or institutional investor that wants to control (hedge) the risk that it will not be paid for its credit due to bankruptcy or business failure of the target. Sellers include securities companies, investment banks, insurance companies, and hedge funds that aim to earn income from buyers' premiums. In addition, the targets of a CDS can include countries as well as companies. The government bonds of OECD member countries, which have a high credit rating, are called sovereign bonds, and in many cases, represent very safe bonds for investment. Similarly, CDSs targeting the government bonds of countries with a high credit rating, such as OECD member countries, are called sovereign CDSs; credit risk related to countries is called sovereign risk. The premium for sovereign CDSs is a measure for the extent to which sovereign risk is rising and should increase as sovereign risk increases.

Although a CDS is a financial product that provides a guarantee for a credit exposure, some use it for speculation because, unlike general insurance, investors can buy and trade a CDS even if they do not actually hold an accounts receivable from the other company. For example, company A can purchase a CDS for target company B from bank C, even it does not hold an accounts receivable credit from company B. If company B goes bankrupt, it can receive a huge payment. The relevant CDS may be sold during the contract period, and it therefore has a characteristic of a speculative product. In a CDS, observers should note the "credit guarantee," which is executed as a contractual guarantee. Before a company defaults, the main lending bank and other lenders may take measures to reduce its debt, such as lowering the interest rate, exempting interest payments, or waiving some part of the debt. However, these will not lead to the execution of a credit guarantee. Since the target of a CDS guarantee is not a specific form of credit, there are many definitions of default and other events that trigger the guarantee. They include not only a company's business failure (bankruptcy) and default (i.e., failure to pay), but also debt restructuring, which may involve lowered interest, payment exemptions, and debt waivers. Thus, in the case of a CDS, a default is recognized at an earlier stage than for an ordinary credit transaction.

The CDS premium can fluctuate, reflecting the market's valuation of the CDS target's creditworthiness, that is, whether or not it can repay its debt. As with general insurance, the CDS premium rate is higher for companies or countries with low creditworthiness and vice versa. Therefore, the CDS premium is an indicator for investors to judge the financial condition and creditworthiness of a company or country, in the same way as a credit rating.

2. The Lehman collapse and CDSs

CDSs were developed in the second half of the 1990s and they began trading in London, the center of international finance. Subsequently, they were used in other major countries, particularly in the U.S. The CDS market expanded rapidly from the year 2000 onwards. Attracted by the convenience of buying and selling a CDS, investors began participating in the CDS market, not only for hedging, but also for speculative purposes, and the market grew exponentially.

According to the International Swaps and Derivatives Association (ISDA; www2.isda.org), in the first half of 2001, the outstanding balance of CDSs was USD 631.50 billion; by the second half of 2007, this reached approximately USD 62,000 billion, showing how rapidly the CDS market expanded. (Please refer to Figure 0.2.)

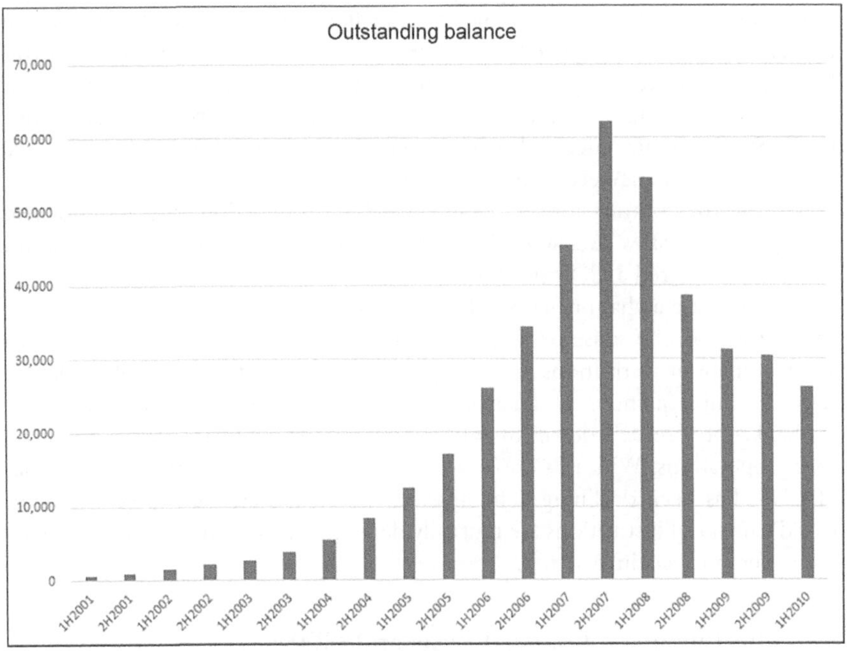

Figure 0.2 Outstanding balance of credit default swaps

Notes: Notional amounts, in billions of U.S. dollars, adjusted for double-counting.

Source: ISDS (2010) Market Surveys Data, 1987–2010
www2.isda.org/functional-areas/research/surveys/market-surveys/

However, the CDS market experienced huge changes in 2007. In the U.S., the business environment for financial institutions deteriorated rapidly against the backdrop of the subprime loan crisis stemming to the mass of home loans to individuals with low credit ratings. In September 2008, Lehman Brothers, a major U.S. securities company, declared bankruptcy, and it became clear thereafter that American International Group (AIG), Inc.'s management was deadlocked and the firm required a bailout from the U.S. government. With the subprime loan crisis as the starting point, the global financial crisis was a series of smaller financial crises worldwide as a chain reaction to the collapse of the housing bubble in the U.S. in 2007, which included the Lehman collapse of 2008.

At that time, CDSs were one of the factors that worsened the situation. If the number of accidents that insurance covers far exceeds the forecast number, then insurance companies' payouts will be so large as to threaten the business. Similarly, a series of sequential large-scale bankruptcies would be a major blow to financial institutions that sell CDSs. AIG had concluded an enormous number of CDS contracts with financial institutions and investors internationally, and had a significant presence in the global CDS market. However, due to the sharp increase in defaults on subprime loan-related securities, AIG's rating decreased drastically. Therefore, AIG had to place very high additional collateral to get the funds to pay CDS buyers and its cash flow worsened rapidly. There was concern that if AIG, as a seller of CDSs, failed, the financial institutions that bought Lehman-related CDSs would not obtain guarantees; they would suffer major losses, and that would likely lead to a string of bankruptcies. Therefore, the U.S. government decided to invest public funds in AIG and implemented a series of emergency economic measures.

Because the contract for a CDS is a matching transaction that does not pass through a securities exchange, it is difficult to obtain information about the parties that entered a CDS and the amount involved. The business failure of the seller may cause a chain reaction of failures for parties with CDS contracts. Due to the turmoil, the sense of caution around counterparty risk rose even higher among financial institutions and companies, which led the financial market to seize up. Subsequently, the financial crisis that began with the Lehman Brothers bankruptcy settled down, in part due to various countries' active monetary easing operations. With this crisis as the turning point, the outstanding balance of CDSs has been declining. The financial crisis exposed the problem that the world's financial institutions are mutually dependent, so an impact on one affects the others in a chain reaction.

3. The European financial crisis and CDSs

Attention once again shifted to CDSs due to the European financial crisis that started in Greece. The country elected a new government in October 2009. Previously, the Greek fiscal deficit ceiling was set at 3.7 percent of gross domestic product (GDP), but the new government led by the Panhellenic Socialist Movement found that the former government run by the New Democracy Party concealed the extent of the budget deficit and that it actually reached 12.7 percent (revised to 13.6 percent in April 2010) of GDP. In January 2010, it was reported that the European Commission pointed out Greece's statistical inadequacies, and the extent of the deterioration in its financial condition became known worldwide (European Commission, 2010). In response, the Greek government announced a three-year fiscal consolidation plan, but it was premised on an overly optimistic economic growth forecast. Therefore, the rating agencies downgraded Greek government bond ratings. Thus, concern spread throughout the financial market that Greece might "default" on its debt because it would be unable to repay the money it borrowed by issuing government bonds, and Greek government bond prices crashed. This triggered the depreciation of the Euro on the foreign exchange market and a decline in stock prices worldwide (the Greek debt crisis).

At that time, financial institutions outside of Greece, such as those in Germany and France, purchased large quantities of Greek government bonds, and each country was trying to support the others' deficits by buying government bonds. Moreover, many sellers of CDSs that targeted Greek government

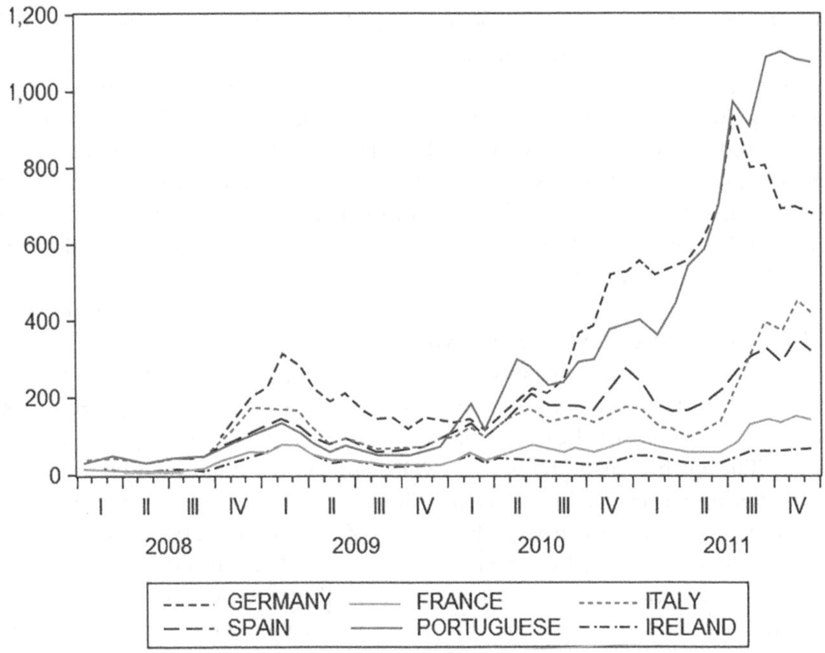

Figure 0.3 CDS premium on five-year sovereign bonds (monthly average)
Source: Bloomberg

bonds were financial institutions outside of Greece. A Greek default would deal a severe blow to these financial institutions. Many feared a potential crisis in which the German and French financial systems would also collapse. Consequently, the financial markets fell into a chaotic state, which worsened after the Greek debt crisis spread to neighboring countries with similar large fiscal deficits. Portugal, Ireland, Italy, and Spain were the countries affected, and along with Greece, became collectively known by the acronym "PIIGS." Figure 0.3 shows the movements in the CDS premiums on five-year sovereign bonds in Germany, France, Italy, Spain, Portugal, and Ireland. The figure clearly shows that the sovereign CDS premium rose rapidly in these countries between 2010 and 2011.

4. Debate about CDS

CDSs have been a controversial subject recently (Stulz, 2010). Indeed, many commentators blamed CDS as a primary cause for the recent financial crises, namely the global financial crisis in 2007–2008 and the European sovereign debt crisis originating in Greece in late 2009. Many blamed CDS for the former because financial institutions such as AIG, who were the main sellers of CDS protection, incurred huge losses on their CDS contracts written on subprime mortgage securities with little or no collateral. Many believed that CDS aggravated the risk of sovereign bonds defaults in the latter crisis because they were allegedly used as speculative instruments. In response, CDS market regulations have proliferated, such as the U.S. introduction of central clearing for CDS transactions and the European Union's (EU) banning of uncovered positions in sovereign CDS. These tighter regulations decreased the popularity of CDS to some extent. Data from the Bank for International Settlements (BIS) shows that the notional amounts of outstanding total global CDS contracts declined from its peak of USD57.4 trillion in 2008 to USD12.3 trillion in 2015.

In contrast, some financial economists and econometricians argue that CDS can enhance social welfare when they are not misused. For example, viewing CDS as term insurance contracts written on traded bonds, Jarrow (2011) highlights the beneficial role of CDS in allocating credit risks to investors who are best equipped to bear it, thus lowering the cost of debt. The author also states that CDS can help reduce market imperfections because they enable short positions on debt without triggering high transaction costs. Similarly, Oehmke and Zawadowski (2017) demonstrate that CDS markets can be larger when the underlying bond issues are fragmented, indicating that CDS markets contribute to liquidity by reducing trading and hedging frictions. Furthermore, other empirical studies show that in terms of price discovery, CDS markets lead bond (e.g., Blanco et al., 2005) and stock markets (e.g., Acharya and Johnson, 2007). Despite these mixed views, we can at least assert that CDS markets are globally important, particularly in the wake of financial crises that focused the attention of traders, policymakers, academics, and other groups on the merits and demerits of CDS instruments.

5. The purpose of this book

Throughout this book, we focus on the characteristics and joint dynamics of the three main segments of CDS markets: sovereign CDS, sector-level CDS, and firm-level CDS. This book is motived by two interesting aspects of CDS markets. First, we focus on the interconnectedness between the sovereign sector and bank sector CDS markets. At the start of the European debt crisis, policymakers saw the banking sector deteriorate, leading them to implement government rescue programs for troubled banks, which exacerbated the fiscal outlook (e.g., Acharya et al., 2011; Alter and Schüler, 2012). The development of financial sector indices such as the banking sector CDS index, which is a highly liquid and standardized instrument, provides a useful indicator to measure sector-level creditworthiness. Uncovering the relationship between sovereign CDS and banking sector CDS will help us understand the subtle mechanism of credit risk transfers between the public and banking sectors, which is critical for identifying the key levers to maintain the soundness of an economy's financial system.

Second, we highlight the spillover effects among several CDS spreads or indices. CDSs are traded in unregulated over-the-counter markets and have significant counterparty risks. In fact, a substantial portion of the gross notional amount of CDS contracts is concentrated in reference entities in the financial sector, and a small number of financial institutions tend to be protection sellers, buyers, and CDS underwriters simultaneously. Therefore, as Jarrow (2011) points out, a significant number of defaults related to some players in CDS markets might prompt the collapse of the entire financial system, indicating some systemic risk. In this respect, studying how the default risks reflected in one CDS spread (or index) spill over into another will provide guidance on using CDS as a hedging and portfolio allocation tool better and to create a more desirable regulatory framework to avoid catastrophic events in the financial system triggered by CDS markets.

The key objective of this book is to provide a comprehensive overview for various segments of global CDS markets. The book pays particular attention to the sovereign CDS markets (Part I), sector-level CDS markets (Part II), and firm-level CDS markets (Part III). Three elements uniquely characterize the contents of the book. First, this is among the first books to conduct an empirical analysis of CDS markets by applying advanced econometric methodologies to time series data. Whilst econometricians published many academic articles about CDS recently, each tends to focus on capturing one particular aspect of these markets. No previously published work offers a helpful introduction to the essence of the findings of these empirical works for broader audiences. Our book can fill this gap. Second, the scope of this book covers not only well-studied sovereign CDS markets, but also sector-level and corporate CDS indices, which remain relatively unexamined in the existing literature. These CDS indices are more liquid than single-name CDSs, and can thus provide reliable and efficient measures of the credit risks faced by a sector or a group of firms in one country. Our book is a good introduction to such important segments of CDS markets. Third, this book investigates causality and co-movements among several CDS markets, or between CDS and other financial markets. The European sovereign debt crisis convinced us that default risks can be transmitted across nations or asset classes, as we saw in the simultaneous increases in CDS spreads among some peripheral countries in the Eurozone and the resulting plummet in stock markets across Europe. Understanding the nature and causes of the complex interconnections of CDS markets is increasingly important for market participants. Our book is full of practical insights in this aspect as well.

We believe that this book has four main target audiences. First, it is useful for policymakers who design and implement regulatory frameworks to ensure properly functioning financial markets, including those for CDSs. Second, it is also relevant to investors who wish to use information about links among CDS markets for speculation, portfolio allocation, and risk management decisions. Third, it serves as a helpful reference for researchers aiming to build a solid knowledge base about CDS markets and the financial crises. Finally, graduate students can use it as supplementary reading material when studying time series analysis or investments. We now provide a brief overview of each chapter.

Part I: Sovereign CDS markets

Chapter 1, *Relationship between sovereign CDS and banking sector CDS*, assesses the causality-in-variance and causality-in-mean between the Eurozone banking sector CDS index and the Greek sovereign CDS spread. We employ Hong's (2001) cross-correlation function approach to analyze daily data, which yields two key findings. First, before the European sovereign debt crisis, a significant unidirectional causality-in-variance and causality-in-mean existed from the bank CDS to the Greek sovereign CDS spreads. Second, during the crisis period, we detected significant causality-in-variance from the Greek sovereign CDS spreads to the bank CDS, implying that Greece's deteriorated solvency might have triggered contagion effects on the area's banking sector credit risks, though Greece accounts for less than 3 percent of the Eurozone's total GDP. This may reflect significant exposure of banks in the Eurozone to Greek sovereign bonds. Our findings suggest that the patterns of mean and volatility spillovers we identify are useful measures for investors pursuing portfolio diversification and risk management related to credit risk exposures. Our results are also relevant for policymakers who want to strengthen control over the relatively unregulated sovereign CDS markets to minimize their impacts on the soundness of financial institutions.

Chapter 2, *Key determinants of sovereign CDS spreads*, examines the main drivers of the movement of sovereign CDS spreads in the U.S. We use Pesaran et al.'s (2001) ARDL bound test approach to identify the existence of cointegration and apply the Dynamic Ordinary Least Squares (DOLS) method (Stock and Watson, 1993) to show the effect of each driver on U.S. sovereign CDSs. We find evidence of cointegration and a positive and significant relationship between the banking sector CDSs and sovereign CDSs, indicating a strong link between a nation's creditworthiness and the banking sector. We also detect that the dummy variable representing the Lehman Brothers bankruptcy shock has a positive and significant relationship with sovereign CDSs. Our findings suggest that traders can use the banking sector CDS index as a risk management tool to hedge exposure to the credit risks of sovereign CDSs. Our empirical results also highlight the need for policymakers to monitor the banking sector CDS index to understand the movement of sovereign CDS spreads thoroughly and take appropriate regulatory actions.

Chapter 3, *Dynamic spillover among sovereign CDS spreads*, examines time-varying spillovers among the sovereign CDS spreads of four ASEAN countries. Employing the Diebold and Yilmaz (2012) spillover index method, we derive several main findings. First, cross-country spillovers explained a substantial portion of the forecast error variances on average, with the total spillover index showing bursts at essentially the timing of crisis events. Second, spillovers across the four countries were bidirectional during the entire sample period. Third, Indonesia, which had few spillovers, became a dominant transmitter of shocks to other countries immediately after the Lehman Brothers collapse. Fourth, the Philippines were net transmitters, while Thailand and Malaysia were mostly net receivers. Our findings are important for traders who need to understand the importance of executing dynamic asset allocations in credit risk trades and incorporate the timing and direction of volatility spillovers across countries. The empirical results are also useful for policymakers keen to understand the cross-country spillover effects of credit risks to maintain the stability of their financial systems.

Part II: Sector-level CDS markets

Chapter 4, *Causality among financial sector CDS indices*, investigates volatility and mean transmissions among the U.S. banking, insurance, and financial services CDS indices at the sector level. We employ the robust cross-correlation function approach and conduct pre-tests for structural breaks in the variances, removing the causality-in-mean effects in the causality-in-variance tests. We find evidence of significant causality-in-mean effects running from the banking sector to the insurance and financial services sector CDS indices and from the financial services to the insurance sector CDS indices, suggesting the leading role of the banking and financial services sectors in price discovery. We also find significant causality-in-variance effects from the financial services sector CDS index to that of the banking sector, implying information transmission from the former, the least regulated of the three markets. Our findings provide insights for traders in terms of pricing credit risks, highlighting the need to incorporate risk migration as reflected in volatility spillovers. In addition, our results should motivate policymakers to monitor the financial services sector as a potential source of contagion among these CDS markets, being mindful of systemic risks potentially triggered by such contagion.

Chapter 5, *Co-movement and spillovers among financial sector CDS indices*, examines the time-varying relationships and volatility spillovers between the three U.K. financial sector CDS indices (banking, life insurance, and other financial sectors) over time. We employ Engle's (2002) DCC-GARCH model to analyze the time-varying correlations, and assess their volatility spillover effects with Diebold and Yilmaz's (2012) spillover index. We find sharp increases in the dynamic conditional correlations (DCCs) for all pairs after the Lehman Brothers bankruptcy, indicating evidence of contagion; and decreases for two pairs (banking-life insurance and life insurance-other financial) after the zenith of the European debt crisis, implying emerging diversification opportunities. Dynamic spillover index measures suggest that, although the banking sector was a dominant net transmitter of volatility, other financial sectors also became net transmitters for some periods. Our findings reveal that traders should pursue dynamic portfolio allocations among financial sector CDS indices or with portfolios exposed to credit risks in these sectors to hedge their risks on a real-time basis. The results also suggest that policymakers should focus on regulating the banking and other financial sectors (i.e., financial services) to reduce the adverse impacts of volatility spillovers from those sectors.

Chapter 6, *Dependence structure of insurance sector CDS indices*, analyzes the non-linear dependence structure and the upper and lower tail dependence behaviors of the U.S., EU, and U.K. insurance sector CDS indices using a copula-GARCH approach. We find substantial increases in dependence during the financial crisis periods. We find various copulas to fit each pair in the pre-crisis period; specifically, we find asymmetric tail dependence for the U.K.–U.S. pair, suggesting the possibility of large simultaneous losses. However, during the crisis periods, the Frank copula fits best, with no significant tail dependence, implying low systemic risks. Our findings imply that traders should concentrate on the risks of substantial simultaneous losses due to extreme co-movements in the value-at-risk calculation of their portfolio exposed to credit risks in the insurance sector. For policymakers, our empirical results suggest that the imminent need to develop a regulatory framework to ameliorate systemic risks may be limited among the insurance sector CDS indices, even during a financial crisis.

Chapter 7, *Time-varying correlation among bank sector CDS indices*, investigates the dynamic relationship among banking sector CDS indices for the EU, the U.K., and the U.S. by employing the asymmetric DCC model proposed by Cappiello et al. (2006). This model allows us to investigate the existence of asymmetric responses in dynamic correlations to negative news. We also examine the potential impacts of the two recent financial crises on the estimated DCCs among the banking sector CDS indices using Yiu et al.'s (2010) method. We find evidence of asymmetric dynamic correlations between the EU and U.K. banking sector CDS indices, and these correlations tend to be higher in response to a joint downward movement. We also find that the DCC estimates of the pairs of the U.S. banking sector CDS and the U.K. and EU banking sector CDSs dropped significantly immediately after the Lehman Brothers collapse, and that the sovereign debt crisis dummy is significantly positive for the pair of U.K. and U.S. banking sector CDSs, as represented by the increased correlations after the onset of the debt crisis. For traders, the significant decrease in the DCCs between U.S. bank sector CDS and U.K. and EU bank sector CDSs imply potential diversification opportunities. Policymakers need to be mindful about the significant increase in the DCCs between U.S. and U.K. bank sector CDSs, as this suggests that cross-border contagion in the creditworthiness of bank sectors may happen in a counterintuitive manner.

Part III: Firm-level CDS markets

Chapter 8, *Dynamic correlation among banks' CDS spreads*, investigates co-movement among the single-name CDS spreads of 15 Eurozone banks using Engle and Kelly's (2012) dynamic equi-correlation (DECO) model. We find a high level of equi-correlation, even prior to the financial crises, suggesting that investors perceived common risks. In addition, we uncover substantial increases in equi-correlation during the crisis events, including the onset of the European debt crisis. Furthermore, our results reveal that the implied volatility measure significantly affected the co-movement of the bank CDS spreads in the period, including during the debt crisis. Our findings are useful for traders and imply that they should be more aware of systemic risks for all banks that had high exposure to the debt of peripheral nations rather than bank-specific risks. Moreover, the results may help policymakers focus more regulatory efforts on monitoring market-wide volatility indicators to prevent systemic failure in the banking system, and to capture signs of deterioration in market conditions that might have adverse effects on a group of banks.

Chapter 9, *Dependence structures among corporate CDS indices*, analyzes the conditional dependence structure of the three corporate CDS indices in Japan (iTraxx.Japan), Europe (iTraxx.Europe), and the U.S. (CDX.NA.IG). We estimate AR-EGARCH models to obtain standardized residuals, transform them into uniform variables, and apply three Archimedean copula (Gumbel, Clayton, and Frank). We find that for the U.S.–Japan pair, the Gumbel copula fit best during the global and European debt crises, implying that exposure to the two corporate CDS indices may trigger a substantial simultaneous loss. We also detect that for all pairwise combinations, the Gumbel copula had the best fit to the data during the post-debt crisis period, meaning that systemic risks reflecting corporate credit risks across the three countries recently become more evident. Our findings help investors pursue timely risk management, recognizing the cross-country transmission of corporate credit risks between Japan and the U.S. in particular, as reflected in the asymmetric dependence structure of their corporate CDS indices. Our results also imply the need for policymakers to identify the signs of potential systemic risks among the corporate CDS indices, even after the European sovereign debt crisis subsided.

Chapter 10, *Interdependence between Corporate CDS Indices: Application of Continuous Wavelet Transform*, empirically analyzes the interdependence between the corporate CDS indices of Japan, Europe, and the U.S. Continuous wavelet transform is employed to analyze the coherence between the corporate CDS indices of the three economies. The power spectrum analysis reveals that the CDS indices had a large power spectrum value during the 2008 global financial crisis. It further reveals that during the subsequent European debt crisis, the power spectrum of the EU CDS index rose, but its impact on the U.S. and Japan was relatively weak. The result of the coherence test to check the interdependency between the CDS indices of the three economies indicates that coherence is stronger for variations with a long-term cycle vis-à-vis a short-term cycle. In addition, the relationship between the markets is in phase, indicating that they move in the same direction.

Acknowledgement

We would like to thank Ms. Xiao Jing Cai for her research assistance. This work was supported by JSPS KAKENHI Grant Number (A) 17H00983 and 17K18564.

References

Acharya, V. V., Drechsler, I., and Schnabl, P. (2011) A pyrrhic victory? Bank bailouts and sovereign credit risk, *NBER Working Paper No. 17136.*

Acharya, V. V. and Johnson, T. (2007) Insider trading in credit derivatives, *Journal of Financial Economics*, **84**, 110–141.

Alter, A. and Schüler, Y. S. (2012) Credit spread interdependencies of European states and banks during the financial crisis, *Journal of Banking & Finance*, **36**, 3444–3468.

Blanco, R., Brennan, S., and Marsh, I. W. (2005) An empirical analysis of the dynamic relation between investment-grade bonds and credit default swaps, *Journal of Finance*, **60**, 2255–2281.

Cappiello, L., Engle, R. F., and Sheppard, K. (2006) Asymmetric dynamics in the correlations of global equity and bond returns, *Journal of Financial Econometrics*, **4**, 537–572.

Diebold, F. X. and Yilmaz, K. (2012) Better to give than to receive: Predictive directional measurement of volatility spillovers, *International Journal of Forecasting*, **28**, 57–66.

Engle, R. (2002) Dynamic conditional correlation: A simple class of multivariate generalized autoregressive conditional heteroskedasticity models, *Journal of Business and Economic Statistics*, **20**, 339–350.

Engle, R. and Kelly, B. (2012) Dynamic equicorrelation, *Journal of Business & Economic Statistics*, **30**, 212–228.

European Commission (2010) *Report on Greek Government Deficit and Debt Statistics*, European Commission, Brussel, pp. 1–30, http://ec.europa.eu/eurostat/documents/4187653/6404656/COM_2010_report_greek/c8523cfa-d3c1-4954-8ea1-64bb11e59b3a.

Hong, Y. (2001) A test for volatility spillover with application to exchange rates, *Journal of Econometrics*, **103**, 183–224.
Jarrow, R. A. (2011) The economics of credit default swaps, *Annual Review of Financial Economics*, **3**, Annual Reviews.
Oehmke, M. and Zawadowski, A. (2017) The anatomy of the CDS market, *The Review of Financial Studies*, **30**, 80–119.
Pesaran, H. M., Shin, Y., and Smith, R. J. (2001) Bounds testing approaches to the analysis of level relationships, *Journal of Applied Econometrics*, **16**, 289–326.
Stock, J. H. and Watson, M. (1993) A simple estimator of cointegrating vectors in higher order integrated systems, *Econometrica*, **61**, 783–820.
Stulz, R. (2010) Credit default swaps and the credit crisis, *Journal of Economic Perspectives*, **24**, 73–92.
Yiu, M. S., Ho, W.-Y. A., and Choi, D. F. (2010) Dynamic correlation analysis of financial contagion in Asian markets in global financial turmoil, *Applied Financial Economics*, **20**, 345–354.

Part I

Sovereign CDS markets

1 Relationship between sovereign CDS and banking sector CDS

1.1 Introduction

The onset of the European sovereign debt crisis, which originated in Greece in late 2009 and spread rapidly across the entire Eurozone, was accompanied by a surge of the Greek sovereign credit default swap (CDS) index. Sovereign CDS indexes are credit derivatives employed to protect against credit events regarding default or restructuring of government debts. The instruments are regarded as measures of sovereign credit risk, as well as tools for credit risk management and speculation. As Delatte et al. (2012) pointed out, the recent debt crisis has strengthened concerns over the use of CDS instruments, because the sudden increases in sovereign CDS prices in several Eurozone peripheral countries have been attributed to speculative trading activities by a few investors, which might have worsened the intensity of the debt crisis. In fact, such concern triggered the European Parliament's adoption of a regulation to ban any entity in the European Union (EU) from entering into uncovered or "naked" CDSs on sovereign debt after November 2012. This regulatory movement might reflect the viewpoint among EU authorities that such uncovered transactions using sovereign CDSs could destabilize the financial market by unnecessarily raising the issuance costs of the underlying sovereign bonds.

An important perspective to investigate in determining why the European sovereign debt crisis worsened so substantially is the connection between sovereign debt and the bank sector in the Eurozone. As Gray et al. (2008) and Acharya et al. (2011) contended, there is a feedback effect in the risk transfer mechanism between the public sector and the bank sector. On one hand, the risks associated with financial distress that occurs in the bank sector might be transmitted to the public sector by increasing the value of the implicit or explicit government guarantee to banks, accompanied by the government's bank bailout programs. In addition, the government faces a worsened fiscal outlook, because the troubled bank sector might contract the EU economy due to the limited credit flow available. On the other hand, the risks associated with fiscal distress of the government in turn might be transmitted to the bank sector, because banks hold a large portion of government debt securities. Indeed, during the European sovereign debt crisis, the surge of sovereign bond yields in peripheral Eurozone countries led several major European banks to suffer from impaired balance sheets. Several stress tests by the European Banking Authority demonstrated that several banks in Europe have huge net exposure to Greek sovereign debts, implying that writing off those debts could trigger substantial losses. Therefore, when we attempt to analyze the sovereign CDS markets that attracted much attention in the context of the recent debt crisis, we consider it important to empirically examine how interconnectedness between sovereign debt and the bank sector can be revealed.

Prior academic studies on the sovereign CDS market from the viewpoint of the impact of financial crises have focused on either the recent co-movement of CDS spreads, including the Greek spread (e.g., Andenmatten and Brill, 2011; Wang and Moore, 2012), or on causal relationships between sovereign debt yields and CDS spreads (e.g., Delis and Mylonidis, 2011; Delatte et al., 2012). Recently, an increasing body of literature has covered the credit spread interrelationships between the public sector and bank sector. For instance, Alter and Schüler (2012) use a vector error correction and a vector autoregressive approach in order to examine the dynamics between the sovereign CDS spreads of seven European countries and the CDS spreads of two banks from each nation. The authors find that after bank bailout programs, contagion from sovereign CDS spreads to bank CDS spreads was permanent, while the spillover effect in the opposite direction, which had been observed predominantly before the government intervention, became transitory. Arnold (2012) employed a panel regression framework to analyze the spillover of sovereign CDS spreads to individual banks' CDS spreads in the EU, incorporating the banks' exposure to the sovereign debt of Greece, Ireland, Portugal, and Spain (GIPS). The results of this study indicate that the CDS spreads of heavily exposed banks, especially those located in GIPS countries, exhibited stronger response to the changes in the sovereign CDS spreads. Bruyckere et al. (2013) employed the factor model in which contagion between bank and sovereign default risk in Europe is defined as having excess correlation, that is, correlation between banks' and sovereign CDS spreads over and above what can be explained by common factors. The authors detected evidence of contagion and found that the contagion effects were higher for banks with low capital adequacy levels, higher reliance on short-term funding, and less focus on traditional banking activities. By calculating spillover effects based on generalized impulse response function analysis, Alter and Beyer (2014) examined the interdependence between sovereign and bank CDS spreads in the Eurozone. Their empirical results showed an increasing level of spillover index from bank to sovereign CDS spreads and from sovereign to bank CDS spreads during the period between October 2009 and July 2012.

In this study, we examine the causality between the spread of the Greek sovereign CDS index over that of Germany and the Eurozone banking sector CDS index,[1] before and during the European sovereign debt crisis. There are three prominent contributions of our study to the existing literature. First, to the best of our knowledge, our study is among the first to examine the spillover effects between banking sector CDS indexes and sovereign CDS spreads. This focus of our investigation is especially relevant in the context of the European sovereign debt crisis, because the substantial amount of Greek government bonds held by financial institutions in the Eurozone might complicate the interrelationships between the two CDS markets.

Second, our research uncovers causality in the conditional mean and causality-in-variance between the two CDS indexes. Assessing causality-in-variance enriches our analysis by clarifying the patterns and timing of information transmission between the variables. As Ross (1989) and Engle et al. (1990) argued, volatility contains useful data on information flows. In fact, volatility spillovers might exist even when two markets do not exhibit apparent causality-in-mean. Third, we use the robust cross-correlation function (CCF) approach, as developed by Hong (2001), to assess causality-in-variance. This modifies the Cheung and Ng (1996) model by weighting lags in a non-uniform manner. Furthermore, unlike the multivariate generalized autoregressive conditional heteroskedasticity (GARCH) framework, Hong's (2001) approach does not depend on simultaneous inter-series modeling and enables flexible specification of innovation processes.

The rest of this chapter is organized as follows. Section 1.2 presents the empirical methodology. Section 1.3 provides an explanation of our dataset and reports our findings from the causality tests. Section 1.4 concludes.

1.2 Empirical methodology

We used the two-stage CCF approach advocated by Hong (2001). Consider two stationary time series, X_t and Y_t. First, univariate models were fitted to each data series, allowing for time variation of conditional means and variances. We selected the best autoregressive, exponential generalized autoregressive conditional heteroskedasticity (AR(k)-EGARCH(p,q)) models:[2]

$$\Delta r_t = a_0 + \sum_{i=1}^{k} a_i \Delta r_{t-i} + \varepsilon_t,\ E_{t-1}(\varepsilon_t) = 0,\ E_{t-1}(\varepsilon_t^2) = \sigma^2, \tag{1.1}$$

$$\log(\sigma_t^2) = \omega + \sum_{i=1}^{q} (\alpha_i |z_{t-i}| + \gamma_i z_{t-i}) + \sum_{i=1}^{p} \beta_i \log(\sigma_{t-i}^2) \tag{1.2}$$

where $z_t = \varepsilon_t/\sigma_t$ has a normal distribution with zero mean and unit variance, and Δr_t represents the first differences of each time series. We determined k (1, 2, . . ., 10), p (1, 2), and q (1, 2) by means of the Schwarz's Bayesian information criterion while conducting residual diagnostics to avoid autocorrelation. The EGARCH models allowed us to capture possible cyclical behavior in volatility because we did not preclude negative coefficients.

Second, causality tests were conducted using weighted CCFs. We calculated the sample cross-correlations of the standardized residuals represented as follows:

$$\hat{u}_t = (X_t - \hat{\mu}_{X,t})^2 / \hat{h}_{X,t}, \tag{1.3}$$

$$\hat{v}_t = (Y_t - \hat{\mu}_{Y,t})^2 / \hat{h}_{Y,t} \tag{1.4}$$

where $\hat{\mu}_{X,t}$, $\hat{\mu}_{Y,t}$ and $\hat{h}_{X,t}$, $\hat{h}_{Y,t}$ are the estimated conditional means and variances of the AR(k)-EGARCH(p,q) models, respectively. The sample CCF of u_t and v_t was defined by

$$\hat{\rho}_{uv}(i) = \{c_{uu}(0)c_{vv}(0)\}^{-1/2} c_{uv}(i) \tag{1.5}$$

$$\text{where } c_{uv}(k) = T^{-1}\sum_{t=1}^{T-k}(\hat{u}_t - \overline{u})(\hat{v}_{t+k} - \overline{v}) \text{ for } k \geq 0$$

$$= T^{-1}\sum_{t=1}^{T-k}(\hat{u}_{t-k} - \overline{u})(\hat{v}_t - \overline{v}) \text{ for } k < 0. \quad (1.6)$$

Note that c_{uu} (0) and c_{vv} (0) represent sample variances of disturbances u_t and v_t, respectively, and T is the sample size.

In order to test the null hypothesis of no causality-in-variance during the first k lags, Cheung and Ng (1996) proposed an *S*-statistic, which follows a null asymptotic χ^2 (k) distribution, as follows:

$$S = T\sum_{i=1}^{k}\hat{\rho}_{uv}^2(i) \xrightarrow{L} \chi^2(k). \quad (1.7)$$

The key weakness of this *S*-statistic is that each lag is weighted uniformly, without differentiation between recent and distant cross-correlations. Hence, the *S*-statistic is inconsistent with the intuition that more recent information should be weighted heavily, and that cross-correlations should decrease to zero as the lag order increases. Hong (2001) overcame this problem by using a new *Q*-statistic for testing one-sided causality:

$$Q = \frac{S-k}{\sqrt{2k}} \xrightarrow{L} N(0,1). \quad (1.8)$$

A *Q*-statistic larger than the upper-tail N (0,1) critical values rejects the null hypothesis of no causality-in-variance during the first k lags. We can conduct the causality-in-mean tests similarly.

1.3 Data and empirical results

Our data were sourced from Thomson Financial Datastream and contain 1,038 daily observations on the Eurozone banking sector CDS index prices (*bkcds*), and the spreads of the five-year Greek sovereign CDS index prices over those of Germany (*grcds*). The sample period ranges from January 2008 to December 2011.[3] As in Kasimati (2011),[4] the sample was divided into two sub-periods, Sample A (pre-crisis period) and Sample B (crisis period), on November 17, 2009, when the Bank of Greece warned that the downgrade of Greek sovereign bonds might reduce the country's prospects for funding from the European Central Bank, triggering a surge in Greek sovereign CDS spreads.

Table 1.1 describes the statistics of level and first-differenced data in Sample A and Sample B. For the two CDS indexes, both means and standard deviations significantly increased throughout the debt crisis. Table 1.1 also indicates that Jarque–Bera tests reject normality for all the time series regardless of the sub-sample periods. In addition, we conducted the augmented Dickey–Fuller (ADF) tests to check for the existence of the unit root. As reported in Table 1.2,

Table 1.1 Summary statistics

Variable	*Mean (b.p.)*	*SD*	*Skewness*	*Kurtosis*	*Jarque–Bera*
Level data					
Sample A: pre-crisis period					
bkcds	144.67	58.78	1.01	3.62	91.67
grcds	88.15	52.58	0.78	2.61	52.62
Sample B: crisis period					
bkcds	276.43	117.89	0.53	2.64	28.46
grcds	1,592.77	1,904.95	2.27	7.87	1,015.08
First-differenced data					
Sample A: pre-crisis period					
bkcds	0.12	6.71	0.02	14.89	2,882.24
grcds	0.24	4.47	-0.07	12.13	1,700.35
Sample B: crisis period					
bkcds	0.73	15.53	0.78	47.55	45,370.68
grcds	17.75	206.62	0.84	39.17	29,928.30

Notes: This table provides the statistics for each time series. The entire sample period was divided into Sample A (from January 1, 2008, to November 16, 2009; n = 490) and Sample B (from November 17, 2009, to December 30, 2011; n = 548).

Table 1.2 Results of the ADF unit root tests

Variable	*ADF test statistics*	
	Constant	*Constant and trend*
Level data		
Sample A: pre-crisis period		
bkcds	-1.832	-1.372
grcds	-1.364	-1.352
Sample B: crisis period		
bkcds	-0.842	-3.220
grcds	3.872	2.201
First-differenced data		
Sample A: pre-crisis period		
bkcds	-19.301***	-19.366***
grcds	-18.724***	-18.712***
Sample B: crisis period		
bkcds	-13.610***	-13.606***
grcds	-20.872***	-21.291***

Notes: Results of the augmented Dickey–Fuller (ADF) unit root tests are reported. This table tests the unit root hypothesis in which the regression contains a constant and no deterministic components, and a constant and a trend.

*** denotes statistical significance at the 1% level.

the results reveal that unit root processes were identified for level data, but not for the first-differenced series of the two variables. Thus, in the subsequent analysis, we used first-differenced data to ensure stationarity of all time series.

Table 1.3 presents the parameter estimates for all selected AR(k)-EGARCH(p,q) models. While the selected lag lengths in the return equations varied, we chose the EGARCH(1,1) model for variance equations of all series. All ARCH (α_i), GARCH (β_i), and asymmetric (γ_i) coefficients were found to be statistically significant at the 5 percent level. The Ljung–Box statistics, $Q(20)$ and $Q^2(20)$, indicate support for the null hypothesis of no autocorrelation up to order 20 for the standardized residuals and squared standardized residuals at the 1 percent significance level. Based on these results, our model specifications are reasonably good.

Table 1.4 reports empirical results on the cross-correlation analysis to test for the null hypothesis of no causality up to lag k (5, 10, 15, 20, 25, and 30), measured in days, for each combination of the series (*bkcds* and *grcds*) in Sample A and Sample B. Our results exhibit markedly different patterns of causal linkages between the two CDS spreads corresponding to the pre-crisis and crisis periods.

In the pre-crisis period, we found significant unidirectional causality-in-mean from the Eurozone banking CDS to the Greek sovereign CDS spreads in all investigated lags. This significant unidirectional causality-in-variance was also detected during this period, which includes the collapse of Lehman Brothers on September 15, 2009. This suggests that the soaring banking sector CDS index might have influenced the increase in the Greek sovereign CDS spreads by transmitting information on the increased exposure of Greece to the surge of credit risks attributable to financial institutions in the Eurozone. Several commentators have argued that the banking CDS index, which is widely traded by speculative investors, might have dried the liquidity of sovereign bond markets in the area. Our empirical results provide support for the need to strengthen regulations over the banking CDS market.

In the crisis period, we observed opposite causality patterns. There was significant unidirectional causality running from the Greek sovereign CDS spreads to the Eurozone banking CDS, although the causality-in-mean effect in this direction was less clear during that period. Interestingly, such causal linkages imply that the sovereign solvency issue of Greece, which accounts for only 2.7 percent of the Eurozone's total gross domestic product, might have exerted contagion effects on credit risks of the banking sector in the area, triggering volatility spillovers through the CDS markets. This presumably reflects the fact that the main financial institutions in the area were significantly exposed to Greek sovereign bonds, and hence, their businesses turned out to be vulnerable to Greece's default risks.

Table 1.3 Results of AR-EGARCH models

	Sample A: pre-crisis period				*Sample B: crisis period*			
	bkcds		*grcds*		*bkcds*		*grcds*	
	AR(10)-EGARCH(1,1)		*AR(5)-EGARCH (1,1)*		*AR(8)-EGARCH(1,1)*		*AR(4)-EGARCH(1,1)*	
	Estimate	*SE*	*Estimate*	*SE*	*Estimate*	*SE*	*Estimate*	*SE*
Return equation								
a_0	0.113	0.192	0.146	0.081	0.469*	0.211	−2.469**	0.408
a_1	0.225**	0.049	0.173**	0.060	0.230**	0.041	0.145**	0.040
a_2	0.030	0.056	0.095	0.054	−0.028	0.054	0.073	0.038
a_3	0.069	0.051	0.063	0.061	−0.078	0.049	−0.027	0.031
a_4	0.029	0.050	−0.014	0.059	−0.060	0.048	−0.013	0.018
a_5	−0.032	0.054	0.024	0.043	0.003	0.050		
a_6	−0.040	0.049			0.027	0.048		
a_7	0.029	0.051			−0.059	0.049		
a_8	−0.057	0.045			−0.054	0.036		
a_9	−0.049	0.049						
a_{10}	0.135**	0.040						
Variance equation								
ω	−0.246**	0.052	−0.116**	0.014	−0.147**	0.042	−0.059**	0.011
α_1	0.395**	0.056	0.204**	0.017	0.477**	0.049	−0.066**	0.009
γ_1	0.094**	0.034	0.036*	0.017	0.162**	0.039	0.258**	0.017
β_1	0.984**	0.011	0.998**	0.002	0.953**	0.010	1.007**	0.001
Log likelihood	−1,457.9		−1,236.8		−1,916.8		−2,915.3	
$Q(20)$	17.045		18.148		19.899		13.300	
p-value	0.650		0.578		0.464		0.864	
$Q^2(20)$	9.428		22.087		14.627		24.554	
p-value	0.977		0.336		0.797		0.219	

Notes: ** and * denote statistical significance at the 1% and 5% levels, respectively. $Q(20)$ and $Q^2(20)$ are the Ljung–Box statistics for the null hypothesis of no autocorrelation up to order 20 for the standardized residuals and squared standardized residuals, respectively.

Table 1.4 Cross-correlation analysis between Eurozone banking sector CDS and Greek CDS spreads

K	*Causality-in-mean*		*Causality-in-variance*	
	bkcds *and* grcds *(−k)*	bkcds *and* grcds *(+k)*	bkcds *and* grcds *(−k)*	bkcds *and* grcds *(+k)*
Sample A: pre-crisis period				
5	0.59	8.62**	-0.95	0.44
10	-0.34	6.10**	-1.65	0.86
15	0.60	5.16**	-1.92	0.35
20	0.30	4.79**	-1.76	1.28
25	0.83	4.54**	0.14	2.54**
30	0.36	3.82**	0.02	1.92*
Sample B: crisis period				
5	0.19	1.03	-0.17	-0.96
10	1.25	0.79	-0.94	-1.45
15	2.13*	0.60	2.06*	-1.61
20	1.24	0.81	2.96**	-1.76
25	1.26	0.70	2.05*	-1.88
30	1.25	0.42	1.48	-2.11

Notes: Table entries indicate the values of the *Q*-statistic, which is used to test the null hypothesis of no causality from lag 1 up to lag k (5, 10, 15, 20, 25, 30). If the test statistic is larger than the critical value of the standard normal distribution, the null hypothesis is rejected.

** and * denote statistical significance at the 1% and 5% levels, respectively. *Q*-statistics are based on one-side tests. Lags are measured in days.

1.4 Conclusion

Using the CCF technique developed by Hong (2001), this study examined causality-in-variance and causality-in-mean between the Eurozone banking sector CDS index and the spreads of the Greek sovereign CDS index over those of Germany using daily data from January 2008 to December 2011.

We document two main findings. (i) Before the sovereign debt crisis, there was significant unidirectional causality-in-variance and causality-in-mean running from the banking sector CDS to the Greek sovereign CDS spreads. (ii) By contrast, during the crisis, we found significant causality-in-variance running from the Greek sovereign CDS spreads to the banking CDS, despite the less clear causality-in-mean effect at that time. The results have especially significant implications for policymakers, who are keen to exert more control over sovereign CDS contracts traded in rather unregulated markets.

Notes

1 We focus on this index, which represents a portfolio of single-name CDSs for selected banks in the area, since market participants are more interested in credit risks at the industry level than at the individual firm level.
2 See Nelson (1991) for details of the EGARCH model.
3 Our choice of start date was constrained by the availability of the Greek sovereign CDS index data through Datastream, which begins only from December 14, 2007.
4 Kasimati (2011) investigated the sovereign debt crisis by analyzing through an error correction model the causality between the increases in the Greek sovereign bond yield over that for German bond, and the devaluation of the euro.

References

Acharya, V., Drechsler, I., and Schnabl, P. (2011) A pyrrhic victory? Bank bailouts and sovereign credit risk, *NBER Working Papers No. 17136.*

Alter, A. and Beyer, A. (2014) The dynamics of spillover effects during the European sovereign debt turmoil, *Journal of Banking & Finance*, **42**, 134–153.

Alter, A. and Schüler, Y. S. (2012) Credit spread interdependencies of European states and banks during the financial crisis, *Journal of Banking & Finance*, **36**, 3444–3468.

Andenmatten, S. and Brill, F. (2011) Measuring co-movements of CDS premia during the Greek debt crisis, *Discussion Papers No. 11–04*, University of Bern, Bern.

Arnold, I. J. M. (2012) Sovereign debt exposures and banking risks in the current EU financial crisis, *Journal of Policy Modeling*, **34**, 906–920.

Bruyckere, V. D., Gerhardt, M., Schepens, G., and Vennet, R. V. (2013) Bank/sovereign risk spillovers in the European debt crisis, *Journal of Banking & Finance*, **37**, 4793–4809.

Cheung, Y. and Ng, L. (1996) A causality-in-variance test and its applications to financial market prices, *Journal of Econometrics*, **72**, 33–48.

Delatte, A.-L., Gex, M., and Lopez-Villavicencio, A. (2012) Has the CDS market influenced the borrowing cost of European countries during the sovereign crisis? *Journal of International Money and Finance*, **31**, 481–497.

Delis, M. D. and Mylonidis, N. (2011) The chicken or the egg? A note on the dynamic interrelation between government bond spreads and credit default swaps, *Finance Research Letters*, **8**, 163–170.

Engle, R. F., Ito, T., and Lin, K. L. (1990) Meteor showers or heat waves? Heteroskedastic intra-daily volatility in the foreign exchange market, *Econometrica*, **58**, 525–542.

Gray, D. F., Merton, R. C., and Bodie, Z. (2008) New framework for measuring and managing macrofinancial risk and financial stability, *NBER Working Papers No. 13607.*

Hong, Y. (2001) A test for volatility spillover with application to exchange rates, *Journal of Econometrics*, **103**, 183–224.

Kasimati, E. (2011) Did the climb on the Greek sovereign spreads cause the devaluation of Euro? *Applied Economics Letters*, **18**, 851–854.

Nelson, D. (1991) Conditional heteroskedasticity in asset returns: A new approach, *Econometrica*, **59**, 347–370.

Ross, S. A. (1989) Information and volatility: No-arbitrage Martingale approach to timing and resolution irrelevancy, *Journal of Finance*, **44**, 1–17.

Wang, P. and Moore, T. (2012) The integration of the credit default swap markets during the US subprime crisis: Dynamic correlation analysis, *Journal of International Financial Markets, Institutions and Money*, **22**, 1–15.

2 Key determinants of sovereign CDS spreads

2.1 Introduction

The outbreak of the European sovereign debt crisis stunned market participants, prompting them to doubt the sustainability of public debt and the default risks of government securities even in advanced economies. Throughout the debt crisis, the surge of sovereign credit default swap (CDS) spreads for peripheral Eurozone economies in particular has attracted attention. According to the Bank for International Settlements (BIS), sovereign CDS markets exhibited rapid growth, from \$1.7 trillion in 2008 to \$3.0 trillion in 2011, but thereafter declined back to \$2.3 trillion in mid-2015.[1] Nonetheless, sovereign CDS is still considered an accurate gauge of the default risk of a country because it is one of the most widely traded credit derivative instruments and is usually more liquid than its reference sovereign bond,[2] as pointed out by Longstaff et al. (2011). In light of this, it is important to identify the key drivers that have significant impacts on the movement of sovereign CDS spreads.

The recent financial turmoil suggests the potential linkages between the sovereigns' creditworthiness and the financial health of their bank sector. The seminal paper by Acharya et al. (2011) asserts that bailouts of banks financed by a government through increased taxation and dilution of existing government debt holders may lead to stagnant economic growth and deterioration of a sovereign's credit risk, which in turn worsens the credit risks of banks holding a substantial amount of government debts. More recently, the empirical study by Avino and Cotter (2015) shows evidence of two-way feedback mechanisms in price discovery between sovereign CDS spreads and an average of single-name CDS for several banks in Eurozone countries. Kallestrup et al. (2016) also show that the exposures of the largest banks to foreign asset holdings have significant effects on not only the CDS prices of the banks themselves but also the sovereign CDS spreads of the countries where the banks reside. Such growing attention to the interconnectedness between a sovereign and bank credit risks indeed motivates us to assess the potential determinants of sovereign CDS spreads, including the creditworthiness of the bank sector serving as one of the explanatory variables explicitly.

The determinants of sovereign CDS spreads have been extensively explored especially for emerging markets, where policymakers feel the need to understand the sources of sovereign default risks more keenly. There have been several studies that have the same scope as ours, including the following. Ismailescu and Kazemi (2010) investigate the impacts of changes in S&P credit rating events on sovereign CDS in 22 emerging countries, and their regression analysis reveals that positive rating announcements affect the CDS spreads immediately, while negative rating events have no impacts. Fender et al. (2012) analyze the determinants of sovereign CDS spreads for 12 emerging countries and uncover that the CDS spreads are more influenced by global and regional risk factors than country-level risk drivers, and this observation is more marked during financial crises. Eyssell et al. (2013) investigate the determinants of sovereign CDS spreads in China and find that not only domestic factors such as the Chinese stock market return and the real interest rate but also global variables including the CBOE Volatility Index (VIX)[3] and the slope of the U.S. yield curve have significant relationships with Chinese sovereign CDS. Aizenman et al. (2016) assess the relationships between sovereign CDS spreads and macroeconomic fundamentals in 20 emerging markets and find that key drivers vary over time, indicating the importance of trade openness and state fragility in the pre-crisis period, and the external debt/GDP ratio and inflation in the financial crisis period.

Recently, there has been a growing body of research that focuses on the determinants of sovereign CDS spreads for multiple countries, including advanced economies in the Eurozone, in the context of the debt crisis. For example, Aizenman et al. (2013) investigate the determinants of sovereign CDS spreads in 50 countries including Portugal, Ireland, Italy, Greece, and Spain, or the so-called PIIGS nations, and uncover that fiscal space[4] is an important predictor for the CDS spreads. Yuan and Pongsiri (2015) use panel data for 36 countries including those in the Eurozone to assess the determinants of sovereign CDS spreads and find that fiscal austerity, debt/GDP ratio, and future output growth play key roles in determining the prices of sovereign default risks. Blommestein et al. (2016) assess the determinants of sovereign CDS spreads for the PIIGS countries, and their regime-switching model indicates that main drivers for the pricing of sovereign CDS are regime dependent, significantly influenced by the contagion from the global financial market.

In this chapter, we investigate the determinants of sovereign CDS spreads in the U.S., which have not been the focus in the strands of previous research. The main contributions of this study to the previous literature are twofold. First, to our knowledge, this is the first study to show that bank sector CDS is one of the key determinants of sovereign CDS spreads. While there is a growing body of literature on the bank sector's substantial roles in the European sovereign debt crisis, this study demonstrates the significant and positive relationship between sovereign CDS and bank sector CDS in the U.S., where sovereign default risks have not been explicitly realized among market participants. Second, in terms of methodologies, we employ the autoregressive distributed lag (ARDL) bounds test approach by Pesaran et al. (2001), which allows for explanatory variables consisting of a mixture of I(0) and I(1) variables. Moreover, after the existence of the cointegration among the variables is confirmed, we apply the dynamic ordinary least squares (DOLS) approach by Stock and Watson (1993), which is applicable to variables that are integrated in different orders, and can deal with dynamic sources of bias as well.

The rest of this chapter is organized as follows. Section 2.2 briefly describes the empirical method used in this study. Section 2.3 explains our dataset. Section 2.4 presents our empirical findings and their implications. Section 2.5 provides the conclusions.

2.2 Empirical methodology

In this study, we take a two-step approach to assess the key determinants of U.S. sovereign CDS spreads. Specifically, we first investigate the existence of cointegration relationships using the ARDL bounds test approach and then employ the DOLS method to analyze to what extent each determinant influences the U.S. sovereign CDS spread.

Our first step, the ARDL bounds test, involves estimating the conditional error correction models (ECMs) for the U.S. sovereign CDS spreads and the six determinants that might affect the sovereign CDS spreads:

Model 1 (constant and no trend)

$$\begin{aligned} \Delta SOVCDS_t = {} & \alpha_0 + \sum\nolimits_{i=1}^{p} \theta_{1i} \Delta SOVCDS_{t-i} + \sum\nolimits_{l=0}^{p} \theta_{2i} \Delta BNKCDS_{t-i} \\ & + \sum\nolimits_{i=0}^{p} \theta_{3i} \Delta STKRTN_{t-i} + \sum\nolimits_{i=0}^{p} \theta_{4i} \Delta VIX_{t-i} + \sum\nolimits_{i=0}^{p} \theta_{5i} \Delta TED_{t-i} \\ & + \sum\nolimits_{i=0}^{p} \theta_{6i} \Delta SLOPE_{t-i} + \sum\nolimits_{i=0}^{p} \theta_{7i} \Delta SPREAD_{t-i} + \delta_1 SOVCDS_{t-1} \\ & + \delta_2 BNKCDS_{t-1} + \delta_3 STKRTN_{t-1} + \delta_4 VIX_{t-1} + \delta_5 TED_{t-1} \\ & + \delta_6 SLOPE_{t-1} + \delta_7 SPREAD_{t-1} + \varepsilon_t, \end{aligned} \tag{2.1}$$

Model 2 (constant and trend)

$$\begin{aligned} \Delta SOVCDS_t = {} & \alpha_0 + \gamma_0 t + \sum\nolimits_{i=1}^{p} \theta_{1i} \Delta SOVCDS_{t-i} \\ & + \sum\nolimits_{i=0}^{p} \theta_{2i} \Delta BNKCDS_{t-i} + \sum\nolimits_{i=0}^{p} \theta_{3i} \Delta STKRTN_{t-i} \\ & + \sum\nolimits_{i=0}^{p} \theta_{4i} \Delta VIX_{t-i} + \sum\nolimits_{i=0}^{p} \theta_{5i} \Delta TED_{t-i} + \sum\nolimits_{i=0}^{p} \theta_{6i} \Delta SLOPE_{t-i} \\ & + \sum\nolimits_{i=0}^{p} \theta_{7i} \Delta SPREAD_{t-i} + \delta_1 SOVCDS_{t-1} + \delta_2 BNKCDS_{t-1} \\ & + \delta_3 STKRTN_{t-1} + \delta_4 VIX_{t-1} + \delta_5 TED_{t-1} + \delta_6 SLOPE_{t-1} \\ & + \delta_7 SPREAD_{t-1} + \varepsilon_t \end{aligned} \tag{2.2}$$

In these equations, *SOVCDS* is the natural logarithm of the U.S. sovereign CDS spread, *BNKCDS* is the natural logarithm of the U.S. bank sector CDS spread, *STKRTN* is the log return of the Dow Jones Industrial Average, *VIX* is the natural logarithm of the implied volatility of the U.S. stock market return from the Chicago Board Options Exchange, *TED* is the TED spread

Table 2.1 Description of the variables

Variable	*Type*	*Description*
SOVCDS	Dependent	Natural logarithm of the U.S. sovereign CDS
BNKCDS	Explanatory	Natural logarithm of the U.S. bank sector CDS
STKRTN	Explanatory	Log return of the Dow Jones Industrial Average
VIX	Explanatory	CBOE Volatility; natural logarithm of the implied volatility of the U.S. stock market return from the Chicago Board Options Exchange
TED	Explanatory	Difference between the USD three-month LIBOR minus the U.S. three-month Treasury Bill rate
SLOPE	Explanatory	Difference between the U.S. 30-year Treasury Bond yield minus the U.S. 2-year Treasury Bond yield
SPREAD	Explanatory	Difference between the U.S. BAA and AAA corporate bond yields

(difference between the USD three-month LIBOR minus the U.S. three-month Treasury Bill rate), *SLOPE* is the slope of the yield curve (difference between the U.S. 30-year Treasury Bond yield minus the U.S. 2-year Treasury Bond yield), *SPREAD* is the spread of the corporate bonds (difference between the U.S. BAA and AAA corporate bond yields), α_0 is the drift component, γ_0 is the time trend component, Δ is the first-difference operator, p is the optimal lag length, and ε_t is the disturbance term. Detailed descriptions of each variable are shown in Table 2.1. We test for the presence of a long-term cointegrating relationship using two statistical tests: an F-test on the joint significance of the lagged level variables (H_0: $\delta_1 = \delta_2 = \delta_3 = \delta_4 = \delta_5 = \delta_6 = \delta_7 = 0$) and a t-test on the significance of the lagged level dependent variables (H_0: $\delta_1 = 0$). The test employs two asymptotic critical value bonds, depending on the unit root properties of the variables (i.e., $I(0)$, $I(1)$, or a mixture of both). A long-run relationship exists if the test statistics exceed their upper critical values, but we cannot reject the null hypothesis of no cointegration if the test statistics are below the lower critical values. If they fall between the bounds, inference would be not conclusive.

If the presence of cointegration is detected, we proceed to the second step, that is, estimating the following regressions using the DOLS method:

Model 1 (constant and no trend)

$$\begin{aligned} SOVCDS_t = \beta_0 &+ \varphi_1 BNKCDS_t + \varphi_2 STKRTN_t + \varphi_3 VIX_t \\ &+ \varphi_4 TED_t + \varphi_5 SLOPE_t + \varphi_6 SPREAD_t + \varphi_7 Dummy \\ &+ \sum\nolimits_{i=-K}^{K} \eta_{1i} \Delta BNKCDS_{t-i} + \sum\nolimits_{i=-K}^{K} \eta_{2i} \Delta STKRTN_{t-i} \\ &+ \sum\nolimits_{i=-K}^{K} \eta_{3i} \Delta VIX_{t-i} + \sum\nolimits_{i=-K}^{K} \eta_{4i} \Delta TED_{t-i} \\ &+ \sum\nolimits_{i=-K}^{K} \eta_{5i} \Delta SLOPE_{t-i} + \sum\nolimits_{i=-K}^{K} \eta_{6i} \Delta SPREAD_{t-i} + \varepsilon_t, \end{aligned} \tag{2.3}$$

Model 2 (constant and trend)

$$
\begin{aligned}
SOVCDS_t = {} & \beta_0 + \gamma_0 t + \varphi_1 BNKCDS_t + \varphi_2 STKRTN_t + \varphi_3 VIX_t \\
& + \varphi_4 TED_t + \varphi_5 SLOPE_t + \varphi_6 SPREAD_t + \varphi_7 Dummy \\
& + \sum_{i=-K}^{K} \eta_{1i} \Delta BNKCDS_{t-i} + \sum_{i=-K}^{K} \eta_{2i} \Delta STKRTN_{t-i} \\
& + \sum_{i=-K}^{K} \eta_{3i} \Delta VIX_{t-1} + \sum_{i=-K}^{K} \eta_{4i} \Delta TED_{t-1} \\
& + \sum_{i=-K}^{K} \eta_{5i} \Delta SLOPE_{t-1} + \sum_{i=-K}^{K} \eta_{6i} \Delta SPREAD_{t-1} + \varepsilon_t .
\end{aligned}
\tag{2.4}
$$

where K is the order of leads and lags for differenced regressors. Here, note that we include *Dummy*, a dummy variable that incorporates the potential impact of a structural break and that takes the value of 1 after the Lehman Brothers collapse on September 15, 2009, and 0 otherwise.

2.3 Data

We employ the daily data from January 1, 2008, to December 30, 2016. The starting date of the dataset is constrained by the availability of the U.S. sovereign CDS spread in our data source, Datastream. We include the U.S. bank sector CDS index as an explanatory variable to capture the default risks of the country's banking system, considering the potential negative effects of bank bailouts by the government on prospects of the country's public finance and thus its sovereign default risks. The other explanatory variables are such financial variables as the stock index return; the VIX, which reflects the market expectations of volatility; the TED spread, which is an indicator of the market assessment of liquidity risk; the slope of the yield curve; and the corporate bond spread, which captures corporate credit risks. These variables are typically included in previous studies analyzing the determinants of sovereign CDS (e.g., Eyssell et al., 2013). With regard to the U.S. sovereign CDS and bank sector CDS data, we select the five-year CDS spreads, because those instruments are the most liquid. Table 2.2

Table 2.2 Summary statistics

Variable	*Mean*	*Max.*	*Min.*	*Std. Dev.*	*Skewness*	*Kurtosis*	*Jarque–Bera*
SOVCDS	3.0264	4.4998	1.7918	0.5348	−0.1840	3.1312	14.91***
BNKCDS	4.6742	6.1072	3.9392	0.4759	0.3338	2.1136	120.30***
STKRTN	0.0002	0.1051	−0.0820	0.0122	−0.0670	13.3093	10386.38***
VIX	2.9664	4.3927	2.3341	0.3785	1.0164	3.8206	469.54***
TED	0.4482	4.5788	0.0876	0.4996	3.6901	20.9245	36714.27***
SLOPE	2.7827	4.0300	1.3752	0.6573	−0.0535	1.9504	108.77***
SPREAD	1.2130	3.5000	0.5300	0.5592	2.2349	8.1435	4536.98***

Notes: Statistics on the daily data for each variable are reported.

*** denotes statistical significance at the 1% level.

reports the descriptive statistics for the dataset. It is notable that the Jarque–Bera test indicates that the null hypothesis of a normal distribution is rejected for all the variables concerned at the 1 percent significance level.

Since the ARDL bound test cannot be applied when the *I*(2) series exist in the variables concerned, we carry out the Augmented Dickey–Fuller (ADF) and the Phillips–Perron (PP) unit root tests. Table 2.3 presents the results from the tests with two sets of assumptions (with a constant and no trend component, and with a constant and trend component). As reported in Table 2.3, our inference on the order of integration for each variable indicates that all the variables are either *I*(0) or *I*(1), although these two tests produce results that are slightly different from each other. This finding is also important because it validates

Table 2.3 Results of the ADF and PP unit root tests

Variable	*ADF test statistics*		*PP test statistics*	
	Constant	*Constant and trend*	*Constant*	*Constant and trend*
SOVCDS	-3.1782**	-3.3376	-3.1589**	-3.3194
ΔSOVCDS	-40.2542***	-40.2527***	-62.8472***	-62.8616***
BNKCDS	-1.8936	-3.2234	-1.9109	-3.6416**
ΔBNKCDS	-25.6792***	-25.6741***	-44.7054***	-44.7000***
STKRTN	-38.2717***	-38.3027***	-54.0215***	-54.1332***
ΔSTKRTN	-21.8710***	-21.8665***	-561.2590***	-561.1387***
VIX	-4.2538***	-5.7646***	-3.8264***	-5.4796***
ΔVIX	-52.7667***	-52.7555***	-58.2108***	-58.1978***
TED	-2.9191**	-3.0863	-3.2682**	-3.3080
ΔTED	-12.3652***	-12.3747***	-36.3727***	-36.3650***
SLOPE	-2.2724	-3.2869	-2.1860	-3.2342
ΔSLOPE	-49.3400***	-49.3788***	-49.4704***	-49.5395***
SPREAD	-1.6671	-2.1951	-1.7306	-2.2731
ΔSPREAD	-15.6205***	-15.6240***	-55.2718***	-55.2520***
Inference on integration based on the above tests				
SOVCDS	I(0)	I(1)	I(0)	I(1)
BNKCDS	I(1)	I(1)	I(1)	I(0)
STKRTN	I(0)	I(0)	I(0)	I(0)
VIX	I(0)	I(0)	I(0)	I(0)
TED	I(1)	I(0)	I(1)	I(0)
SLOPE	I(1)	I(1)	I(1)	I(1)
SPREAD	I(1)	I(1)	I(1)	I(1)

Notes: The results of the Augmented Dickey–Fuller (ADF) and Phillips–Perron (PP) unit root tests are reported. The unit root hypothesis in which the regression contains a constant and no trend component, and a constant and trend component, are tested.

*** and ** denote statistical significance at the 1% and 5% levels, respectively.

Table 2.4 Results of the unit root tests with a structural break

Variable	*Test statistics*	*Structural break point*
SOVCDS	-6.7017***	2008/10/6
ΔSOVCDS	-14.0314***	2008/12/4
BNKCDS	-4.1995	2011/5/31
ΔBNKCDS	-15.6385***	2008/8/1
STKRTN	-13.4704***	2009/3/5
ΔSTKRTN	-17.3866***	2008/10/9
VIX	-5.3411**	2009/3/9
ΔVIX	-53.4257***	2015/8/24
TED	-7.4907***	2008/10/10
ΔTED	-16.9869***	2008/10/10
SLOPE	-4.4275	2008/12/26
ΔSLOPE	-9.7647***	2008/2/14
SPREAD	-6.7824***	2009/4/13
ΔSPREAD	-18.2252***	2008/10/17

Notes: The results of the unit root tests allowing for a structural break in the intercept and trend based on Perron (1989) are reported. The table indicates that SOVCDS, STKRTN, VIX, TED, and SPREAD are stationary at level, while BNKCDS and SLOPE are only stationary in first-differences.

*** and ** denote statistical significance at the 1% and 5% levels, respectively.

our choice of the ARDL bounds test approach, which is applicable even when the regressors are a mixture of $I(0)$ and $I(1)$.

However, Perron (1989) suggests that conventional unit root tests such as the ADF and PP tests may be biased toward a false unit root null, if the data are trend stationary with a structural break. Hence, we also conduct the unit root test allowing for a structural change in the intercept and the trend based on Perron (1989). The results of the test are reported in Table 2.4. We find that SOVCDS, STKRTN, VIX, TED, and SPREAD are stationary at level, while BNKCDS and SLOPE are only stationary in first-differences. It should be also noteworthy that structural break points identified through the unit root tests in most cases seem to be concentrated between August and October 2008, which corresponds to the timing of the Lehman Brothers collapse.[5] These results provide additional support for our application of the ARDL bounds test, given the presence of a mixture of $I(0)$ and $I(1)$ variables even in consideration of structural breaks.

2.4 Empirical results

ARDL cointegration tests

First, we employ the ARDL bounds test approach to investigate whether there is a cointegrating relationship between the U.S. sovereign CDS spread and its six potential determinants. To derive the optimal number of lags for the conditional

Table 2.5 Results of the ARDL cointegration tests

Model type	*F-statistic*	*1% lower bound*	*1% upper bound*	*t-statistic*
Model 1 (constant)	8.6104***	3.1500	4.4300	–2.5846***
Model 2 (constant and trend)	10.2708***	3.6000	4.9000	–3.8739***

Notes: The first column denotes the models with an intercept and no trend (Model 1) and with an intercept and a trend (Model 2). The second column indicates the results of an *F*-test on the joint null hypothesis that the coefficients on level variables are jointly equal to zero. The third and fourth columns include critical values of the *F*-statistic from Pesaran et al. (2001) for the lower and upper bounds at the 1% level. The fifth column indicates the results of a *t*-test on the null hypothesis that the coefficient on SOVCDS(–1) is equal to zero.

*** denotes statistical significance at the 1% level.

ECM, we use the Schwarz-Baysian criteria, ensuring that no evidence of serial correlation is identified. Table 2.5 indicates the results of the ARDL cointegration tests for both Model 1 (with constant and no trend) and Model 2 (with constant and trend). For both models, the values of the *F*-statistics and *t*-statistics show that the null hypothesis of no cointegration relationship is rejected, and hence, that there is a long-run relationship between the variables.

DOLS estimation

Now that the presence of a cointegrating relationship is confirmed, we carry out the DOLS estimation developed by Stock and Watson (1993). The main advantage of this methodology is that it allows for variables to be integrated in different orders and hence is suitable for analyzing the effects of key determinants, which consist of a mixture of $I(0)$ and $I(1)$ variables, on the sovereign CDS in our analysis. Furthermore, the DOLS method can correct for the endogeneity issue that may arise between regressors, as it includes several leads and lags of first-differences of the regressors. Here, we set K to be between 1 and 5 to see the sensitivity around the orders of leads and lags.

We can derive three key findings from the results of the DOLS estimation, which are reported in Table 2.6. First and foremost, the estimation results reveal a positive and significant relationship between SOVCDS and BNKCDS for both Model 1 and Model 2 and for both orders of leads and lags (i.e., $K = 1$ and $K = 5$). This finding may imply subtle linkages of credit risks between the bank sector and public debt. On one hand, a deteriorated credit quality of the bank sector of an economy leads the government to finance a bailout of troubled banks, resulting in fiscal imbalances. On the other hand, the increases in sovereign credit risks may provide negative feedback effects on the bank sector because of guarantees and holdings of sovereign bonds by the bank sector. While previous studies such as that by Acharya et al. (2011) touch upon the relationship between sovereign CDS spreads and a portfolio of single-name CDS spreads of several banks, our finding suggests that the credit risks of the bank

Table 2.6 Results of the dynamic OLS estimation

Orders of leads and lags	*K = 1*			*K = 5*		
Variable	*Estimate*	*SE*	*p-value*	*Estimate*	*SE*	*p-value*
Model 1 (constant)						
Constant	−0.9230***	0.2537	0.0003	−1.1382***	0.2570	0.0000
BNKCDS	0.4474***	0.0563	0.0000	0.5176***	0.0561	0.0000
STKRTN	−1.0070	4.5954	0.8266	−0.0195	8.3761	0.5491
VIX	0.0011	0.0884	0.9902	−0.0324	0.0931	0.7276
TED	−0.1373**	0.0587	0.0194	−0.0508	0.0682	0.4565
SLOPE	0.1539***	0.0323	0.0000	0.1471***	0.0320	0.0000
SPREAD	0.2568***	0.0633	0.0001	0.1648**	0.0696	0.0180
Dummy	1.2751***	0.0789	0.0000	1.3585***	0.0804	0.0000
Adjusted R-squared	0.7186			0.7447		
Model 2 (constant and trend)						
Constant	−0.4810	0.4492	0.2844	−0.6666	0.4555	0.1435
Trend	−0.0001	0.0001	0.2340	−0.0001	0.0001	0.2109
BNKCDS	0.4137***	0.0629	0.0000	0.4834***	0.0622	0.0000
STKRTN	−0.8081	4.5837	0.8601	−4.5523	8.3482	0.5856
VIX	−0.0289	0.0916	0.7522	−0.0699	0.0974	0.4732
TED	−0.1457**	0.0590	0.0135	−0.0591	0.0683	0.3871
SLOPE	0.0999*	0.0557	0.0730	0.0909*	0.0551	0.0991
SPREAD	0.2309***	0.0667	0.0005	0.1404*	0.0720	0.0512
Dummy	1.3858***	0.1218	0.0000	1.4726***	0.1213	0.0000
Adjusted R-squared	0.7198			0.7460		

Notes: The results of the dynamic OLS estimation by Stock and Watson (1993) with orders of 1 and 5 leads and lags are reported, respectively. SE denotes the standard errors adjusted by using the Newey–West (1987) method.

***, **, and * denote statistical significance at the 1%, 5%, and 10% levels, respectively.

sector collectively reflected in the U.S. bank sector CDS index are positively associated with the sovereign default risks of the country. Second, other conventional financial variables such as TED, SLOPE, and SPREAD exhibit significant relationships with SOVCDS in some models or some orders of leads and lags, but not necessarily in all cases, at the 5 percent significance level, indicating the lack of robustness of the relationships. This result further confirms our view that the bank sector CDS may be a more important determinant of sovereign CDS spreads in the U.S. Third, Dummy consistently has a positive and significant relationship with SOVCDS for both Model 1 and Model 2 and for both orders of leads and lags. This result intuitively makes sense because the outbreak of financial crises after the Lehman Brothers collapse may have led investors to call for a higher level of compensation for bearing sovereign credit risks, resulting in higher sovereign CDS spreads.

Our main findings may provide important implications for both traders and policymakers. Our empirical results imply that not only conventional financial variables such as TED, SLOPE, and SPREAD but also the credit risks of the bank sector can be key determinants of sovereign CDS spreads. In light of this, our findings suggest that the bank sector CDS index can provide traders with a useful instrument for managing their exposures to sovereign default risks in their portfolio. For policymakers, it is important to note that the positive and significant relationship between the sovereign CDS and the bank sector CDS was uncovered in the U.S., where treasury bonds were rather seen as safe haven assets during the financial turmoil and the sovereign default risk has not been keenly realized. Apparently, the U.S. has had different experiences from those of peripheral European countries in which the government bailout on the troubled bank sector resulted in sudden increases in sovereign default risks, and thus, a clear interconnectedness between public debt and the bank sector was observed with the advent of the European sovereign debt crisis. Our findings interestingly indicate that even in the U.S., the bank sector CDS index can become a leading indicator for policymakers to monitor in order to foresee sovereign creditworthiness and potential negative effects of the surge of sovereign CDS spreads on their economy.

2.5 Conclusion

In this chapter, we examined the factors that help us determine sovereign CDS spreads in the U.S. The sample period spans from January 1, 2008, to December 30, 2016. The variables we considered as potential determinants include several conventional variables such as the stock return, VIX, TED spread, slope of the yield curve, spread of the corporate bonds, and most notably, the U.S. bank sector CDS index. The ARDL bounds test approach was used to investigate the existence of a cointegrating relationship between the sovereign CDS spread and its determinants, and then Stock and Watson's (1993) DOLS method was employed to analyze how the determinants affect the sovereign CDS spreads.

Our results reveal the following three main findings: (i) There is a cointegration relationship between the sovereign CDS and the six key determinants. (ii) There is strong evidence that among the factors considered, the bank sector CDS is a key driving factor of the sovereign CDS, and the positive and significant relationship identified between the two implies the strong linkage between sovereign creditworthiness and the financial health of the bank sector. (iii) The dummy variable representing the occurrence of the Lehman Brothers collapse also has a positive and significant relationship with the sovereign CDS, suggesting its substantial impacts on the sovereign default risk of the U.S. Our empirical findings indicate that traders can use the bank sector CDS index as a tool for risk management, particularly regarding their exposures to credit risks associated with the sovereign CDS. Our findings also imply that policymakers should closely monitor the bank sector CDS index to understand the movement of the sovereign CDS spreads thoroughly and thus anticipate sovereign creditworthiness in the future.

Notes

1 See BIS (2015) for details of the CDS market statistics.
2 CDS contracts are traded synthetically in the relatively unregulated over-the-counter market, while the bond market trades physical bonds. Also, CDS markets are not constrained by limited supply, unlike bond markets.
3 VIX represents the implied volatility for the U.S. stock market return from the Chicago Board Options Exchange.
4 Fiscal space is defined as the ratio of the public debt divided by the tax base.
5 Lehman Brothers filed for bankruptcy on September 15, 2008.

References

Acharya, V. V., Drechsler, I., and Schnabl, P. (2011) A pyrrhic victory? Bank bailouts and sovereign credit risk, *NBER Working Paper No. 17136.*

Aizenman, J., Hutchison, M., and Jinjarak, Y. (2013) What is the risk of European sovereign debt defaults? Fiscal space, CDS spreads and market pricing of risk, *Journal of International Money and Finance*, **34**, 37–59.

Aizenman, J., Jinjarak, Y., and Park, D. (2016) Fundamentals and sovereign risk of emerging markets, *Pacific Economic Review*, **21**, 151–177.

Avino, D. and Cotter, J. (2015) Sovereign and bank CDS spreads: Two sides of the same coin? *Journal of International Financial Markets, Institutions and Money*, **32**, 72–85.

Bank for International Settlements (2015) OTC derivatives statistics at end-June 2015, *Monetary and Economic Department*, November 2015.

Blommestein, H., Eijffinger, S., and Qian, Z. (2016) Regime-dependent determinants of Euro area sovereign CDS spreads, *Journal of Financial Stability*, **22**, 10–21.

Eyssell, T., Fung, H.-G., and Zhang, G. (2013) Determinants and price discovery of China sovereign credit default swaps, *China Economic Review*, **24**, 1–15.

Fender, I., Hayo, B., and Neuenkirch, M. (2012) Daily pricing of emerging market sovereign CDS before and during the global financial crisis, *Journal of Banking & Finance*, **36**, 2786–2794.

Ismailescu, I. and Kazemi, H. (2010) The reaction of emerging market credit default swap spreads to sovereign credit rating changes, *Journal of Banking & Finance*, **34**, 2861–2873.

Kallestrup, R., Lando, D., and Murgoci, A. (2016) Financial sector linkages and the dynamics of bank and sovereign credit spreads, *Journal of Empirical Finance*, **38**, 374–393.

Longstaff, F. A., Pan, J., Pedersen, L. H., and Singleton, K. J. (2011) How sovereign is sovereign credit risk? *American Economic Journal: Macroeconomics*, **3**, 75–103.

Newey, W. K. and West, K. D. (1987) A simple, positive semi-definite, heteroskedasticity and autocorrelation consistent covariance matrix, *Econometrica*, **55**, 703–708.

Perron, P. (1989) The great crash, the oil price shock and the unit root hypothesis, *Econometrica*, **57**, 1361–1401.

Pesaran, M. H., Shin, Y., and Smith, R. J. (2001) Bounds testing approaches to the analysis of level relationships, *Journal of Applied Econometrics*, **16**, 289–326.
Stock, J. H. and Watson, M. W. (1993) A simple estimator of cointegrating vectors in higher order integrated systems, *Econometrica*, **61**, 783–820.
Yuan, C. and Pongsiri, T. J. (2015) Fiscal austerity, growth prospects, and sovereign CDS spreads: The Eurozone and beyond, *International Economics*, **141**, 50–79.

3 Dynamic spillover among sovereign CDS spreads

3.1 Introduction

Southeast Asian countries, severely affected by the Asian financial crisis triggered in Thailand in 1997, had manifested signs of recovery in terms of their economic growth during the early to mid-2000s. Nevertheless, after the global credit crisis that originated in the U.S. mortgage market and, in particular, culminated with the bankruptcy of Lehman Brothers in September 2008, the countries did not find relief from the adverse impacts of the financial meltdown. Interestingly, the credit crisis amplified, spreading to several Southeast Asian countries whose direct exposures to the U.S. sub-prime mortgages were rather limited. In fact, after the Lehman shock, countries in the region, particularly Indonesia and the Philippines, not only experienced sharp devaluations of their local currencies against the U.S. dollar, but were also confronted with simultaneous increases in their sovereign credit default swaps[1].

Pan and Singleton (2008) demonstrated that, on some occasions, a substantial portion of the co-movement among the term structures of sovereign CDS spreads across countries is more likely to be triggered by changes in the appetites of market participants for credit risk exposure at a global level rather than by reassessments of the fundamental strengths of the countries concerned. Indeed, according to Kim et al. (2010), the amplification of the global financial crisis to Asia described above may have been largely caused by valuation losses that occurred globally because of the repricing of credit risks, triggered by the collapse of the credit bubble. Such spillovers of credit risks at a global or regional level may be of great concern for policymakers because of the possibility that the stability of their countries' financial system can be threatened and even impaired, regardless of the fundamental macroeconomic conditions. Thus, they may have a keen interest in monitoring the degrees and directions of cross-country spillovers. This understanding led us to investigate the specific question of how the linkages among the sovereign CDS markets in the Southeast Asian region actually changed over time.

Historically, not many studies have examined the interrelationships between sovereign CDS markets. However, that is changing now. Chen et al. (2011) applied the copula method to the sovereign CDS quotes of four Latin American nations and found that their dependence levels had increased. Moreover, the dependence structures were asymmetric during the financial turmoil. Conducting a dynamic conditional correlation (DCC) analysis for the CDS spreads of 38 countries with the U.S. market, Wang and Moore (2012) found a significant increase in the dynamic correlation after the Lehman collapse, particularly for developed countries. Kalbaska and Gatkowski (2012), who adopted the exponentially weighted moving average (EWMA) correlation analysis and the Granger causality test, identified the presence of contagion in the CDS markets of eight EU countries after the global financial crisis, with Spain and Ireland particularly triggering substantial impacts. Fong and Wong (2012) used the conditional value at risk (CoVAR) measure to analyze sovereign CDS data of 11 Eurozone countries, Japan, the U.S., and the U.K. They found that Greece had the highest conditional risk, followed by Portugal. Moreover, Greece exerted a larger spillover effect on Portugal and Ireland. Gorea and Radev (2014) investigated the default region of the distribution of sovereign CDS rates for 13 Euro-area nations and documented an increase in the joint probabilities of default after the Lehman Brothers collapse and the outbreak of the European debt crisis.

In the present chapter, we analyze the dynamic interrelationships among the sovereign CDS spreads of four ASEAN (Association of Southeast Asian Nations) countries, namely, Indonesia, Malaysia, the Philippines, and Thailand, during the sample period between 2005 and 2010. Our contributions to the literature are twofold. First, to the best of our knowledge, we are among the first to examine spillover effects across sovereign CDS rates, with particular emphasis on Southeast Asia. Although much research has been conducted on financial market integration in ASEAN countries with regard to equity markets (e.g., Azman-Saini et al., 2002; Click and Plummer, 2005), bond markets (e.g., Plummer and Click, 2005), and currency markets (e.g., Hurley and Santos, 2001), little is known about how shocks on sovereign risks are transmitted to the burgeoning sovereign CDS markets in the region, which are more liquid than the underlying government bond markets. Our study attempts to fill this gap.

Second, the easily interpretable spillover measures proposed by Diebold and Yilmaz (2012) allow a clear view on the directions and degrees of spillovers among the CDS spreads over time, and identify the existence of contagion, specifically prior to and during the global financial crisis. This methodology is based on the variance decomposition analysis, which allows us to assess what proportion of the forecast error variance of one variable can be explained by shocks to other variables. Moreover, the method is superior to the model originally proposed by Diebold and Yilmaz (2009) in two aspects: (i) it does not depend on variable orderings, owing to the application of a generalized vector autoregression (VAR) approach, and (ii) it offers novel concepts of directional spillovers and net (directional) spillovers to detect whether the variables (markets) are transmitters or receivers of spillover effects at a specific point of time.

In summary, our estimation on the total spillover index reveals that, on average, a substantial portion of the forecast error variance is explained by cross-country spillovers among the four countries' sovereign CDS markets. Our rolling-window analysis documents the evidence of contagion, with the total spillover plot exhibiting bursts in August 2007 and October 2008, consistent with the episodes of the global credit crisis. Directional spillover plots indicate that substantial spillover effects exist between any pairs of the four nations in both directions, exhibiting their bidirectional nature. Net spillover plots suggest that Indonesia is a dominant transmitter of shocks, particularly during the crisis period. Furthermore, throughout the sample period, the Philippines is a net transmitter of spillovers, while Thailand and Malaysia are primarily net receivers.

The remainder of this chapter is organized as follows. Section 3.2 briefly describes the empirical method used in this study. Section 3.3 explains our dataset. Section 3.4 presents our empirical findings and their implications. Finally, Section 3.5 concludes.

3.2 Empirical methodology

In this paper, we adopt the model developed by Diebold and Yilmaz (2012) to investigate time-varying linkages among the Southeast Asian sovereign CDS spreads. Consider the following *p*th order *N*-variable vector autoregression (VAR):

$$r_t = \sum_{i=1}^{p} \Theta_i r_{t-i} + \varepsilon_t, \tag{3.1}$$

where $r_t = (r_1 t, \ldots, r_{Nt})$ is a vector of N endogenous variables, with each variable representing the first differences of each country's sovereign CDS spreads, Θ_i is an $N \times N$ parameter matrix, and $\varepsilon \sim (0, \Sigma)$ is a vector of independently and identically distributed disturbances. The moving average representation is provided by $r_t = \sum_{i=0}^{\infty} A_i \varepsilon_{t-i}$, where the $N \times N$ coefficient matrix A_i obeys $A_i = \Theta_1 A_{i-1} + \ldots + \Theta_p A_{i-p}$, with A_0 being an $N \times N$ identity matrix and $A_i = 0$ for $i < 0$. Diebold and Yilmaz (2012) utilized the generalized VAR approach of Koop et al. (1996) and Pesaran and Shin (1998) in order to derive variance decompositions that are invariant to the variable ordering. According to their method, the H-step-ahead forecast error variance decomposition can be defined as

$$\theta_{ij}^{g}(H) = \frac{\sigma_{jj}^{-1} \sum_{h=0}^{H-1} (e_i' A_h \Sigma e_j)^2}{\sum_{h=0}^{H-1} (e_i' A_h \Sigma A_h' e_i)}, \tag{3.2}$$

where Σ is the variance matrix of the error vector ε, σ_{jj} is the standard deviation of the error term for the *j*th equation, and e_i is the selection vector with 1 as the *i*th element and 0 otherwise. The sum of each row in the variance decomposition matrix does not equal one, because the shocks to each variable are not orthogonalized in the generalized VAR approach. Thus, each entry of the variance decomposition matrix is normalized by dividing by its row sum, so that

$$\tilde{\theta}_{ij}^{g}(H)=\frac{\theta_{ij}^{g}(H)}{\sum_{j=1}^{N}\theta_{ij}^{g}(H)}, \tag{3.3}$$

with $\sum_{j=1}^{N}\tilde{\theta}_{ij}^{g}(H)=1$ and $\sum_{i,j=1}^{N}\tilde{\theta}_{ij}^{g}(H)=N$ by construction. This leads us to define what Diebold and Yilmaz (2012) referred to as the *total spillover index*:

$$S^{g}(H)=\frac{\sum_{i,j=1,i\neq j}^{N}\tilde{\theta}_{ij}^{g}(H)}{\sum_{i,j=1}^{N}\tilde{\theta}_{ij}^{g}(H)}\times 100=\frac{\sum_{i,j=1,i\neq j}^{N}\tilde{\theta}_{ij}^{g}(H)}{N}\times 100. \tag{3.4}$$

Distilling the information from variance decompositions into a single value, the total spillover index measures the fraction of cross-country spillovers that are captured by the share of cross-country error variance relative to the total error variance. In this approach, we can derive the time-varying behavior of the spillover index using the rolling-window estimation technique.

Further, Diebold and Yilmaz (2012) developed the concept of *directional spillovers* to examine the spillover effects from or to a particular country. Specifically, the directional spillovers received by country i from all other countries j are defined as

$$S_{i\leftarrow j}^{g}(H)=\frac{\sum_{j=1,j\neq i}^{N}\tilde{\theta}_{ij}^{g}(H)}{\sum_{i,j=1}^{N}\tilde{\theta}_{ij}^{g}(H)}\times 100, \tag{3.5}$$

and the directional spillovers transmitted from country i to all other countries j are defined as

$$S_{i\to j}^{g}(H)=\frac{\sum_{j=1,j\neq i}^{N}\tilde{\theta}_{ji}^{g}(H)}{\sum_{i,j=1}^{N}\tilde{\theta}_{ji}^{g}(H)}\times 100. \tag{3.6}$$

Moreover, we subtract Equation (3.5) from Equation (3.6) to obtain the *net (directional) spillovers* from country i to all other countries j as follows:

$$S_{i}^{g}(H)=S_{i\to j}^{g}(H)-S_{i\leftarrow j}^{g}(H). \tag{3.7}$$

The concept of net spillovers enables us to analyze whether a particular country is a net receiver or transmitter of shocks.

3.3 Data

The data used in this study contain daily five-year[2] CDS spreads, quoted in basis points (b.p.), of the sovereign bonds of four Southeast Asian countries – Indonesia, Malaysia, the Philippines, and Thailand. The data are collected from CMA through Datastream over the sample period from January 3, 2005, to September 30, 2010. As the daily sovereign CDS data are known to be relatively scanty, we take the weekly series (i.e., end of Friday data points) to eliminate irregularities of daily CDS movements, which results in 299 observations. We chose the above four nations because they are among the original members of the ASEAN[3] and have established more developed local bond markets than other emerging countries in the region, such as Brunei Darussalam, Cambodia, Laos, Myanmar, and Vietnam; thus, they are suitable from the viewpoint of analyzing the interrelationships and contagions among sovereign CDS markets in the region. Our choices of both the beginning and ending dates are constrained by data availability, as CDS price data of reasonable quality are seldom available before 2004 for the selected nations. Furthermore, CMA stopped providing CDS data through Datastream from October 1, 2010, onwards.

Figure 3.1 provides a visual representation of the raw sovereign CDS data series for the four Southeast Asian nations. Note that the CDS spreads of the Philippines and Indonesia were at a higher level as compared to the other two countries even during 2005–2006, ranging from approximately 115 b.p. to 480 b.p. It is also notable that all the nations' CDS spreads simultaneously began to exhibit increasing trends since mid-2007 and showed bursts immediately after September 2008, when the American investment bank Lehman Brothers collapsed. In fact,

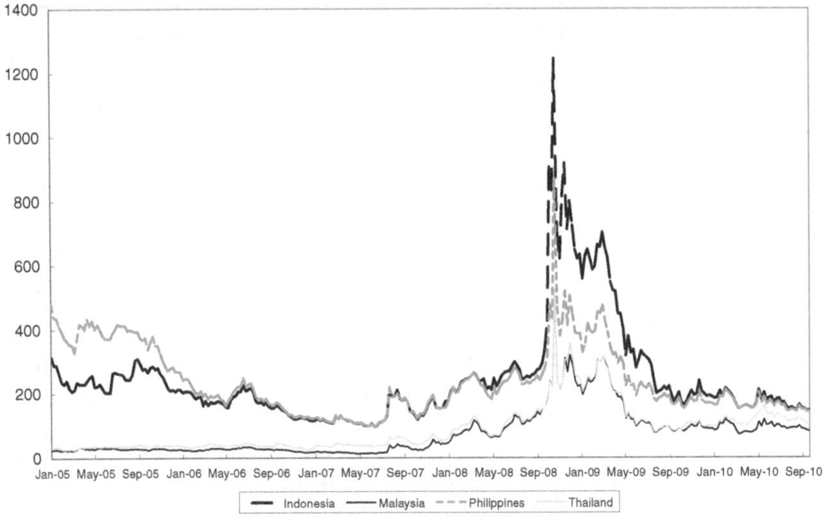

Figure 3.1 CDS spreads of the Southeast Asian countries

Notes: Time-varying paths of the level data for the CDS series are presented above.

such similar movements of the series among the four countries continued to be observed until the end of our sample period, September 30, 2010.

Table 3.1 displays key statistics of the weekly data for the CDS spreads. The highest value was observed for Indonesia (1245.00 b.p.), followed by the Philippines (870.00 b.p.). The volatility represented by the standard deviation is also largest for Indonesia (159.74). All the series are characterized by a positive value of skewness and a high value of kurtosis, suggesting deviations from normality assumptions. Indeed, the Jarque–Bera statistics indicate that the null hypothesis of a normal distribution is rejected at the 1 percent significance level. Before applying the VAR-based spillover method, we conduct the augmented Dickey–Fuller (ADF) and Phillips and Perron (PP) tests to check for the existence of the unit root. Table 3.2 reports the results of these tests. They show

Table 3.1 Summary statistics

Variable	*Mean (b.p.)*	*Maximum (b.p.)*	*Minimum (b.p.)*	*SD*	*Skewness*	*Kurtosis*	*Jarque–Bera statistics*
Indonesia	246.51	1245.00	96.90	159.74	2.70	11.54	1271.93***
Malaysia	75.52	520.20	12.00	72.22	2.10	8.97	664.33***
Philippines	236.97	870.00	97.00	108.27	1.33	5.90	192.42***
Thailand	88.41	524.20	24.20	71.13	2.05	8.84	634.43***

Notes: Statistics on weekly level data are reported.

*** denotes statistical significance at the 1% level.

Table 3.2 Results of the ADF and PP unit root tests

Variable	*ADF test statistics*		*PP test statistics*	
	constant	*constant and trend*	*constant*	*constant and trend*
Level data				
Indonesia	-2.072	-2.078	-2.361	-2.379
Malaysia	-1.645	-1.800	-1.999	-2.362
Philippines	-2.343	-2.292	-2.714	-2.681
Thailand	-1.771	-2.052	-2.105	-2.650
First-differenced data				
Indonesia	-11.153***	-11.150***	-31.939***	-31.926***
Malaysia	-9.544***	-9.548***	-30.231***	-30.240***
Philippines	-14.659***	-14.664***	-31.973***	-32.047***
Thailand	-15.817***	-15.815***	-31.251***	-31.250***

Notes: Results of the Augmented Dickey–Fuller (ADF) and Phillips–Perron (PP) unit root tests are reported. The unit root hypothesis in which the regression contains a constant and no deterministic components, and a constant and a trend are tested.

*** denotes statistical significance at the 1% level.

that the CDS series for all the four countries are I(1) variables. Therefore, we employ the first differences of the raw CDS data in our subsequent analysis.[4]

3.4 Empirical results

Spillover table

In Table 3.3, we present the spillover indices within and across the four countries' sovereign CDS spreads over the entire sample. The results are derived from 10-week ahead forecast error variance decompositions in our VAR model of order 2, where the order is selected based on the Bayesian–Schwarz information criterion (BIC). The *ij*th entry in this table represents the estimated contribution to the forecast error variance of country *i* arising from innovations to the CDS spreads of country *j*. The diagonal elements indicate own-country spillovers, whilst the off-diagonal elements represent cross-market spillover effects between the two countries. Moreover, the total spillover index reported in the lower right corner measures the fraction of all the cross-country spillovers over the sample.

According to Table 3.3, own-country spillovers occupy the highest share of forecast error variance, ranging from 25.3 percent for Thailand to 32.7 percent for Indonesia. Nonetheless, cross-country spillovers in the off-diagonal elements also play a major role in explaining the forecast error variance. For instance, innovations to the CDS spreads of Indonesia account for 24.6 percent, 26.7 percent, and 25.4 percent of the error variance in forecasting those of Malaysia, the Philippines, and Thailand, respectively. In fact, we find quite a high value of the total spillover index (71.8 percent), which implies that a large fraction of the forecast error variance is explained by cross-country spillovers. This indicates a high level of interconnectedness of sovereign default risks, an aspect policymakers in the region perhaps need to pay particular attention to. In addition, Table 3.3 shows that in terms of net spillover values reported in the last column, Indonesia and the Philippines are the primary transmitters of spillovers (9.4 percent and 1.4 percent, respectively), whilst Thailand and Malaysia are at the receiving ends of spillovers (–9.0 percent and –1.8 percent, respectively).

Table 3.3 Spillover table for the Southeast Asian CDS spreads

To (i) Sector	*From (j) Indonesia*	*Malaysia*	*Philippines*	*Thailand*	*Directional from others*
Indonesia	32.7	21.9	25.7	19.7	67.3
Malaysia	24.6	26.9	24.1	24.5	73.2
Philippines	26.7	23.7	28.1	21.5	71.9
Thailand	25.4	25.8	23.5	25.3	74.7
Directional to others	76.7	71.4	73.3	65.7	287.1
Directional including own	109.4	98.3	101.4	91.0	Total spillover index = 71.8%
Net spillovers	9.4	-1.8	1.4	-9.0	

The results are consistent with the fact that Indonesia and the Philippines exhibited higher means and higher volatilities in terms of the sovereign CDS spreads than Thailand and Malaysia throughout the sample period. Thus, sharp increases in the sovereign risks of the former countries were initially realized by market participants, which may have resulted in spillovers of the perceived risks to the latter countries, given the geographical proximity and strong linkages of the economies cultivated through regional free trade and investment activities.

Total spillover plot

Although we capture the average level of spillover indices over the entire sample in Table 3.3, the spillovers may vary substantially over time, because our sample includes the global financial crisis period. Therefore, in order to analyze the evolution of the spillovers among the sovereign CDS spreads over time, we conduct a rolling-window analysis using 50-week subsamples, and derive time-varying estimates of spillover indices. We then obtain the total spillover plot described in Figure 3.2.

Figure 3.2 indeed shows large fluctuations of the indices over time. Interestingly, the timings of bursts of the indices coincide with a couple of crucial incidences associated with the global financial crisis. Specifically, the indices exhibit sharp increases in early August 2007. At this time, BNP Paribas had announced that it would cease the activities of its hedge funds specializing in mortgage-backed securities. This event is usually regarded as the trigger for the outbreak of the global credit crisis. Moreover, another hike in the indices occurs around October 2008, immediately after Lehman Brothers filed for bankruptcy on September 15, 2008. After the peak, the indices remained high compared

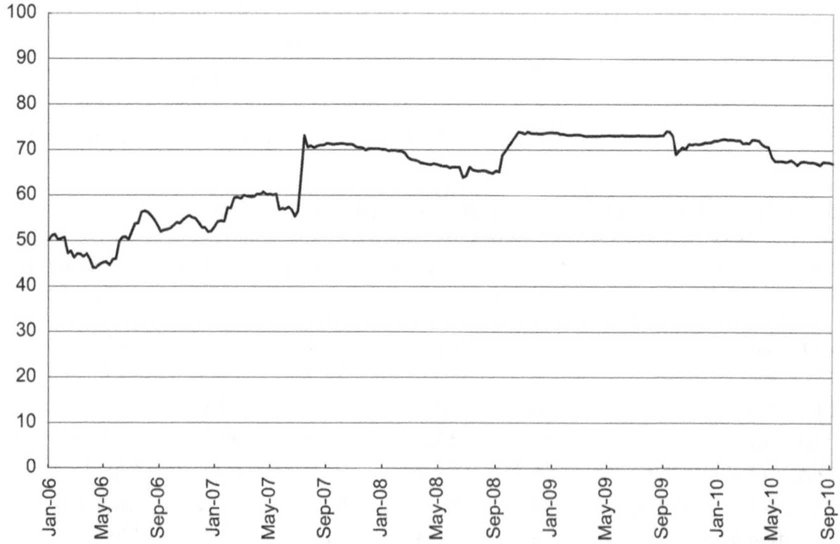

Figure 3.2 Total spillover plot (estimated using a 50-week rolling window)

to the pre-crisis period, ranging from approximately 65 percent to 75 percent. These results suggest the existence of contagion among the sovereign CDS markets of the ASEAN nations, primarily driven by the global credit crunch.

Directional spillover plots

Next, we focus on evaluating the spillover effects from or to a particular country. In this regard, we display the directional spillovers *from* each country (which correspond to $S^g_{i\to j}(H)$ in Equation (3.6)) in Figure 3.3 and the directional

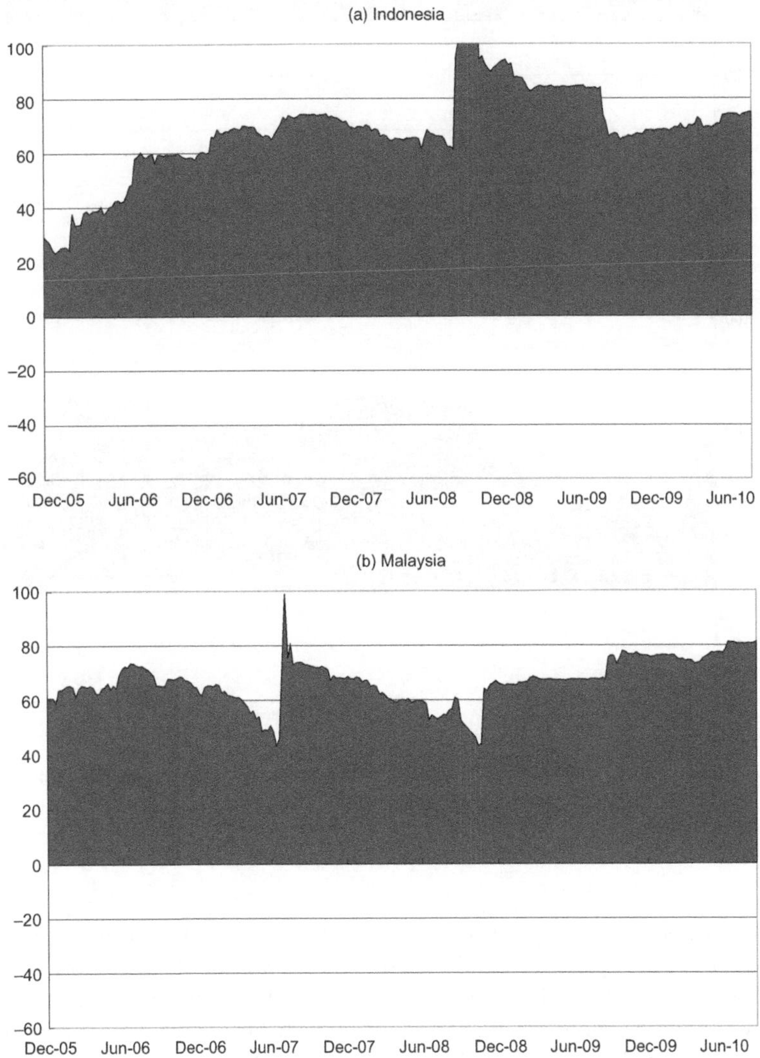

Figure 3.3 Directional spillovers from each country to other countries (estimated using a 50-week rolling window)

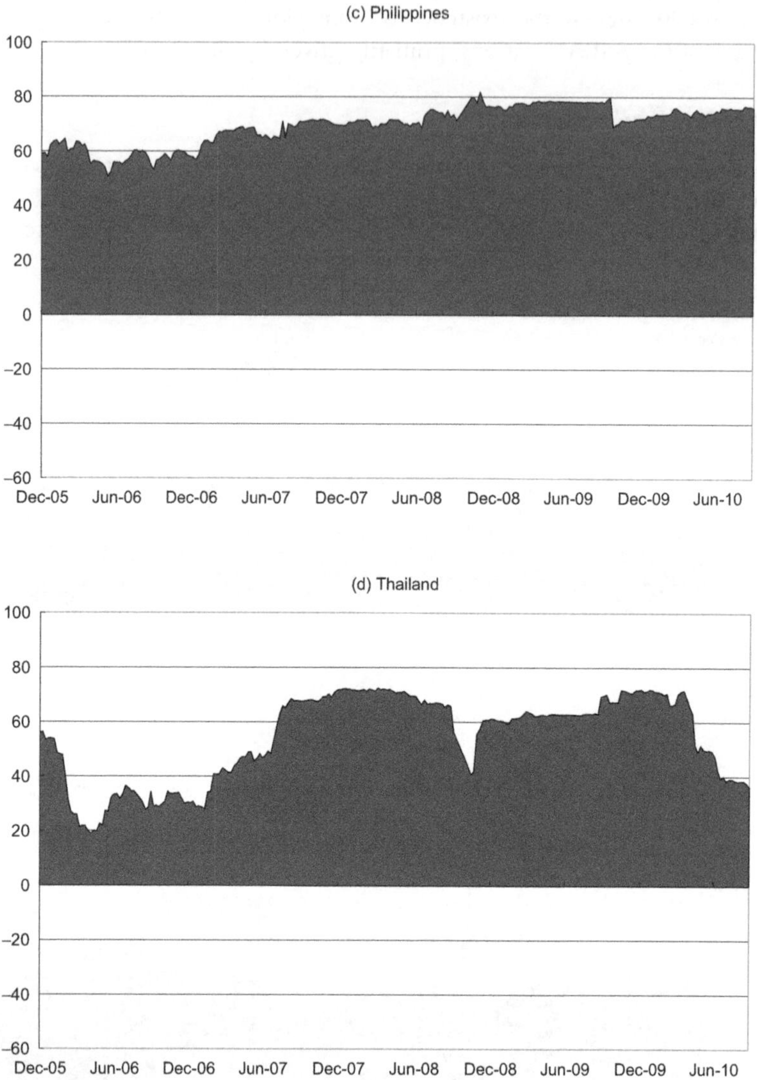

Figure 3.3 (Continued)

spillovers *to* each country (which correspond to $S^{g}_{i\leftarrow j}(H)$ in Equation (3.5)) in Figure 3.4. These plots are obtained using the 50-week rolling window analysis.

These figures show the bidirectional nature of the spillovers, namely spillovers in both directions, fluctuating at substantially high levels (i.e., at least above 20 percent) in the case of all the four countries. Notably, on most plots, the directional spillovers show visible increases in their levels, particularly after 2007.

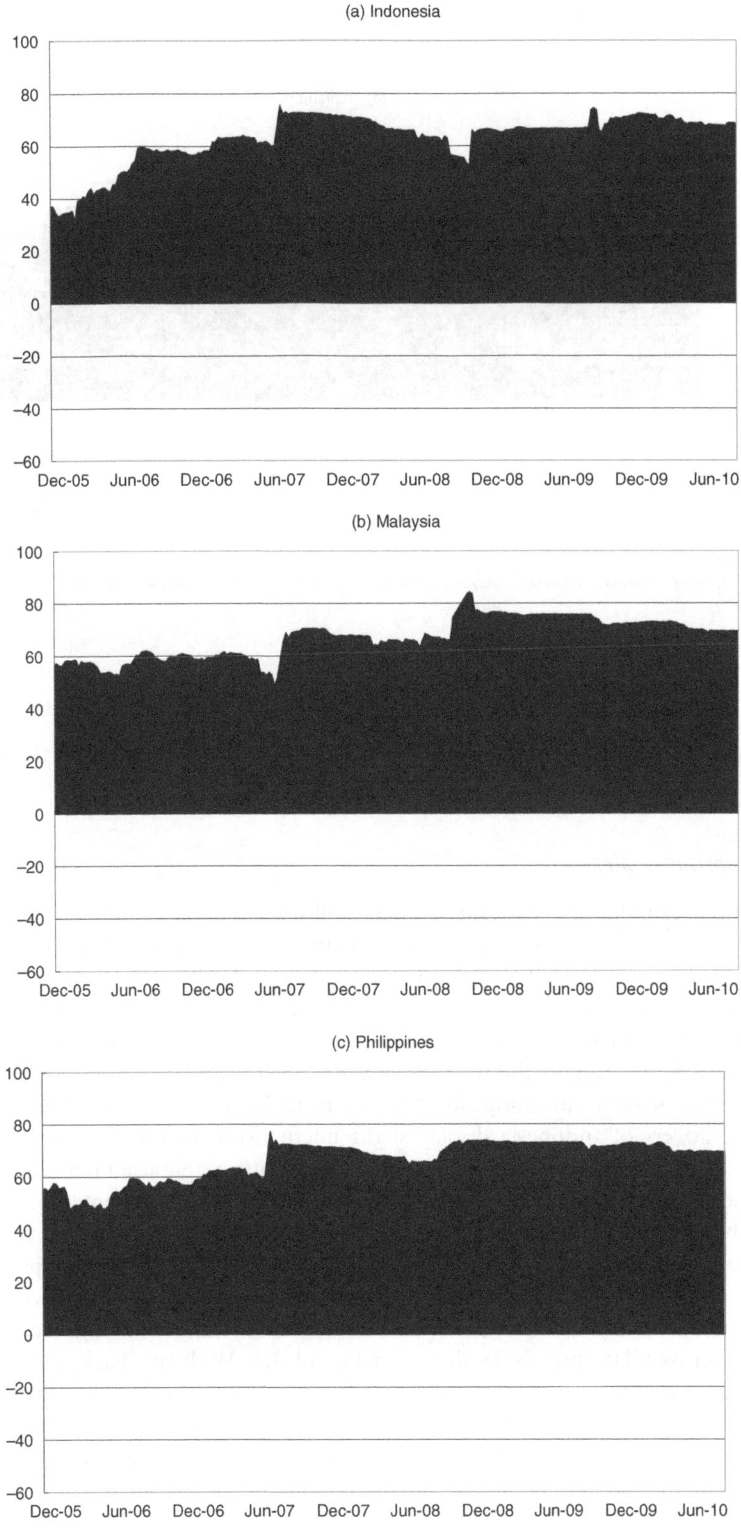

Figure 3.4 Directional spillovers from other countries to each country (estimated using a 50-week rolling window)

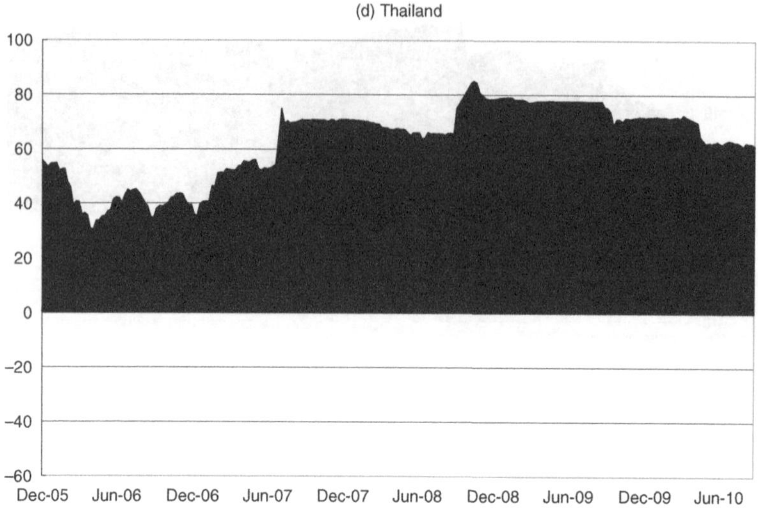

Figure 3.4 (Continued)

This provides further evidence for the existence of contagion among the sovereign CDS spreads in the region during the recent financial turmoil.

Net spillover plots

We then examine the net (directional) spillovers (corresponding to $S_i^g(H)$ in Equation (3.7)), namely the difference between the directional spillovers by a specific country transmitted to and received from all other countries concerned. A positive (negative) value of the net spillover indicates that the country is a net transmitter (receiver) of shocks in the CDS spreads at a point of time. In Figure 3.5, we present the time-varying net spillovers.

We find several intriguing observations from Figure 3.5. First, although the net spillovers of Indonesia display slight fluctuations for most of the periods, they exhibit sudden bursts, with the nation becoming a significant net transmitter of shocks only during the period between October 2008 and September 2009. Furthermore, Indonesia experienced a substantial devaluation of its nominal exchange rate against the U.S. dollar after the Lehman Brothers collapse. This resulted in soaring levels of external debt, and increased perceived concerns over the country's sovereign default risks, which may have triggered sharp spikes in its CDS spreads, as shown in Figure 3.1. With this background, it is not surprising to observe that Indonesia became a major source of transmission of shocks among the CDS spreads in the region, despite the relatively small size of its government debt market. Second, the Philippines has mostly been a net transmitter of shocks throughout the sample period, particularly the global financial crisis period. It is worthwhile to mention that the Philippines is similar to Indonesia, in that both have relatively high exposure to external debts in net terms. For instance, according to the statistics provided by the CEIC Global

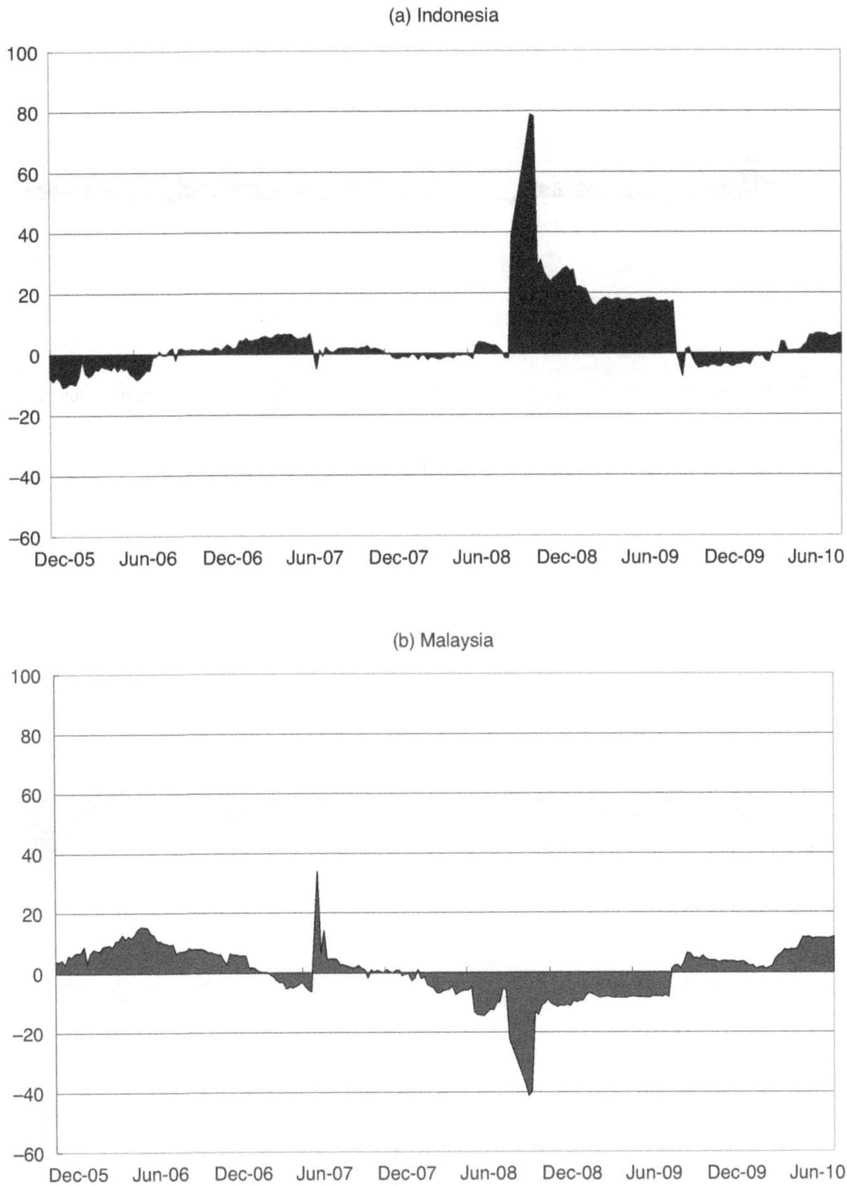

Figure 3.5 Net spillovers (estimated using a 50-week rolling window)

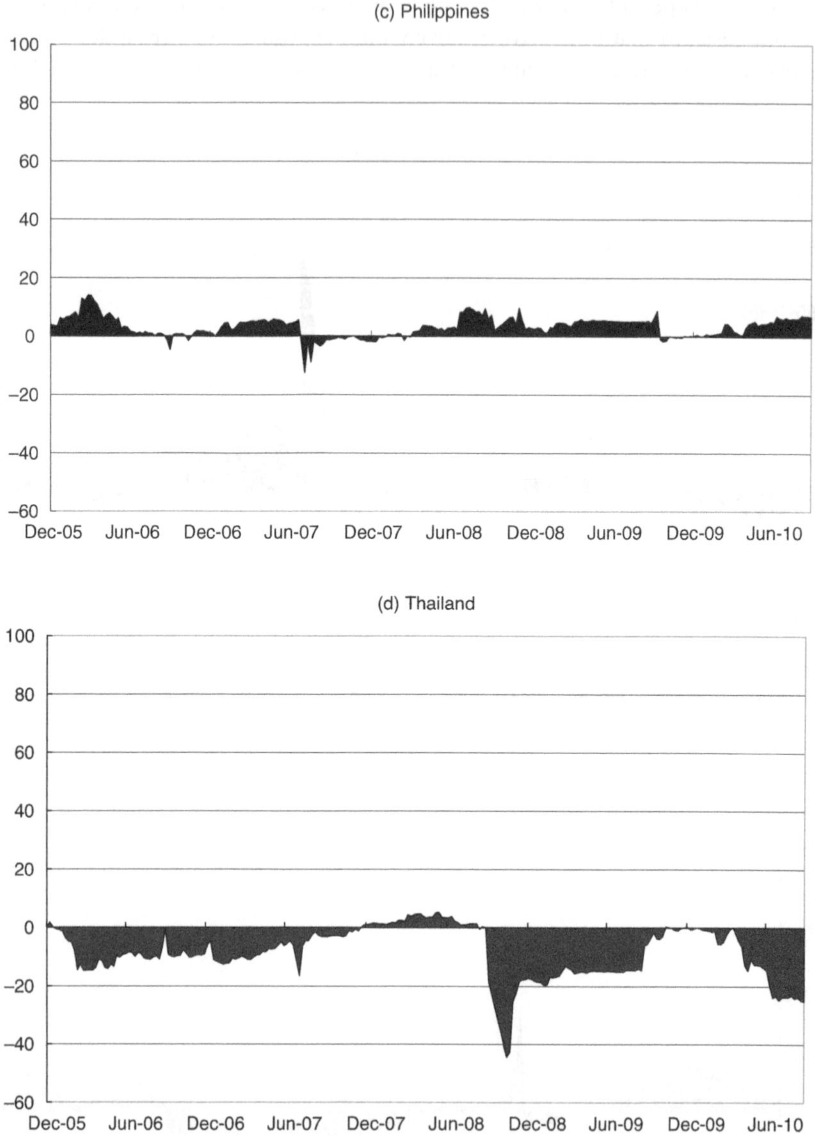

Figure 3.5 (Continued)

Database, the percentage of the net external asset over GDP for the Philippines in 2007 was −9.0 percent (compared to −21.3 percent for Indonesia, 6.7 percent for Malaysia, and 11.8 percent for Thailand).[5] Such dependence on external debt may have made the nation vulnerable to fluctuations in its sovereign CDS spreads, which in turn transmitted the shocks to other countries. Third and contrastively, Thailand and Malaysia have mostly been net receivers of shocks, particularly during the crisis period, having exerted little spillover effect on the CDS spreads in other countries. The results may imply that the two nations at the receiving ends should be cautious about the potential propagation of shocks from the credit risks of other nations in the region, regardless of their fundamental creditworthiness.

Discussion

The empirical results based on Diebold and Yilmaz's (2012) dynamic spillover indices clearly show how the shocks were spread over time among the sovereign CDS spreads of the Southeast Asian nations. Our findings can provide two primary implications to policymakers. First, our evidence of the increased total spillover indices, particularly during the market turbulences, suggests the existence of contagion in the sovereign CDS markets, highlighting the importance of spillovers as key determinants for the changes in a country's sovereign default risk. In particular, policymakers of countries such as Thailand and Malaysia, which were found to be the net receivers of shocks in the region, should make more efforts to prevent spillovers from the CDS spreads in neighboring nations, despite the sound macroeconomic fundamentals and the relatively high intrinsic creditworthiness of their own countries.

Second, our findings on the large fluctuations of the directional spillover indices from or to a particular country underline the importance of closely monitoring how the direction and degree of spillovers among the sovereign CDS markets change over time. Specifically, our results show that Indonesia, which had triggered a limited degree of spillovers to the CDS spreads of other nations, suddenly emerged as the most contagious nation in the region after the bankruptcy of Lehman Brothers. Furthermore, Malaysia, which had been a net transmitter of shocks prior to the crisis, turned into a net receiver, particularly after the Lehman Brothers collapse. These results imply that policy responses to minimize the adverse spillover effects among the sovereign CDS spreads should be as flexible as possible, based on the solid understanding of the time-varying nature of the transmissions of shocks.

Robustness check

In order to check the robustness of our empirical results, we carry out the following additional analyses: (i) in addition to a VAR lag of 2 assumed in our baseline model, we calculate the spillover tables with VAR lags of 1, 3, 4, and 5, respectively, and (ii) besides the 50-week forecast horizon in our baseline assumption, we compute the total spillover plot, directional spillover plots, and net spillover plots, employing 25-week, 75-week, and 100-week rolling windows, respectively. Although we do not report the empirical results to save space, we confirm that the results turn out to be qualitatively similar, and therefore our findings are robust to these modifications of the assumptions.

3.5 Conclusion

This article investigated the dynamic spillover effects among sovereign CDS spreads of four ASEAN countries (Indonesia, Malaysia, the Philippines, and Thailand) from 2005 to 2010, using the econometric model newly developed Diebold and Yilmaz (2012). The forecast error variance decompositions in a generalized VAR framework allowed us to derive the total spillover index, capturing all cross-country spillover effects as a single measure. Further, it allowed us to produce the total, directional, and net spillover plots to visualize the time-varying behaviors of the spillovers.

We summarize our main findings as follows. (i) Cross-country spillovers account for 71.8 percent of the forecast error variances among the four countries in the entire sample, thus revealing the importance of spillovers. (ii) The time-varying path of the total spillover index exhibits sharp increases at the timings of several events symbolizing the onset and deepening of the global financial crisis, indicating the existence of contagion. (iii) Directional spillover plots suggest the bidirectional nature of spillover effects among the CDS markets. (iv) Net spillover plots indicate that Indonesia, which had caused little spillover effect prior to the crisis, quickly became a dominant transmitter after the Lehman Brothers collapse. (v) The Philippines has consistently been a net transmitter of shocks, whilst Thailand and Malaysia have primarily been net receivers over the sample period.

Our findings are of great relevance for policymakers who are interested in preventing their countries' sovereign CDS markets from destabilization due to potential contagion, which might occur during market turbulences. This study presents a clear picture of how cross-country spillovers were transmitted among the countries concerned over time, prior to, and during the global financial crisis. However, it does not necessarily uncover the concrete channels through which the crisis, which originated in the U.S. subprime loan market, triggered the patterns of spillovers explained above among the Southeast Asian sovereign CDS markets. This topic will form the basis for future research.

Notes

1 See Stulz (2010) for a detailed review of the mechanics of CDS.
2 We select five-year CDS contracts because they are the most actively traded in the markets.
3 Unfortunately, Singapore – another original member of the ASEAN – is not included in our scope, owing to the lack of its sovereign CDS data availability in our data source. We also exclude the U.S., the origin of the global financial crisis, because the country's CDS data are available only for a limited time period (i.e., from December 11, 2007, to September 30, 2009).
4 We do not take log differences to express as percentage points, because the CDS spreads are already expressed in b.p. (i.e., one b.p. is equal to 0.01 percent.)
5 This calculation is based on the assumption that external debts include foreign investment in the form of equities, bonds, and loans, but exclude direct investment.

References

Azman-Saini, W. N. W., Azail, M., Habibullah, M. S., and Matthews, K. G. (2002) Financial integration and the ASEAN-5 equity markets, *Applied Economics*, **34**, 2283–2288.

Chen, Y. H., Wang, K., and Tu, A. H. (2011) Default correlation at the sovereign level: Evidence from some Latin American markets, *Applied Economics*, **43**, 1399–1411.

Click, R. W. and Plummer, M. G. (2005) Stock market integration in ASEAN after the Asian financial crisis, *Journal of Asian Economics*, **16**, 5–28.

Diebold, F. X. and Yilmaz, K. (2009) Measuring financial asset return and volatility spillovers, with application to global equity markets, *The Economic Journal*, **119**, 158–171.

Diebold, F. X. and Yilmaz, K. (2012) Better to give than to receive: Predictive directional measurement of volatility spillovers, *International Journal of Forecasting*, **28**, 57–66.

Fong, T. P. W. and Wong, A. Y. T. (2012) Gauging potential sovereign risk contagion in Europe, *Economics Letters*, **115**, 496–499.

Gorea, D. and Radev, D. (2014) The Euro area sovereign debt crisis: Can contagion spread from the periphery to the core? *International Review of Economics and Finance*, **30**, 78–100.

Hurley, D. T. and Santos, R. A. (2001) Exchange rate volatility and the role of regional currency linkages: The ASEAN case, *Applied Economics*, **33**, 1991–1999.

Kalbaska, A. and Gatkowski, M. (2012) Eurozone sovereign contagion: Evidence from the CDS market (2005–2010), *Journal of Economic Behavior and Organization*, **83**, 657–673.

Kim, D. H., Loretan, M., and Remolona, E. M. (2010) Contagion and risk premia in the amplification of crisis: Evidence from Asian names in the global CDS market, *Journal of Asian Economics*, **21**, 314–326.

Koop, G., Pesaran, M. H., and Potter, S. M. (1996) Impulse response analysis in nonlinear multivariate models, *Journal of Econometrics*, **74**, 119–147.

Pan, J. and Singleton, K. (2008) Default and recovery implicit in the term structure of sovereign CDS spreads, *Journal of Finance*, **63**, 2345–2384.

Pesaran, M. H. and Shin, Y. (1998) Generalized impulse response analysis in linear multivariate models, *Economics Letters*, **58**, 17–29.

Plummer, M. G. and Click, R. W. (2005) Bond market development and integration in ASEAN, *International Journal of Finance and Economics*, **10**, 133–142.

Stulz, R. (2010) Credit default swaps and the credit crisis, *Journal of Economic Perspectives*, **24**, 73–92.

Wang, P. and Moore, T. (2012) The integration of the credit default swap markets during the US subprime crisis: Dynamic correlation analysis, *Journal of International Financial Markets, Institutions and Money*, **22**, 1–15.

Part II

Sector-level CDS markets

4 Causality among financial sector CDS indices

4.1 Introduction

The 2007–2008 global financial crisis, which originated in the U.S. subprime mortgage market, immediately had devastating effects on the financial sectors in the country and then worldwide, as seen by the bankruptcy of Lehman Brothers, failure of Washington Mutual, and government bailout of AIG. As substantial concerns about the solvency of financial institutions were being raised in the aftermath of the credit crisis, many scholars began to pay attention to the growing issuance and trading of credit default swaps (CDS). On the one hand, as Stulz (2010) contends, CDS is a useful measure that contains important information on credit risks at their prices and a tool that enables such risks to be borne by the most suitable recipients. On the other hand, CDS is accused of serving as a trigger for the financial meltdown during the crisis. In fact, banks and other financial institutions were spurred to hold a vast amount of mortgage securities, which finally incurred large losses, by the regulations that allowed them to put forward less regulatory capital if the protection was bought with CDS.

In this study, we use daily data from January 1, 2004, to December 31, 2011, to examine the causality-in-mean and causality-in-variance among the CDS indices of three U.S. financial sectors,[1] namely banking, insurance, and financial services. Investigating the causal relationships among financial sector CDS indices at the sector level is worthy of scholarly attention because these indices are accurate measures of the credit risks of these three important sectors that, despite being subject to different regulations, are vital to sustain the health of financial markets.

Specifically, the findings of our analysis offer practical implications to traders and policymakers. For traders, knowing the lead-lag relationships among sector-level CDS indices would help them formulate not only their arbitrage and hedging strategies involving CDS but also their broader level of portfolio allocation based on a solid understanding of evolving credit risks in financial sectors. For policymakers, knowledge on the above-described causal relationships would allow them to understand contagions in financial sector CDS indices and consider the appropriate regulatory frameworks for different sectors.

Testing for causality-in-variance is as important as analyzing causality-in-mean because, as Ross (1989) argues, volatility is concerned with the extent to which market participants assimilate information. From this perspective, volatility in asset price changes contains important data on information transmission across markets. Engle et al. (1990) also support the view that volatility reflects the time market participants take to assimilate new information and call volatility spillover effects from one market to another "meteor showers." Given this theoretical importance of volatility, it is natural to investigate causality at the variance level as well, because our primary interest lies in extracting useful information about the transmission of risks as revealed in these three financial sector CDS indices.

Indeed, a recent proliferation of academic studies has analyzed the interrelationships among sovereign CDS spreads (e.g., Dooley and Hutchison, 2009; Wang and Moore, 2012) or CDS spreads at the individual firm or bank level (e.g., Kim et al., 2010; Eichengreen et al., 2012). However, only a few studies have focused on the relationships among financial sector CDS indices.

For example, Hammoudeh and Sari (2011) use the ARDL approach to investigate the dynamic relations among the three U.S. financial sector CDS indices examined herein (banking, insurance, and financial services), S&P 500 index, and Treasury securities rates. The authors find weaker cointegrating relationships among these variables during the global credit crisis compared with the entire study period. Their generalized variance decomposition and impulse response analyses also show that in the short run cross-shock effects are the highest within the three financial sector CDS indices, suggesting the existence of contagion.

By employing the momentum-threshold autoregression approach, Chen et al. (2011) examine the asymmetric behaviors of the same three U.S. financial sector CDS indices under the presence of a threshold effect and find the existence of asymmetric cointegration for all pairs of indices. Moreover, their results indicate that the speeds of adjustment to the long-term equilibrium are much faster during widenings than narrowings for all CDS index pairs, implying that market participants that use these indices become more active when facing negative events.

Moreover, Hammoudeh et al. (2013) apply vector error correction models to these three CDS indices. Their empirical results demonstrate that in terms of adjustment to the long-run equilibrium, insurance sector CDS is the highest, whereas banking sector CDS is not error correcting. In addition, they identify significant bidirectional linkages among the three indices and show that the strongest (weakest) impacts come from shocks in the banking (insurance) sector CDS index.

Finally, Arouri et al. (2014) explore the short- and long-run relationships among the three CDS indices by employing the smooth transition error-correction models (STECMs) in order to show whether there exist non-linearity and asymmetry in the adjustment process of the CDS indices to their long-run equilibrium, specifically. They find that the only two pairs of the three CDS indices (banking–financial services and banking–insurance) indicate the evidence of cointegration and their adjustment process to the long-run equilibrium can indeed be characterized by non-linearity and asymmetry.

Our study differs from these previous works by exploring short-term causality at both the variance and the mean levels. Methodologically, this paper employs the cross-correlation function (CCF) approach proposed by Hong (2001)[2] to assess volatility and mean spillovers, which has three main advantages. First, these tests make no distributional assumptions and therefore tend to show higher power than conventional Granger causality tests. Second, they do not rely on the simultaneous modeling of inter-series dynamics and thus are typically less complex than multivariate GARCH models. Third, Hong's (2001) tests overcome the weakness of Cheung and Ng's (1996) approach that relies on a counterintuitive assumption of weighting each lag uniformly. Nonetheless, the recent literature has pointed out that Hong's causality-in-variance tests may suffer from size distortion when there is a structural break in the variance series or when causality-in-mean effects are left unaccounted for. In this study, we address these issues by employing a state-of-the-art framework that includes implementing pre-tests for multiple structural breaks and incorporating the identified causality-in-mean effects into the causality-in-variance tests.

We organize the remainder of this paper as follows. Section 4.2 explains our empirical framework. Section 4.3 describes the data used in this study, and Section 4.4 reports the empirical results. Finally, our conclusions are provided in Section 4.5.

4.2 Empirical methodology

Hong's (2001) CCF methodology is an extension of the tests first proposed by Cheung and Ng (1996). While conventional Granger causality tests deal with only causality at the mean level, Cheung and Ng (1996) introduce the notion of causality-in-variance. Their test is described as follows. Suppose that X_t and Y_t are two stationary time series that follow the AR(k)-EGARCH(p,q) processes[3]:

$$\begin{cases} X_t = a_{X,0} + \sum_{i=1}^{k} a_{X,i} X_{t-i} + \varepsilon_{X,t} \\ \log(\sigma^2_{X,t}) = \omega_X + \sum_{i=1}^{q} (\alpha_{X,i} \, | z_{X,t-i} | + \gamma_{X,i} z_{X,t-i}) + \sum_{i=1}^{p} \beta_{X,i} \log(\sigma^2_{X,t-i}) \end{cases} \tag{4.1}$$

$$\begin{cases} Y_t = a_{Y,0} + \sum_{i=1}^{k} a_{Y,i} Y_{t-i} + \varepsilon_{Y,t} \\ \log(\sigma^2_{Y,t}) = \omega_Y + \sum_{i=1}^{q} (\alpha_{Y,i} \, | z_{Y,t-i} | + \gamma_{Y,i} z_{Y,t-i}) + \sum_{i=1}^{p} \beta_{Y,i} \log(\sigma^2_{Y,t-i}) \end{cases} \tag{4.2}$$

where $\varepsilon_{X,t}$ ($\varepsilon_{Y,t}$) is the error term with E_{t-1} ($\varepsilon_{X,t}$) = 0 (E_{t-1} ($\varepsilon_{Y,t}$) = 0) and $E_{t-1}(\varepsilon^2_{X,t}) = \sigma^2_{X,t}$ ($E_{t-1}(\varepsilon^2_{Y,t}) = \sigma^2_{Y,t}$). We assume that the random variables $z_{X,t} = \varepsilon_{X,t} / \sigma_{X,t}$ and $z_{Y,t} = \varepsilon_{Y,t} / \sigma_{Y,t}$ have a generalized error distribution. We select k (= 1, 2, . . ., 10), p (= 1, 2), and q (= 1, 2) on the basis of the Schwarz Bayesian information criterion. We then define two information sets by

$$I_t = \{X_{t-j}; j \geq 0\} \text{ and } J_t = \{X_{t-j}, Y_{t-j}; j \geq 0\} \tag{4.3}$$

Y_t is said to cause X_t in variance if

$$E[(X_t - \mu_{X,t})^2 \mid I_{t-1}] \neq E[(X_t - \mu_{X,t})^2 \mid J_{t-1}] \tag{4.4}$$

where $\mu_{X,t}$ represents the mean of X_t conditioned on I_t. Suppose that $h_{X,t}$ and $h_{Y,t}$ represent the conditional variances of the EGARCH(p,q) models; thus, we denote the squares of the standardized innovations by

$$u_t = (X_t - \mu_{X,t})^2 / h_{X,t} \tag{4.5}$$

$$v_t = (Y_t - \mu_{Y,t})^2 / h_{Y,t}. \tag{4.6}$$

Then, the S-statistic developed by Cheung and Ng (1996) to test for the null hypothesis of no causality-in-variance at the first M lag is calculated as

$$S = T\sum_{j=1}^{M} \hat{\rho}^2(j) \xrightarrow{L} \chi^2 \tag{4.7}$$

where

$$\hat{\rho}_{uv}(i) = \{\hat{c}_{uu}(0)\hat{c}_{vv}(0)\}^{-1/2}\hat{c}_{uv}(i) \tag{4.8}$$

$$\hat{c}_{uv}(j) = \begin{cases} T^{-1}\sum_{t=j+1}^{T} \hat{u}_t \hat{v}_{t-j} \text{ (for j} \geq 0\text{)} \\ T^{-1}\sum_{t=-j+1}^{T} \hat{u}_{t+j} \hat{v}_t \text{ (for j} < 0\text{)} \end{cases} \tag{4.9}$$

with $\hat{c}_{uu}(0)$ and $\hat{c}_{vv}(0)$ representing the sample variances of disturbances u_t and v_t.

A key drawback of the S-statistic is that it places equal weighting on each lag, with no differentiation between recent cross-correlations and distant ones. Hence, the S-statistic may be inefficient when M becomes large. Hong (2001) modifies the CCF approach by developing the following Q-statistic to overcome this shortcoming. Specifically, the Q-statistic employs a non-uniform kernel weighting function[4]

$$Q = \{T\sum_{j=1}^{T-1} k^2(j/M)\hat{\rho}_{uv}^2(j) - C_{1T}(k)\} / \{2D_{1T}(k)\}^{1/2} \tag{4.10}$$

where

$$C_{1T}(k) = \sum_{j=1}^{T-1}(1 - j/T)k^2(j/M) \tag{4.11}$$

$$D_{1T}(k) = \sum_{j=1}^{T-1}(1 - j/T)\{1 - (j+1)/T\}k^4(j/M) \tag{4.12}$$

$$k(z) = \begin{cases} 1, & |z| \leq 1 \\ 0, & otherwise. \end{cases} \tag{4.13}$$

Hong (2001) shows that $Q \to N(0,1)$ in distribution. The *Q*-statistic is a one-sided test. If the *Q*-statistic is larger than the critical values of the upper-tailed normal distribution, we reject the null hypothesis of no causality-in-variance during the first *M* lags.[5]

Despite its growing popularity, recent research has detected limitations in Hong's (2001) CCF approach. A major complication is pointed out by Van Dijk et al. (2005), who demonstrate that the causality-in-variance test is subject to severe size distortions if structural breaks exist in the variances of the time series of interest. Therefore, conducting pre-testing for structural breaks is recommended to overcome this drawback. In this regard, we test for volatility breaks by applying Bai and Perron's (1998, 2003) approach to the absolute values of the demeaned series. Bai and Perron's test enables us to estimate multiple structural changes endogenously and generalize specifications in terms of selecting heterogeneity and autocorrelation in the residuals.

The structural breaks in the variance are identified through the following equation:

$$\sqrt{\pi/2}\,|\hat{\varepsilon}_t| = c + u_t \tag{4.14}$$

where the left-hand side represents the unbiased estimators of the standard deviation of ε_t from the conditional mean equation. We employ a sequential application of the *Sup* FT$(k+1|k)$ statistics to identify $k+1$ breaks conditional on identifying k breaks and search for up to five breaks with a trimming parameter of 0.15.[6]

Further, Hong's test may suffer from size distortions when the existence of causality-in-mean effects is left unaccounted for, as Pantelidis and Pittis (2004) contend. Thus, the final step in our approach consists of eliminating causality-in-mean effects by including the lagged values[7] of the variable *X* in the conditional mean equation of another variable *Y* in cases when *X* is found to Granger-cause *Y*.

4.3 Data

Similar to the approach taken by Hammoudeh et al. (2013), we use daily data on five-year CDS indices[8] for the U.S. banking (BNK), insurance (INS), and financial services (FIN) sectors. Our data range from January 1, 2004, to December 31, 2011, and consist of 2,087 observations in total. They are retrieved from Datastream. The beginning of the period is constrained primarily by the availability of sector-level CDS index data.

Table 4.1 reports the descriptive statistics for our dataset. Note that the banking sector CDS index has a lower mean and standard deviation than those for the insurance and financial services sectors, which may reflect the fact that banks are more regulated than insurance and financial services institutions. The

Table 4.1 Summary statistics

Variable	*Mean (b.p.)*	*Maximum (b.p.)*	*Minimum (b.p.)*	*SD*	*Skewness*	*Kurtosis*	*Jarque–Bera*
BNK	94.925	595.986	10.200	85.342	1.197	4.689	746.135**
INS	345.878	3182.448	17.242	401.538	1.646	7.679	2846.309**
FIN	306.719	2015.214	21.360	355.134	1.516	4.939	1126.117**

Notes: Level data are presented for all the variables.

** denotes statistical significance at the 1% level.

positive skewness values for all three indices indicate that large increases are more likely than decreases. The high level of kurtosis shows that extreme changes in these indices tend to occur frequently, suggesting the existence of fat tails in the distribution. Furthermore, the Jarque–Bera tests reject normality for the series at the 1 percent significance level. We also conducted augmented Dickey–Fuller unit root tests with intercept and intercept plus trend for all CDS indices and found that they are I(1) variables.[9] Therefore, we used first-differenced data[10] in our subsequent analysis, in line with previous research on CDS indices.

4.4 Empirical results

We first fit univariate models to each data series by selecting the best of the AR(k)-EGARCH(p,q) models. Table 4.2 presents the estimates of the coefficients of each of the selected AR-EGARCH models. Based on our selection criteria, we chose the AR(2)-EGARCH(1,1) model for the insurance sector CDS index and AR(1)-EGARCH(1,1) models for the banking and financial services CDS indices. Notably, both the mean and the variance equations display good fits for all indices. In the mean equations, all the coefficients for the lagged terms are statistically significant at the 1 percent level. In the variance equations, all the parameters are significant at the 1 percent level as well. Moreover, the Ljung–Box statistics $Q(20)$ and $Q^2(20)$ indicate that we can accept the null hypothesis of no autocorrelation up to order 20 for the standard residuals and standard residuals squared. These results demonstrate the adequacy of our model specification.

Our next step is to use Hong's (2001) approach to test for the causality-in-mean effects among the three investigated financial sector CDS indices. Since this approach allows us to analyze only two variables at a time and is typically applied to investigate the causal relationships in a bivariate framework, we present the empirical results up to M (= 10, 15, 20) lags, measured in days, for each pair of CDS indices (Table 4.3).

We find significant unidirectional causality-in-mean effects running from the banking to the insurance and financial services sector CDS indices and from the financial services sector CDS index to the insurance sector CDS index. This finding suggests that the banking (financial services) sector CDS spreads play leading roles in the price discovery of credit risks for those of the insurance and financial services sectors (insurance sector) in the short run. An important

Table 4.2 Results of the AR-EGARCH models

	BNK		*INS*		*FIN*	
	Estimate	*SE*	*Estimate*	*SE*	*Estimate*	*SE*
Return equation						
a_0	-0.005	0.010	-0.047**	0.007	-0.055**	0.009
a_1	0.082**	0.018	0.135**	0.012	0.150**	0.013
a_2			0.045**	0.012		
Variance equation						
ω	-0.199**	0.016	-0.184**	0.016	-0.124**	0.013
α_1	0.292**	0.024	0.351**	0.027	0.187**	0.020
γ_1	0.094**	0.017	-0.063**	0.018	0.092**	0.014
β_1	0.995**	0.002	0.990**	0.002	0.998**	0.001
GED parameter	0.998**	0.037	0.707**	0.014	0.806**	0.021
$Q(20)$	21.098		21.998		24.859	
p-value	0.391		0.341		0.207	
$Q^2(20)$	20.402		0.519		3.389	
p-value	0.433		1.000		1.000	

Notes: $Q(20)$ and $Q^2(20)$ are the Ljung–Box statistics for the autocorrelation test.

** denotes statistical significance at the 1% level.

Table 4.3 Causality-in-mean tests among the CDS indices in U.S. financial sectors

Direction of causality	*Hong's Q-statistic*		
	M=*10*	M=*15*	M=*20*
BNK→INS	4.70**	5.31**	4.81**
INS→BNK	-0.55	-1.01	-0.99
INS→FIN	0.64	0.26	-0.24
FIN→INS	8.11**	7.41**	6.69**
FIN→BNK	1.98	1.36	0.89
BNK→FIN	7.43**	6.02**	4.85**

Notes: The Q-statistic is used to test the null hypothesis of no causality from lag 1 up to lag M (=10, 15, 20). Q-statistics are based on one-sided tests. Lags are measured in days.

** denotes statistical significance at the 1% level.

implication for traders is thus that they can use the information on the pricing of credit extracted from the banking sector CDS index with the insurance and financial services sector CDS indices and that from the financial services sector CDS index with the insurance sector CDS index when constructing arbitrage or hedging strategies. The above finding is generally in line with the results of Hammoudeh et al. (2013), who conduct generalized impulse response analyses under a vector error correction model framework and show that the highest (lowest) cross-sector shock impacts come from the banking (insurance) sector CDS index.

Before conducting the causality-in-variance tests, we need to investigate the existence of structural breaks in volatility, which may undermine the validity of the presented tests, as explained earlier. In this regard, we apply Bai and Perron's (1998, 2003) multiple structural break tests to the absolute values of the demeaned series. Our approach to testing for volatility breaks differs from that of Van Dijk et al. (2005), who employ the sup-Wald statistic developed by Andrews (1993), which aims to identify the existence of only one structural break point in the series. As indicated in Table 4.4, our sequential application of the *Sup* FT(*k*+1|*k*) statistics to identify *k*+1 breaks conditional on identifying *k* breaks indicates that the null hypothesis of no structural change in the variances for all three CDS indices cannot be rejected at the 1 percent level.

Because we identified some significant causality-in-mean effects (see Table 4.3), we carry out the causality-in-variance tests after eliminating these effects as

Table 4.4 Results of the Bai and Perron (1998, 2003) structural break tests in volatility

<table>
<tr><td colspan="4">Panel A: BNK</td></tr>
<tr><td colspan="4">Tests</td></tr>
<tr><td>SupFT(2|1):</td><td>SupFT (3|2):</td><td>SupFT (4|3):</td><td>SupFT (5|4):</td></tr>
<tr><td>1.8441</td><td>1.6252</td><td>0.4230</td><td>–</td></tr>
<tr><td colspan="4">Number of breaks selected</td></tr>
<tr><td colspan="4">0 break</td></tr>
<tr><td colspan="4">Break date</td></tr>
<tr><td colspan="4">–</td></tr>
<tr><td colspan="4">Panel B: INS</td></tr>
<tr><td colspan="4">Tests</td></tr>
<tr><td>SupFT(2|1):</td><td>SupFT (3|2):</td><td>SupFT (4|3):</td><td>SupFT (5|4):</td></tr>
<tr><td>2.1357</td><td>2.1357</td><td>0.3079</td><td>–</td></tr>
<tr><td colspan="4">Number of breaks selected</td></tr>
<tr><td colspan="4">0 break</td></tr>
<tr><td colspan="4">Break date</td></tr>
<tr><td colspan="4">–</td></tr>
<tr><td colspan="4">Panel C: FIN</td></tr>
<tr><td colspan="4">Tests</td></tr>
<tr><td>SupFT(2|1):</td><td>SupFT (3|2):</td><td>SupFT (4|3):</td><td>SupFT (5|4):</td></tr>
<tr><td>0.8148</td><td>0.6704</td><td>0.5188</td><td>–</td></tr>
<tr><td colspan="4">Number of breaks selected</td></tr>
<tr><td colspan="4">0 break</td></tr>
<tr><td colspan="4">Break date</td></tr>
<tr><td colspan="4">–</td></tr>
</table>

Notes: We sequentially test for the hypothesis of k breaks vs. k + 1 breaks at the 1% level, employing the Sup FT (k + 1|k) statistics.

much as possible by including in the conditional mean equations of the AR-EGARCH framework the lagged values of the variables found to Granger-cause each explained variable at the mean level.[11] Table 4.5 reports the results of the causality-in-mean tests after the re-estimation of mean equations that additionally include the significant lagged explanatory variables. We confirm that the causality-in-mean effects identified in Table 4.3 become insignificant, except that effect running from the financial services to the insurance sector CDS index, implying the appropriate removal of the causality-in-mean effects through this re-estimation procedure. Thus, we believe that this approach additionally supports the adequacy of the subsequent causality-in-variance analysis.

Table 4.6 presents the results of the causality-in-variance tests applied to the squares of the standardized innovations derived from the new AR-EGARCH

Table 4.5 Causality-in-mean tests among the CDS indices in U.S. financial sectors (after the re-estimation procedure)

Direction of causality	*Modified* Q*-statistic*		
	M=*10*	M=*15*	M=*20*
BNK→INS	0.86	1.57	1.63
INS→BNK	-0.57	-0.94	-0.92
INS→FIN	0.44	0.28	0.02
FIN→INS	4.84**	4.20**	4.07**
FIN→BNK	1.83	1.30	0.80
BNK→FIN	1.35	0.55	0.08

Notes: The modified *Q*-statistic is used to test the null hypothesis of no causality from lag 1 up to lag *M* (=10, 15, 20). *Q*-statistics are based on one-sided tests. Lags are measured in days.

** denotes statistical significance at the 1% level.

Table 4.6 Causality-in-variance tests among the CDS indices in U.S. financial sectors (after the re-estimation procedure)

Direction of causality	*Modified* Q*-statistic*		
	M=*10*	M=*15*	M=*20*
BNK→INS	-1.88	-0.69	-1.20
INS→BNK	-2.06	-2.52	-2.85
INS→FIN	-2.16	-2.61	-3.04
FIN→INS	-2.05	-2.56	-2.98
FIN→BNK	25.68**	20.32**	17.00**
BNK→FIN	-1.52	-2.05	-2.25

Notes: The modified *Q*-statistic is used to test the null hypothesis of no causality from lag 1 up to lag *M* (=10, 15, 20). *Q*-statistics are based on one-sided tests. Lags are measured in days.

** denotes statistical significance at the 1% level.

models. Interestingly, we find significant causality-in-variance effects running from the financial services sector CDS index to that of the banking sector. As shown in Table 4.3, we find significant unidirectional causality-in-mean effects running in the opposite direction between these two indices. According to Ross (1989) and Engle et al. (1990), such causality-in-variance effects reflect the extent of information transmission and contagion across markets. In this regard, we can draw the following implications of the above finding for traders and policymakers.

For traders, the results suggest that the banking sector CDS spread can be used for pricing credit risks in the financial services sector in the short-term. However, traders must be aware of potential contagion and the transmission of risks from the latter to the former when formulating their trading strategies. In fact, the financial services sector typically has higher risk tolerability than the banking sector because of the presence of weaker regulations and hence it may react more quickly to new information on serious credit events and increases in credit risks. Traders can thus utilize the presented empirical results to build a portfolio of assets that might be protected from volatility spillovers across financial sectors. Our findings also highlight the importance of investigating causality not only at the mean level but also at the variance level as well as becoming more mindful of the contagion effects among financial CDS markets, as identified by the causality-in-variance analysis presented in this paper.

The key implications for policymakers are twofold. First, they should study the financial services sector as a potential source of contagion among these CDS markets. Regulatory authorities tend to pay closer attention to the banking sector given its role as a financial intermediary in the economy. Nonetheless, our findings suggest that the financial services sector, the least regulated of the three financial sector CDS indices examined herein, may transmit risks to other sectors such as banking in the case of serious credit events, which may cause financial instability. This finding confirms the significance of determining the level of regulatory capital in the financial services industry and designing regulations for CDS contracts in the sector carefully.

Second, policymakers should be aware that such volatility spillovers among financial sector CDS spreads as those identified in our analysis might trigger potential systemic risks. CDS contracts are traded on over-the-counter markets, meaning that counterparty risk (i.e., the risk that one of the parties may default) is a major issue. According to the Depository Trust and Clearing Corporation, approximately 40 percent of the gross notional amount of single-name CDS contracts is concentrated on reference entities in the financial sector. Moreover, a small number of players in that sector are protection sellers, buyers, and CDS underwriters at the same time. Hence, there exists the risk that CDS, which was originally designed as a tool for hedging default risks, may result in the collapse of the financial system owing to the overexposure of interconnected players. In this regard, regulators must strive to manage counterparty risks in financial CDS markets, for instance, by monitoring the bilateral commitments of major dealers closely and improving market transparency through the standardization of CDS contracts in the financial sector.

4.5 Conclusion

This study examines causality-in-variance and causality-in-mean among the CDS indices of the banking, insurance, and financial services sectors in the United States from January 2004 to December 2011. Investigating the causality-in-variance effects among these three important indices is crucial because it enables us to clarify the directions and lags of volatility spillovers in the U.S. financial sector that was severely affected by the financial crisis and suggest patterns of information transmission.

We use Hong's (2001) version of the CCF approach, which is suitable for analyzing short-term bivariate volatility and mean transmissions among series. Moreover, we follow the recent development of Hong's methodology by pre-testing for the presence of structural breaks in the variances of CDS index series and testing for causality-in-variance while removing causality-in-mean effects.

Our empirical results indicate evidence of unidirectional causality-in-mean effects running from the banking to the insurance and financial services sector CDS indices and from the financial services sector CDS index to the insurance sector CDS index. This finding implies the leading role of the banking (financial services) sector in the short-run price discovery of credit for those of the insurance and financial services sectors (insurance sector). In addition, we find evidence of significant unidirectional causality-in-variance effects running from the financial services sector CDS index to that of the banking sector. This finding may indicate that at least over short time horizons, the CDS index of the financial services sector, which is the least tightly regulated, is a source of information flows for the other sectors and can serve as a leading indicator of capturing volatility spillovers.

Our results offer valuable insights for both traders, who use financial sector CDS indices as tools for speculation and portfolio allocation, and policymakers, who wish to regulate these three financial sectors and the growing CDS market more broadly. While financial traders may refer to the banking (financial services) sector CDS spread when pricing credit risks in the financial services and insurance sectors (insurance sector), they should also incorporate the migration of risks reflected in the causality-in-variance effects running from the financial services sector CDS index to that of the banking sector. Policymakers should place more emphasis on monitoring and regulating the financial services sector as a potential source of contagion among these CDS markets. Moreover, regulatory authorities should recognize that such contagion may cause systemic risks because of the over-concentration of exposures in financial CDS markets and therefore formulate and implement initiatives to manage the operation of counterparty risks in a more effective manner.

Notes

1 These financial sector CDS indices incorporate an average mid-spread calculation of a portfolio of a single-name CDS for several financial institutions that represent each sector.
2 With regard to the application of Hong's test, some recent examples include Li et al. (2008), Atukeren et al. (2012), and Tamakoshi and Hamori (2013).
3 Unlike GARCH, the EGARCH model ensures the non-negativity of the conditional variance and hence we are not constrained by the signs of the coefficients. Moreover, the coefficients of the ARCH terms in the EGARCH model can capture the asymmetric effects caused by positive and negative shocks, which tend to be observed in the case of financial time series such as CDS index spreads. See Nelson (1991) for more details of the EGARCH model.
4 We selected the truncated kernel, which can provide compact support. Hong (2001) demonstrates that for a smaller M, this kernel provides approximately similar power to non-uniform kernels such as the Bartlett kernel and the Daniell kernel.
5 We follow a similar process to conduct the causality-in-mean tests by using the CCF values of standardized residuals instead of squared standardized residuals.
6 For the implementation, we used the Matlab code written by Yohei Yamamoto based on Bai and Perron's Gauss code. The code is available at http://people.bu.edu/perron/code.html.
7 We selected the optimal number of lags included based on the Schwarz Bayesian information criterion.
8 We chose five-year CDS indices because these are the most actively traded among CDS indices that range in maturity from one to 10 years.
9 The results of the unit root tests are available upon request.
10 We did not take the logarithmic first differences, because the units of the CDS indices are expressed in basis points and thus it does not necessarily make sense to convert them into the logarithmic form.
11 The estimation results of the new AR-EGARCH models are not reported here to save space but they are available upon request.

References

Andrews, D. W. (1993) Tests for parameter instability and structural change with unknown change point, *Econometrica*, **61**, 821–856.

Arouri, M., Hammoudeh, S., Jawadi, F., and Nguyen, D. K. (2014) Financial linkages between US sector credit default swaps markets, *Journal of International Financial Markets, Institutions, and Money*, **33**, 223–243.

Atukeren, E., Korkmaz, T., and Cevik, E. (2012) Spillovers between business confidence and stock returns in Greece, Italy, Portugal, and Spain, *International Journal of Finance and Economics*, **18**, 205–215.

Bai, J. and Perron, P. (1998) Estimating and testing linear models with multiple structural changes, *Econometrica*, **66**, 47–78.

Bai, J. and Perron, P. (2003) Computation and analysis of multiple structural change models, *Journal of Applied Econometrics*, **18**, 1–22.

Chen, L. H., Hammoudeh, S., and Yuan, Y. (2011) Asymmetric convergence in US financial credit default swap sector index markets, *The Quarterly Review of Economics and Finance*, **51**, 408–418.

Cheung, Y. and Ng, L. (1996) A causality-in-variance test and its applications to financial market prices, *Journal of Econometrics*, **72**, 33–48.

Dooley, M. and Hutchison, M. (2009) Transmission of the U.S. subprime crisis to emerging markets: Evidence on the default swap spreads, *Journal of International Money and Finance*, **28**, 1131–1149.

Eichengreen, B., Mody, A., Nedeljkovic, M., and Sarno, L. (2012) How the subprime crisis went global: Evidence from bank credit default swap spreads, *Journal of International Money and Finance*, **31**, 1299–1318.

Engle, R., Ito, T., and Lin, W. L. (1990) Meteor showers or heat waves? Heteroskedastic intra-daily volatility in the foreign exchange market, *Econometrica*, **58**, 525–542.

Hammoudeh, S., Nandha, M., and Yuan, Y. (2013) Dynamics of CDS spread indexes of US financial sectors, *Applied Economics*, **45**, 213–223.

Hammoudeh, S. and Sari, R. (2011) Financial CDS, stock market and interest rates: Which drives which? *North American Journal of Economics and Finance*, **22**, 257–276.

Hong, Y. (2001) A test for volatility spillover with application to exchange rates, *Journal of Econometrics*, **103**, 183–224.

Kim, D., Loretan, M., and Remolona, E. M. (2010) Contagion and risk premia in the amplification of crisis: Evidence from Asian names in the global CDS market, *Journal of Asian Economics*, **21**, 314–326.

Li, G., Refalo, J., and Wu, L. (2008) Causality-in-variance and causality-in-mean among European government bond markets, *Applied Financial Economics*, **18**, 1709–1720.

Nelson, D. (1991) Conditional heteroskedasticity in asset returns: A new approach, *Econometrica*, **59**, 347–370.

Pantelidis, T. and Pittis, N. (2004) Testing for Granger causality in variance in the presence of causality in mean, *Economic Letters*, **85**, 201–207.

Ross, S. A. (1989) Information and volatility: No-arbitrage Martingale approach to timing and resolution irrelevancy, *Journal of Finance*, **44**, 1–17.

Stulz, R. (2010) Credit default swaps and the credit crisis, *Journal of Economic Perspectives*, **24**, 73–92.

Tamakoshi, G. and Hamori, S. (2013) Volatility and mean spillovers between sovereign and banking sector CDS markets: A note on the European sovereign debt crisis, *Applied Economics Letters*, **20**, 262–266.

Van Dijk, D., Osborn, D. R., and Sensier, M. (2005) Testing for causality in variance in the presence of breaks, *Economic Letters*, **89**, 193–199.

Wang, P. and Moore, T. (2012) The integration of the credit default swap markets during the US subprime crisis: Dynamic correlation analysis, *Journal of International Financial Markets, Institutions, and Money*, **22**, 1–15.

5 Co-movement and spillovers among financial sector CDS indices

5.1 Introduction

The global financial crisis of 2007–2008 caused the sudden spread of instability in the global financial industry as several major institutions sought government bailouts or collapsed. The financial sector in the United Kingdom was no exception, with its first bank run observed in the case of Northern Rock in September 2007. Moreover, the government bailed out three banks, acquiring substantial equity stakes in the Royal Bank of Scotland, Lloyds TSB, and HBOS. Bank of England (2011) reported that, by the end of 2010, output in the financial sector was 10 percent lower than the peak levels before the crisis. In late 2009, the crisis in Europe entered a new phase as market participants cast doubt on the solvency of several peripheral countries, resulting in the outbreak of the European sovereign debt crisis. The U.K. financial system was not completely excluded from these adverse developments because U.K. banks were heavily exposed to the sovereign debt of Ireland, which faced the collapse of its banking system and received 85 billion euros in financial support from the Eurozone and International Monetary Fund.

This study contributes to the strand of literature on financial crises and their effects by focusing on the credit default swap (CDS) indexes of three financial industries: banking, life insurance, and other financial sectors (i.e., investment funds, finance leasing, and non-bank credit grantors). The financial sector is crucial to the smooth functioning of an economy because of its role in providing credit, liquidity, and risk management services to non-financial sectors (Baily and Elliott, 2013). Against this background, understanding the relationships among financial sector CDS indexes is significant for investors who seek diversification or hedging opportunities at the sector level and for regulators concerned about setting appropriate regulations for each sector.

The financial sector CDS indexes adopted in this study reflect an average mid-spread calculation of their constituents, that is, several financial institutions' single-name CDS spreads in each sector. These indexes are thus considered to be efficient measures of the credit risks faced by each financial sector (Hammoudeh et al., 2013a). These three sector CDS indexes may move in parallel, reflecting the underlying factors affecting the creditworthiness of the whole financial system in an economy. However, they may also respond differently to changes in credit market conditions because of the diverse characteristics of the three sectors in question, such as the degree of regulation and typical position in CDS markets (i.e., protection buyer or seller).

A growing number of recent studies have addressed the dynamics of financial sector CDS indexes, the majority of which focus on banking, life insurance, and financial services in the United States. Hammoudeh and Sari (2011) used the autoregressive distributed lag approach and examined the relationships between these CDS indexes, the stock price index, and Treasury security rates. They found that the three CDS spreads exhibit the highest short-run cross-shock effects. Chen et al. (2011) employed the momentum threshold autoregression approach and assessed the adjustment of the three CDS indexes to the long-run equilibrium. They uncovered that the speed of adjustment was faster during divergences than convergences, providing support for the presence of asymmetric co-movement. By implementing a vector error correction model to analyze the causalities among the three CDS indexes, Hammoudeh et al. (2013a) demonstrated that the insurance sector CDS index exhibits the highest adjustment in the long run, whereas the banking sector plays a leading role in the price discovery process in the short run. Hammoudeh et al. (2013b) also applied a vector error correction model to analyzing the interrelationships of the three financial sector CDS indices, other measures of risk, and inflation expectations. They found evidence of not only the contagion effects among the three CDS indices and other risk measures but also the significant effects of QE1 on those risk measures. By using the smooth transition error-correction models (STECMs), Arouri et al. (2014) found that for two pairs of the three CDS indexes (banking–financial services and banking–insurance), the adjustment process to the long-term equilibrium is characterized by asymmetry and non-linearities. Tamakoshi and Hamori (2014), who studied return and volatility spillovers among the three CDS indexes with a cross-correlation function approach, detected significant causality-in-variance running from the financial services sector CDS index to that of the banking sector, suggesting the existence of information transmission and contagion from financial services to the banking sector.

In contrast to these U.S. market-focused studies, this work is among the first to investigate the dynamic relationships among U.K. financial sector CDS indexes. Our sample period ranges from January 1, 2008, to December 31, 2013, and includes the global financial crisis and European sovereign debt crisis, both of which heavily affected the financial markets of the United Kingdom. While Benbouzid and Mallick (2013) used the U.K. banking sector CDS index, the authors primarily analyzed its main determinants including housing prices.

The main contribution of our study is thus the examination of time-varying co-movement and volatility spillovers among financial sector CDS indexes. According to Ross' (1989) seminal paper, volatility is related to information flow, implying that changes in the rates of information flow among markets may trigger different volatility transmission patterns. Hence, studying the nature of volatility spillovers clarifies the mutual transmission of risks among (and perhaps triggered contagion effects on) the above three financial sectors in response to various credit events during financial crises. Therefore, our analysis of the time variations of volatility spillovers among CDS indexes, combined with that of co-movement, will affect decisions on dynamic portfolio allocation, risk management, and regulation establishment in the U.K. financial sector.

We employ a two-step approach[1] to analyze time-varying co-movement and volatility spillovers among financial sector CDS indexes. We examine the dynamic conditional correlations (DCCs) by using the DCC-GARCH model developed by Engle (2002). Then, with the estimated conditional volatilities from the DCC-GARCH model, we investigate volatility spillovers by employing the spillover index measures advocated by Diebold and Yilmaz (2012). We base this novel methodology on the variance decomposition in a generalized vector autoregressive (VAR) approach and, hence, it is invariant to variable orderings. Moreover, the methodology shows the degrees and directions of volatility spillover effects *over time*, clarifying whether each sector is a net transmitter or receiver of spillovers at each point in time.

In summary, the main findings from our empirical analyses are fivefold. First, we find evidence of contagion among the three sector CDS indexes, as evidenced by the sharp increases in the DCCs for all pairs after the Lehman Brothers bankruptcy. Second, we detect a substantial decrease in the DCCs for the banking–life insurance and life insurance–other financial pairs after the summit of the European debt crisis in September 2011, triggering potential diversification opportunities. Third, the total volatility spillover index indicates that the spillover effects across the three sector CDS indexes account for a substantial proportion of the forecast error variances on average. Moreover, the spikes coincide with major crisis events during the recent period of financial turmoil. Fourth, the net volatility spillover plots show that the directions of volatility spillovers from or to each of the three CDS indexes substantially alter over time, implying that it is crucial to hedge the credit risks underlying these financial sectors on a real-time basis. Finally, we find that other financial sectors are net transmitters of volatility spillovers during some periods, underscoring the importance of appropriate regulatory policies for that specific sector as well as the banking sector, which is consistently a net transmitter. We discuss the relevance of these findings to the trading and hedging strategies of portfolio managers and regulatory framework development by policymakers.

The remainder of this article is organized as follows. Section 5.2 explains the empirical framework. Section 5.3 describes the data. Section 5.4 reports our empirical findings and their implications. Section 5.5 provides concluding remarks.

5.2 Empirical methodology

The empirical approach employed is composed of two main steps. We first assess the DCCs among the three financial sector CDS indexes by applying Engle's

(2002) DCC-GARCH model. We then analyze the spillovers in the estimated conditional volatilities, as obtained from the DCC-GARCH model, by using the spillover index measures proposed by Diebold and Yilmaz (2012).

In the first step, we consider the following DCC-GARCH framework:

$$r_t = \varphi_0 + \varphi_1 r_{t-1} + \varepsilon_t, \ \varepsilon_t \,|\, \Omega_{t-1} \sim N(0, H_t), \tag{5.1}$$

$$h_{i,t} = \omega + \alpha_1 \varepsilon_{i,t-1}^2 + \beta_1 h_{i,t-1}, \ (\text{for } i = 1,\ 2,\ 3) \tag{5.2}$$

$$\varepsilon_t = H_t^{1/2} u_t, \ u_t \sim N(0, I), \tag{5.3}$$

$$H_t = D_t R_t D_t \tag{5.4}$$

where $r_t = [r_{1t}, r_{2t}, r_{3t}]'$ is a 3 × 1 vector including each first-differenced CDS index with a conditional mean assumed to follow an AR(1) model, $\varepsilon_t = [\varepsilon_{1t}, \varepsilon_{2t}, \varepsilon_{3t}]'$ is a 3 × 1 vector of the error term, $u_t = [u_{1t}, u_{2t}, u_{3t}]'$ is a 3 × 1 vector of the standardized residuals, and Ω_{t-1} is the information set at time $t - 1$. $h_{i,t}$ is the conditional variance, which is assumed to follow a GARCH(1,1) model, H_t is the conditional covariance matrix, D_t is the diagonal matrix of the conditional standard deviations, and R_t is the time-varying correlation matrix. We represent the DCC model as

$$Q_t = (1 - a_1 - b_1)\overline{Q} + a_1 u_{t-1} u_{t-1}' + b_1 Q_{t-1}, \tag{5.5}$$

where $\overline{Q}$ is the unconditional covariance matrix of u_t. Here, non-negative scalar variables, a_1 and b_1, must satisfy the condition $a_1 + b_1 + < 1$ to ensure the stability of the conditional variances. The matrix containing the time-varying conditional correlations is derived by

$$R_t = Q_t^{*-1} Q_t Q_t^{*-1}, \tag{5.6}$$

where Q_t^* is a diagonal matrix including the square root of the diagonal entries of Q_t.

In the second step, we investigate the spillovers among the volatilities of the three sector CDS indexes by using the generalized version of the spillover index advocated in Diebold and Yilmaz (2012). This approach adopts the generalized VAR system of Koop et al. (1996) and Pesaran and Shin (1998), where variance decompositions are invariant to the variable ordering. To illustrate the methodology, we suppose the *p*th order, *N*-variable VAR as follows:

$$x_t = \sum_{i=1}^{p} \Theta_i x_{t-i} + \varepsilon_t \tag{5.7}$$

where x_t is a vector of N endogenous variables (containing the estimated conditional volatility obtained from Equation (5.2)), Θ_i is an $N \times N$ parameter matrix, and ε_t is a vector of independently and identically distributed errors. The moving average representation is denoted as $x_t = \sum_{i=0}^{\infty} A_i \varepsilon_{t-i}$, where the coefficient matrices A_t are derived by the recursion $A_i = \Theta_1 A_{i\text{-}1} + \ldots + \Theta_p A_{i\text{-}p}$ with A_0 being an $N \times N$ identity matrix and $A_i = 0$ for $i < 0$. Then, the H-step-ahead forecast error variance decomposition is given by

$$\theta_{ij}^{g}(H) = \frac{\sigma_{jj}^{-1} \sum_{h=0}^{H-1} (e_i' A_h \Sigma e_j)^2}{\sum_{h=0}^{H-1} (e_i' A_h \Sigma A_h' e_i)}, \tag{5.8}$$

where Σ is the variance matrix for ε, σ_{jj} is the standard deviation of the error term for the jth equation, and e_i is the selection vector, with one as the ith element and zero otherwise. We normalize each entry of the variance decomposition matrix by the row sum, which yields

$$\tilde{\theta}_{ij}^{g}(H) = \frac{\theta_{ij}^{g}(H)}{\sum_{j=1}^{N} \theta_{ij}^{g}(H)}, \tag{5.9}$$

where $\sum_{j=1}^{N} \tilde{\theta}_{ij}^{g}(H) = 1$ and $\sum_{i,j=1}^{N} \tilde{\theta}_{ij}^{g}(H) = N$ by construction. According to Diebold and Yilmaz (2012), we construct the total spillover index as follows:

$$S^{g}(H) = \frac{\sum_{i,j=1,i\neq j}^{N} \tilde{\theta}_{ij}^{g}(H)}{\sum_{i,j=1}^{N} \tilde{\theta}_{ij}^{g}(H)} \cdot 100 = \frac{\sum_{i,j=1,i\neq j}^{N} \tilde{\theta}_{ij}^{g}(H)}{N} \cdot 100. \tag{5.10}$$

This index captures the contribution of the spillovers of shocks across all variables to the total forecast error variance. Another important concept developed by Diebold and Yilmaz (2012) is net spillover, which identifies whether a particular variable is a net receiver or transmitter of shocks. The net spillovers from sector i to all other sector j ($S_i^{g}(H)$) is derived by subtracting the directional spillovers received by variable i from all other variables j ($S_{i\leftarrow j}^{g}(H)$) from the directional spillovers transmitted from variable i to all other variables j ($S_{i\rightarrow j}^{g}(H)$), so that

$$S_i^{g}(H) = S_{i\rightarrow j}^{g}(H) - S_{i\leftarrow j}^{g}(H), \tag{5.11}$$

where the directional spillovers are denoted as

$$S_{i\leftarrow j}^{g}(H) = \frac{\sum_{j=1,j\neq i}^{N} \tilde{\theta}_{ij}^{g}(H)}{\sum_{i,j=1}^{N} \tilde{\theta}_{ij}^{g}(H)} \times 100 \text{ and} \tag{5.12}$$

$$S_{i\rightarrow j}^{g}(H) = \frac{\sum_{j=1,j\neq i}^{N} \tilde{\theta}_{ji}^{g}(H)}{\sum_{i,j=1}^{N} \tilde{\theta}_{ji}^{g}(H)} \times 100. \tag{5.13}$$

5.3 Data

We use weekly data (end of Friday data points) on the five-year CDS indexes of the three U.K. financial sectors, ranging from January 1, 2008, to December 31, 2013. The data are extracted from the sub-sector CDS indexes of Thomson Reuters Datastream. The five-year CDS indexes are the most liquid term among the indexes traded in the market (i.e., from one to 10 years). We select the beginning of the period based on the availability of U.K. sector CDS index data. We also use weekly data because they are less prone to noise than daily CDS index data, which can be unreliable.

Figure 5.1 presents the level data for the three U.K. financial sector CDS index series. Not surprisingly, all the CDS indexes, particularly those for life insurance and other financial sectors, exhibited bursts after the collapse of Lehman Brothers on September 15, 2008, suggesting severe effects from the global financial crisis on the creditworthiness of the U.K. financial sector. The indexes rose sharply again after September 2011, when the European debt crisis triggered a loss of confidence in the financial markets in Eurozone countries as well as in Asia, the United Kingdom, and the United States with global stock markets plummeting simultaneously.

Table 5.1 reports the basic statistics for the weekly level data for the three financial sector CDS indexes. The standard deviation is the lowest for the banking sector and the highest for the other financial sectors, perhaps reflecting the greater degree of regulation in the former and lack of regulation in the latter. The high level of kurtosis, particularly for the life insurance and other financial sectors,

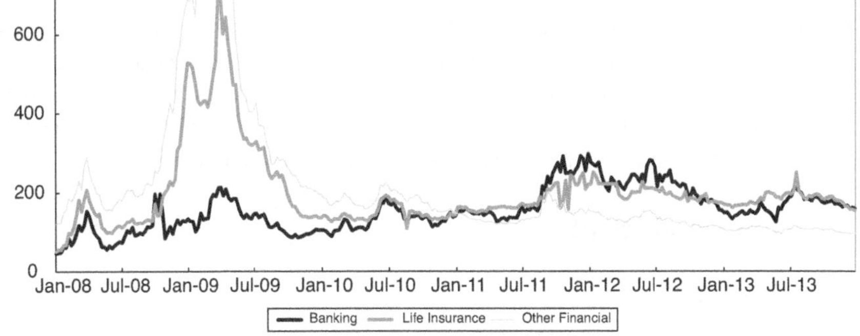

Figure 5.1 U.K. financial sector CDS indexes

Notes: Weekly data for the CDS indexes of the three sectors in the United Kingdom are presented (unit: basis points).

Table 5.1 Summary statistics

Variable	*Mean (b.p.)*	*Maximum (b.p.)*	*Minimum (b.p.)*	*SD*	*Skewness*	*Kurtosis*	*Jarque–Bera*
Banking	156.42	296.92	46.05	53.86	0.48	2.74	12.67***
Life Insurance	200.59	705.00	50.13	100.08	2.54	10.30	1031.61***
Other Financial	217.60	1026.42	94.33	181.20	2.71	10.05	1030.68***

Notes: Statistics on weekly level data are reported.

*** denotes statistical significance at the 1% level.

Table 5.2 Results of the ADF and PP unit root tests

Variable	*ADF test statistics*	*PP test statistics*
	constant and trend	*constant and trend*
Level data		
Banking	-2.705	-2.962
Life Insurance	-3.224	-2.697
Other Financial	-3.004	-2.621
First-differenced data		
Banking	-21.095***	-21.176***
Life Insurance	-7.393***	-15.899***
Other Financial	-5.470***	-17.822***

Notes: Results of the Augmented Dickey–Fuller (ADF) and Phillips–Perron (PP) unit root tests are reported. The unit root hypothesis in which the regression contains a constant and a trend components are tested.

*** denotes statistical significance at the 1% level.

indicates that extreme changes in these CDS indexes often occur. Moreover, the Jarque–Bera tests reject the null hypothesis of a normal distribution for all indexes at the 1 percent significance level. We employ the augmented Dickey–Fuller and Phillips and Perron tests and find that all the CDS indexes are I(1) variables at the 1 percent significance level, as reported in Table 5.2. Hence, we use the first-differenced series of the indexes in the subsequent analysis.[2]

5.4 Empirical results

DCC analysis

We first fit the DCC-GARCH framework to the first-differenced series of the CDS index data. Table 5.3 reports the results of the model estimation. We find a good fit of the variance equations to the data for the univariate AR(1)-GARCH(1,1) models applied to each series of the CDS indexes, reflected by both

Table 5.3 Results of the DCC-GARCH models

	Banking		*Life Insurance*		*Other Financial*	
	Estimate	*SE*	*Estimate*	*SE*	*Estimate*	*SE*
First step: GARCH model estimation						
Mean equation						
φ_0	−0.1132	0.7604	0.0000	0.0000	−0.9104***	0.0991
φ_1	−0.0812	0.0964	0.0000	0.0000	0.1005***	0.0127
Variance equation						
ω	7.5201	5.3525	26.3204	17.7612	1.0049	0.7828
α_1	0.1771***	0.0671	0.4607***	0.1488	0.2442***	0.0433
β_1	0.8073***	0.0639	0.5383***	0.1666	0.7548***	0.0314
GED parameter	1.1476***	0.1697	0.6381***	0.0699	1.0569***	0.1118
$Q(20)$	15.3030		23.0310		26.8040	
p-value	0.7590		0.2870		0.1410	
$Q^2(20)$	4.8961		11.1140		5.9498	
p-value	1.0000		0.9430		0.9990	
Second step: DCC model estimation						
A	0.0249*	0.0149				
B	0.9589***	0.0278				

*** and * indicate statistical significance at the 1% and 10% levels, respectively.

the coefficients of the squared error terms and the lagged conditional volatility (α_1 and β_1), which are statistically significant at the 1 percent level.[3] Additionally, the p-values of the Ljung–Box statistics indicate no autocorrelation up to order 20 for the standardized residuals and standard residuals squared. Moreover, the estimation results of the DCC model reported in Table 5.3 show that the coefficients of the standardized residuals (a_1) and of innovations in the dynamics of the conditional correlation matrix (b_1) are significant at the 10 percent level and that the condition $a_1 + b_1 < 1$ is satisfied. Based on these estimation results, we conclude that the DCC-GARCH model employed in our analysis is well specified.

Figure 5.2 presents the evolution of the estimated DCCs between each pair of the CDS indexes. Several interesting observations are drawn from these graphs. First, the DCCs for all pairs increased to 0.7–0.8 during the global financial crisis period, with the first peak occurring immediately after the Lehman Brothers bankruptcy. This finding is consistent with the empirical results of previous studies that have used a DCC framework, which have found evidence of contagion during financial crises, typically defined as sudden increases in the estimated DCCs (e.g., Chiang et al., 2007).

Second, since late 2009, when market participants' concerns about the increased sovereign risks of some peripheral European countries magnified, the correlations

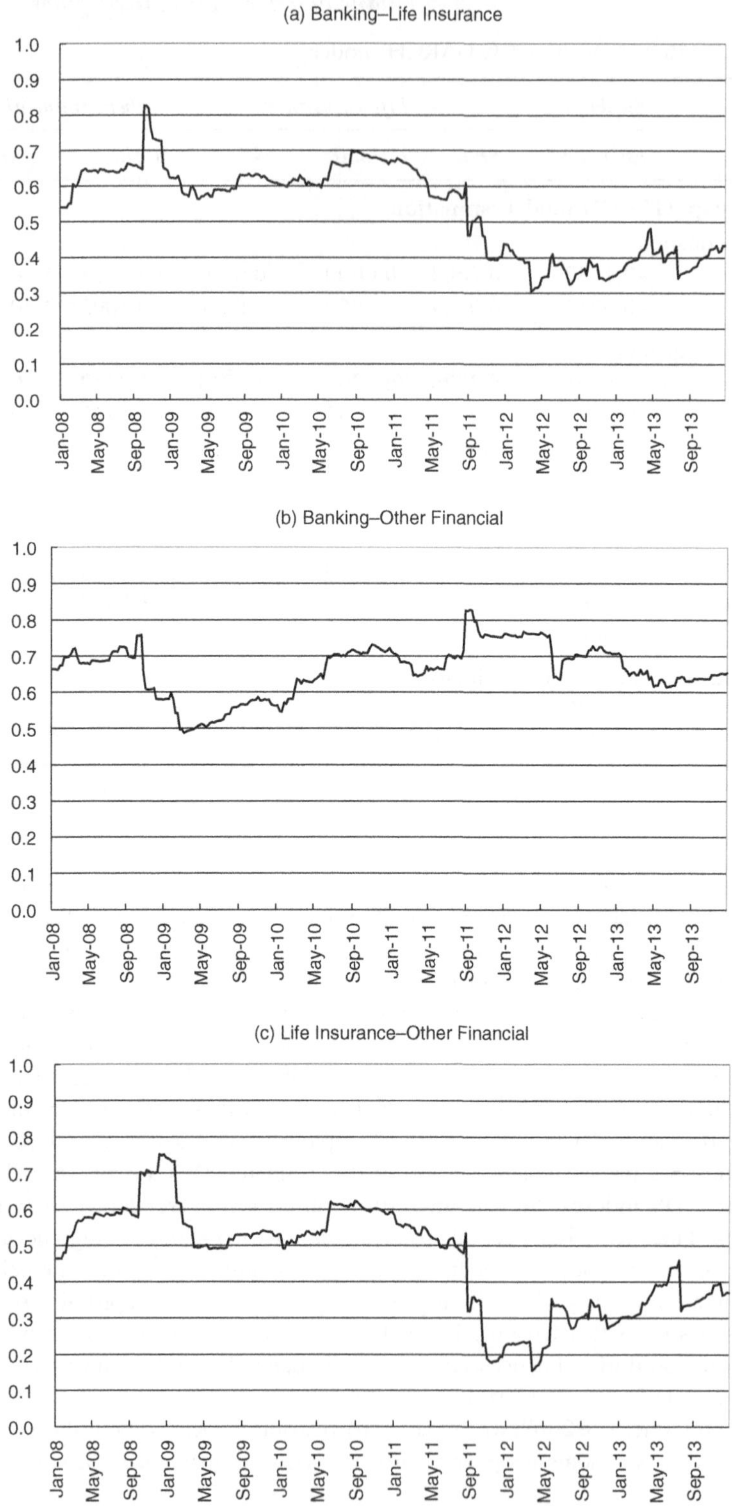

Figure 5.2 Estimated DCCs between U.K. financial sector CDS indexes

are even higher for the banking–other financial pair. This finding implies that the debt crisis affected the credit risk exposure of the U.K. banking and other financial sectors similarly, triggering simultaneous increases in the CDS indexes of both sectors. Since financial service firms rely heavily on banks in terms of the deposits and borrowing needed to run their operations, U.K. banks were first hit by the debt crisis through their exposure to debt from peripheral economies such as Greece, which may have also affected the perceived credit risks of other financial sectors.

Third, and more interestingly, the DCCs for the other two pairs (banking–life insurance and life insurance–other financial) exhibited declining trends during the debt crisis, particularly after September 2011, which was the zenith of the turmoil. The effects of the debt crisis on credit risks in the U.K. life insurance sector, which tends to be a protection seller of CDS contracts, may have been different in nature from those of protection buyers such as banks and financial service firms. Moreover, the operations of insurance firms may be less dependent on banks than are the operations of financial service firms. Therefore, divergent behaviors between the life insurance and banking sector CDS indexes may have been triggered upon the debt crisis, from which banks particularly suffered because of the subtle relationships between the sovereign debt and banks in Europe.[4]

Volatility spillover analysis

The next step is to present the empirical results on volatility spillovers, employing the Diebold and Yilmaz (2012) methodology. The approach uses variables that are the estimated conditional volatilities series derived from the DCC-GARCH model. By using the Bayesian–Schwarz information criterion, we chose order 1 for the VAR model. Table 5.4 presents the estimation results.

In Table 5.4, the *ij*th entry indicates the estimated contribution from innovations to sector *j* in the 10-step forecast error variance of sector *i*. Cross-sector volatility spillovers are represented by the off-diagonal elements, whereas the diagonal elements show own-sector volatility spillovers. We derive two main findings. First, the magnitude of the volatility spillovers among the three sector CDS indexes is substantial, as shown by the total spillover index of 17.2 percent in the lower-right row. This finding implies that cross-sector volatility spillovers in the off-diagonal elements explain a large proportion of the forecast error variance. The three financial sectors are different with respect to the nature of the businesses, degree of regulation, and involvement in CDS markets. Nonetheless,

Table 5.4 Volatility spillover table for U.K. financial sector CDS indexes

To (i) *Sector*	*From (j)* *Banking*	*Life* *Insurance*	*Other* *Financial*	Directional from others
Banking	96.7	0.9	2.4	3.3
Life Insurance	12.8	70.9	16.3	29.1
Other Financial	8.8	10.3	80.9	19.1
Directional to others	21.6	11.2	18.7	51.5
Directional including own	118.3	82.1	99.6	Total spillover
Net spillovers	18.3	-17.9	-0.4	index = 17.2%

our finding on the high total volatility index suggests that the CDS indexes of these sectors, despite the aforementioned differences, are related and that they exert a mutual influence, thus posing systemic risks in times of market turbulence.

Second, the values in the "net spillovers" row show that the banking sector is a net transmitter of volatility spillovers (18.3 percent), whereas the life insurance and other financial sectors are net receivers (–17.9 percent and –0.4 percent, respectively). The high volatility transmission from the banking sector may be driven by the fact that our sample period spans these two recent financial crises. Considering that European banks (including those in the United Kingdom) were heavily affected by the 2007–2008 banking crisis and European debt crisis, we suggest that the banking sector CDS index became a primary source of volatility spillovers, thereby playing a leading role in transmitting information on credit risk surges.

Table 5.4 only captures the average spillovers over the study period; therefore, we must also examine the time-varying behaviors of volatility spillovers. In this regard, we perform a rolling window analysis with 50-week subsamples, which yields the total volatility spillover index plot shown in Figure 5.3.

As expected, this figure illustrates several hikes in the total volatility spillover index coinciding with the European debt crisis episodes, such as the surge in Greek sovereign risks from late 2009 to early 2010 and the spread of concern about sovereign risks in Italy and Spain in August and September 2011. Overall, such patterns provide additional support for the evidence of contagion in the three financial sector CDS indexes during the debt crisis.

We then analyze the time-varying net spillovers, defined as the difference between the directional spillovers by one sector transmitted to and received from all the other sectors over time. Figure 5.4 shows that the level of net spillovers

Figure 5.3 Total volatility spillover index plot estimated by using a 50-week rolling window

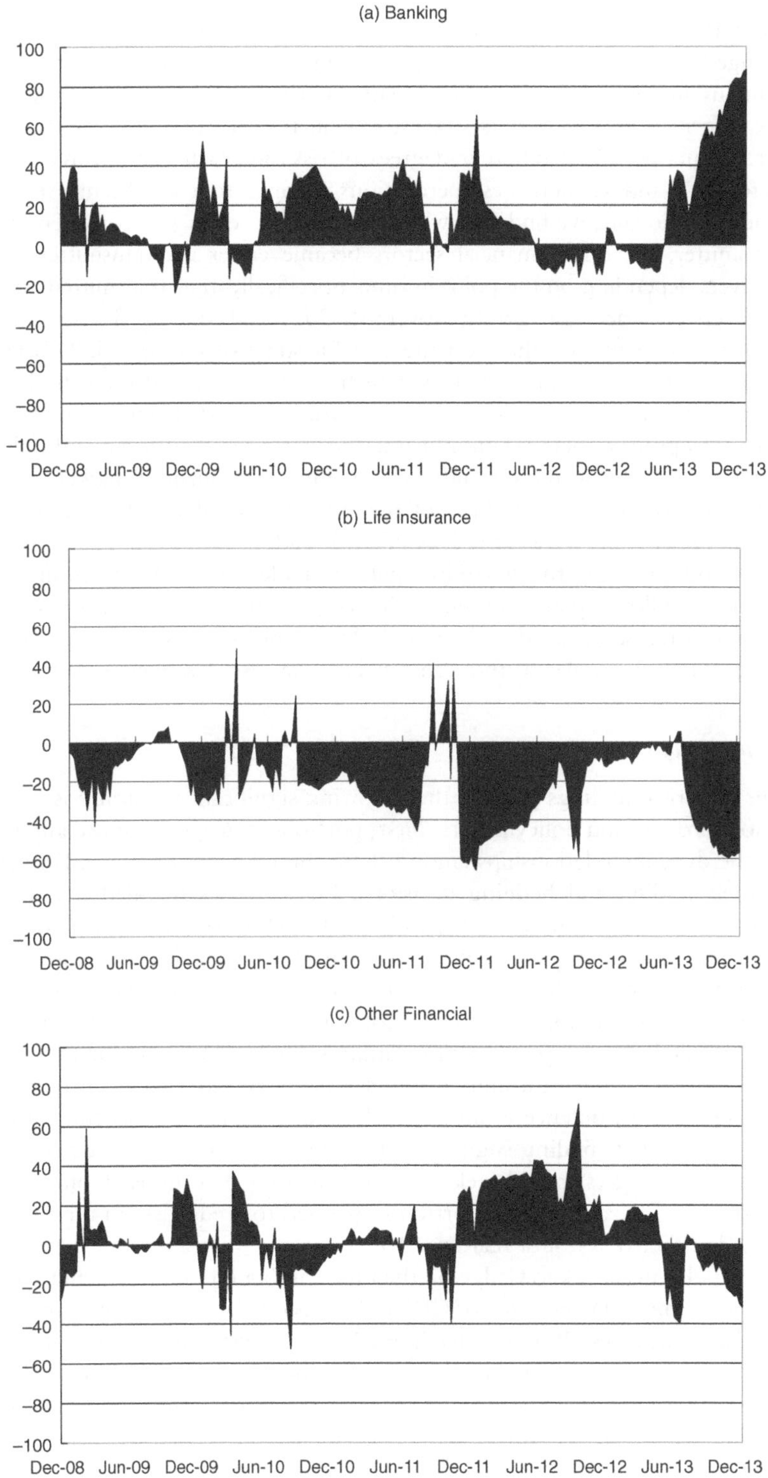

Figure 5.4 Net spillovers estimated by using a 50-week rolling window

for all the sector CDS indexes as well as the direction of spillovers across sectors changed significantly over the sample period. As Ross (1989) argues, volatility contains important data on the extent to which market participants assimilate information. Our results suggest that in the face of credit events, market participants perceived different degrees of risks for each of the three financial sector CDS indexes and these perceptions changed to a significant extent over time. Additionally, we find that while the banking sector was consistently a net transmitter, the other financial sectors became either net transmitters or net receivers depending on the point in time. Specifically, they transmitted volatility spillovers on a net basis during November 2011 and May 2013 when even the banking sector was on the receiving end for some of the period. This finding implies that other financial sectors, which are less regulated than the banking sector, became a major source of risk transmission when the crisis spread to large European Monetary Union member countries such as Spain and Italy, and hence cast doubt on the overall health of European financial markets.

Finally, we check the validity of our empirical results under the following assumptions. First, we assume lags of 2, 3, and 4 (instead of 1) for the VAR framework to yield the volatility spillover tables. Second, we compute the volatility spillover plots assuming 25-week, 75-week, and 100-week rolling window forecasts (instead of 50-week). The results of these additional analyses are qualitatively similar to those in our baseline case described earlier.

Implications

Our empirical findings provide the following significant implications for portfolio managers and policymakers. First, portfolio managers can use knowledge on the dynamic relationships among these three financial sector CDS indexes in their trading and hedging decisions. Our analyses revealed that for two pairs of sector CDS indexes, the estimated DCCs exhibited drastic decreases after September 2011 as concerns over the European debt crisis intensified. After that time, portfolio managers could benefit from diversification effects by investing in combinations of sector CDS indexes. Moreover, our results also revealed that the patterns of volatility spillover shown by the three sector CDS indexes changed throughout our sample period in parallel with the examined financial turbulence events (i.e., the global financial crisis and European debt crisis). This finding suggests that, from a risk management perspective, portfolio managers should seek dynamic portfolio allocations among financial sector CDS indexes (or with portfolios exposed to credit risks in these sectors) to hedge their risks on a real-time basis.

For policymakers, knowledge on the time-varying co-movement and volatility spillovers among financial sector CDS indexes is crucial for designing appropriate regulatory schemes. We found that immediately following the collapse of Lehman Brothers, the DCCs sharply increased for the bivariate combinations of all three sector CDS indexes, indicating evidence of contagion. This finding highlights the importance of preparing for the materialization of systemic risks in which the surge of credit risks for all three sectors concerned could simultaneously emerge, despite their apparent differences. Additionally, we detected that the banking sector was consistently a net transmitter of volatility spillovers during the sample period, while other financial sectors also became a net transmitter of risks for some of the period (i.e., during November 2011 and May 2013). This fact underscores the need for policymakers in the United Kingdom to devote their regulatory focus toward the banking sector and other financial sectors (i.e., financial services) to avoid adverse spillover effects in times of market stress. This finding is consistent with the results of Tamakoshi and Hamori (2014) who studied volatility spillovers among U.S. financial sector CDS indexes before and during the global financial crisis.

5.5 Conclusion

This work is the first to examine the time-varying relationships among the United Kingdom's three financial sector CDS indexes (banking, life insurance, other financial sectors). We employed Engle's (2002) DCC-GARCH model to analyze the DCCs among the indexes and the extracted conditional volatilities for each index to assess their volatility spillover effects, using the most recent spillover index by Diebold and Yilmaz (2012). This approach enabled us to track the evolution of volatility spillovers across the three CDS indexes over time. We used weekly data for 2008–2013, which included the recent periods of financial turbulence faced by the United Kingdom.

Our analyses revealed several interesting findings. First, the DCCs for the pairs of all three CDS indexes increased substantially after the Lehman shock in September 2008, indicating the existence of contagion in terms of credit risks across sectors. Second, while the DCCs for the banking–other financial pair peaked again in September 2011 at the zenith of the European debt crisis, those for the banking–life insurance and life insurance–other financial pairs fell sharply, suggesting the emergence of diversification opportunities for investors. Third, the total spillover index measure, which exhibited bursts in conjunction with several episodes of the European debt crisis, revealed that cross-sector spillovers explained 17.2 percent of the forecast error variances on average, showing that the degree of volatility spillovers was substantial among the three CDS indexes over the sample period. Fourth, the patterns and directions of volatility transmission from or to the three CDS indexes greatly changed over time, calling for the need to hedge the portfolios exposed to credit risks in these financial sectors dynamically in real time. Fifth, the banking sector was mostly a net transmitter of volatility spillovers and other financial sectors became a net transmitter only occasionally, emphasizing the importance of developing appropriate regulatory frameworks to ameliorate volatility spillover effects with a focus on other financial sectors as well as the banking sector during periods of financial turmoil.

Our empirical results have significant implications for portfolio managers for trading and hedging purposes and policymakers in the formulation of regulatory policies. One limitation of our study is that it does not incorporate in its scope the CDS spreads for non-financial industries such as manufacturing and services. However, assessing the interconnectedness of several of those sectors and financial sectors and their time variations is an interesting empirical research topic. Further research opportunities relate to the examination of CDS indexes at the sector level.

Notes

1 For examples of studies applying such two-step approaches in other fields of study, refer to Antonakakis (2012) and Apostolakis and Papadopoulos (2014).
2 Because the CDS indexes are expressed in basis points (b.p.), we do not take the log differences to express percentages.
3 The coefficients in the mean equations are not significant, except for the other financial sector CDS index. However, we do not consider this to be a major problem because our focus is on understanding the index correlations. Hence, we are interested in the adequacy of our specification for the variance equations.
4 These "subtle interrelationships" imply that bank rescues placed a heavy burden on public finances after the onset of the global financial crisis, while banks were exposed to large government debt holdings.

References

Antonakakis, N. (2012) Exchange return co-movements and volatility spillovers before and after the introduction of Euro, *Journal of International Financial Markets, Institutions, and Money*, **22**, 1091–1109.

Apostolakis, G. and Papadopoulos, A. P. (2014) Financial stress spillovers in advanced economies, *Journal of International Financial Markets, Institutions, and Money*, **32**, 128–149.

Arouri, M., Hammoudeh, S., Jawadi, F., and Nguyen, D. K. (2014) Financial linkages between US sector credit default swaps markets, *Journal of International Financial Markets, Institutions, and Money*, **33**, 223–243.

Baily, M. N. and Elliott, D. J. (2013) The role of finance in the economy: Implications for structural reform of the financial sector, *Working Paper*, The Brooking Institution, 1–34.

Bank of England (2011) Measuring financial sector output and its contribution to UK GDP, *Quarterly Bulletin*, 2011 Q3.

Benbouzid, N. and Mallick, S. (2013) Determinants of bank credit default swap spreads: The role of the housing sector, *North American Journal of Economics and Finance*, **24**, 243–259.

Chen, L. H., Hammoudeh, S., and Yuan, Y. (2011) Asymmetric convergence in US financial credit default swap sector index markets, *The Quarterly Review of Economics and Finance*, **51**, 408–418.

Chiang, T. C., Jeon, B. N., and Li, H. (2007) Dynamic correlation analysis of financial contagion: Evidence from Asian markets, *Journal of International Financial Markets, Institutions, and Money*, **26**, 1206–1228.

Diebold, F. X. and Yilmaz, K. (2012) Better to give than to receive: Predictive directional measurement of volatility spillovers, *International Journal of Forecasting*, **28**, 57–66.

Engle, R. (2002) Dynamic conditional correlation: A simple class of multivariate generalized autoregressive conditional heteroskedasticity models, *Journal of Business & Economic Statistics*, **20**, 339–350.

Hammoudeh, S., Bhar, R., and Liu, T. (2013b) Relationships between financial sectors' CDS spreads and other gauges of risk: Did the Great Recession change them? *The Financial Review*, **48**, 151–178.

Hammoudeh, S., Nandha, M., and Yuan, Y. (2013a) Dynamics of CDS spread indexes of US financial sectors, *Applied Economics*, **45**, 213–223.

Hammoudeh, S. and Sari, R. (2011) Financial CDS, stock market and interest rates: Which drives which? *North American Journal of Economics and Finance*, **22**, 257–276.

Koop, G., Pesaran, M. H., and Potter, S. M. (1996) Impulse response analysis in nonlinear multivariate models, *Journal of Econometrics*, **74**, 119–147.

Pesaran, M. H. and Shin, Y. (1998) Generalized impulse response analysis in linear multivariate models, *Economics Letters*, **58**, 17–29.

Ross, S. A. (1989) Information and volatility: No-arbitrage Martingale approach to timing and resolution irrelevancy, *The Journal of Finance*, **44**, 1–17.

Tamakoshi, G. and Hamori, S. (2014) Spillovers among CDS indexes in the US financial sector, *North American Journal of Economics and Finance*, **27**, 104–113.

6 Dependence structure of insurance sector CDS indices

6.1 Introduction

The announcement of the U.S. government's bailout of the American International Group (AIG) on September 16, 2009, gave the financial market the impression that the insurance company was too big to fail. Similar governmental support was also provided to several other large insurance firms such as Prudential and Hartford. Following such bailouts, some scholars started to observe "systemic risk" in the insurance sector. Systemic risk is widely believed to be a problem when the collapse of one financial institution triggers the potential failure of others or spreads instability throughout the financial system. Indeed, banking businesses run by insurance companies (e.g., credit derivative transactions and securities lending programs) and their multinational activities have the potential to generate systemic risk.

Previous findings on the influence of systemic risk in the insurance sector are mixed. For example, while Harrington (2009) considers such systemic risks to be relatively low owing to the large amount of capital employed by insurance companies, Acharya et al. (2009) describe the specific types of systemic risks that might arise in the insurance sector.[1] They also emphasize its "too interconnected to fail" nature as a key issue and propose that a federal regulator must exercise some control over large insurance firms.

Given the diversity of research opinions on this topic, analyzing empirically the interconnectedness among the credit risks of insurance sectors across countries is necessary. In this study, we thus investigate the dependence structure of the credit default swap (CDS[2]) indices of the insurance sectors in the United States, the European Union (EU), and the United Kingdom, using daily data from January 2, 2004, to June 30, 2013. CDS indices, which consist of a portfolio of single-name swaps, provide the liquid market prices of credit risks in different sectors. Hence, insurance sector CDS indices can be regarded as accurate measures of the default risk premium in this sector. Analyzing these indices is therefore important for policymakers who wish to identify and monitor interconnectedness across countries and for investors who wish to take advantage of the diversification opportunities at the sector level.

Recent empirical studies of insurance sector CDS indices have focused on their linkages with other financial sector CDS indices and other financial assets. For example, by using the autoregressive distributed lag approach, Hammoudeh and Sari (2011) analyze the relationships between the CDS indices of the banking, insurance, and financial services sectors; stock price index; and Treasury security rates in the United States. They detect evidence of contagion effects between the CDS indices of these financial sectors and observe that their short-run cross-shock effects are the highest. By using the momentum threshold autoregression approach, Chen et al. (2011) demonstrate that for all three financial sector CDS indices, the speed of adjustment to the long-term equilibrium is faster during divergences than convergences, implying the presence of asymmetric cointegration. By using a vector error correction model, Hammoudeh et al. (2013a) show significant bidirectional causality between these three financial sector indices and find that the largest impacts stem from shocks in the banking sector CDS index. Hammoudeh et al. (2013b) also employ a vector error correction model for the three financial sector CDS indices, other measures of risk, and inflation expectations and find evidence of contagion as well as significant QE1 effects on most risk measures. Chen et al. (2013) apply a linear and non-linear Granger test to firm-level CDS spread data in the insurance and banking sectors and find that, after controlling for conditional heteroskedasticity, the causality running from banks to insurers is stronger than that in the opposite direction. Arouri et al. (2014) investigate the dynamic linkages between the financial sector CDS indices for the banking, insurance, and financial services sectors over the recent period covering the global financial crisis by employing the smooth transition error-correction models (STECMs). They uncover the existence of a cointegrating relationship for the two pairs of the three CDS indexes (banking–financial services and banking–insurance), which is marked by asymmetry and non-linearity in the adjustment process to the long-term equilibrium.

The present study makes two primary contributions to the above strand of the literature. First, to our knowledge, we are among the first to study the relationships among insurance sector CDS indices across countries. Specifically, we examine whether the degree of co-movements changed during the global credit crisis that originated in the United States and the European sovereign debt crisis that originated in Greece. As the CDS indices may inherently pose the risk of large simultaneous losses when the credit quality of their reference entities deteriorates, it is intriguing to investigate the potential impacts of financial turmoil on their interconnectedness.

Second, our research methodology differs from that of previous studies in that we use a copula-GARCH[3] framework. This copula approach has two primary analytical advantages. The first is that it allows for the non-linear portions of the dependence structure of variables, to which applying linear correlation measures may result in misspecification. This fact is important because normality assumptions tend to be challenged for credit assets such as the studied CDS indices. Second, the copula technique enables us to identify the existence of tail dependence – whether symmetric or asymmetric – that arises from occasional extreme co-movements. Therefore, our method is useful to assess the existence of systemic risks that may manifest in the tail behaviors of insurance sector CDS indices.

The remainder of this paper is organized as follows. Section 6.2 describes our empirical methodology. Section 6.3 briefly explains the data used, and Section 6.4 provides our empirical results. Finally, Section 6.5 concludes.

6.2 Empirical methodology

In this study, we use a two-step estimation approach for copula models, following the methodology adopted by Aloui et al. (2013).[4] We first introduce the copula function and then describe our empirical model for marginal distributions. We next present several alternative copula models of conditional dependence structures and explain their estimation and testing methods.

Copula function

Copula functions were first introduced by Sklar (1959), who shows that if the joint distribution of two continuous random variables X and Y ($F_{XY}(x, y)$) has margins $F_X(x)$ and $F_Y(y)$, there exists a copula C such that for all x and y in R,

$$F_{XY}(x,y) = C(F_X(x), F_Y(y)) . \tag{6.1}$$

In other words, a copula is a joint distribution function of marginal distributions, which are uniform in the interval [0, 1]. The copula function allows us to model the marginal distribution and dependence structure separately; that is, we construct a multivariate joint distribution by first specifying the univariate marginal distributions and then choosing a copula to capture the dependence structure.

Tail dependence, which some copula specifications have, describes the probability that two random variables are in the lower or upper joint tails of bivariate distributions. The coefficients of the lower (λ_L) and upper tail dependence (λ_U) can be written in terms of the copula between the random variables X and Y as follows:

$$\lambda_L = \lim_{u \to 0} \Pr[X \leq F_X^{-1}(u) \mid Y \leq F_Y^{-1}(u)], \tag{6.2}$$

$$\lambda_U = \lim_{u \to 1} \Pr[X > F_X^{-1}(u) \mid Y > F_Y^{-1}(u)], \tag{6.3}$$

where F_X^{-1} and F_Y^{-1} are marginal quantile functions. If $\lambda_L = \lambda_U$, we assume that there is symmetric tail dependence and asymmetric tail dependence otherwise.

Specifications of the marginal distributions

Our first step is to fit a univariate model to set the margins. We adopt the maximum likelihood method and choose the best AR(k)-EGARCH(p,q) models, specified as follows:

$$\Delta r_t = \phi_0 + \sum_{i=1}^{k} \phi_i \Delta r_{t-i} + \varepsilon_t, \tag{6.4}$$

$$\log(\sigma_t^2) = \omega + \sum_{i=1}^{q} (\alpha_i |z_{t-i}| + \gamma_i z_{t-i}) + \sum_{i=1}^{p} \beta_i \log(\sigma_{t-i}^2), \tag{6.5}$$

where Δr_t represents the first difference of each CDS index series, ε_t is the error term with $E_{t-1}(\varepsilon_t) = 0$ and $E_{t-1}(\varepsilon_t^2) = \sigma_t^2$, and k (= 1, 2, . . ., 10), p (= 1, 2), and q (= 1, 2) are selected on the basis of the Schwarz–Bayesian information criterion. We assume that a random variable $z_t = \varepsilon_t/\sigma_t$ has a generalized error distribution. Unlike the standard GARCH model employed by Aloui et al. (2013), we use the EGARCH model to capture the asymmetric movement in the volatility caused by past shocks, which is usually observed in financial assets such as CDS indices. Further, we contend that the EGARCH model is preferred to other classes of asymmetric volatility models such as Glosten–Jagannathan–Runkle's (1993) GJR-GARCH model and Zakoian's (1991) threshold GARCH model in that it is not constrained by the signs of the coefficients because its logarithm form ensures the non-negativity of conditional variance.

Specifications of the conditional dependence structure

Our next step is to extract the standardized residuals from each of the univariate EGARCH models and transform them into uniform variables to enable us to obtain the filtered series used to estimate the copula parameters. Here, we use several copula models to examine the various patterns of dependence between the insurance sector CDS indices. Specifically, two elliptical copulas (Normal and Student-t) and three Archimedean copulas (Gumbel, Clayton, and Frank) are considered for the comparison.

The Normal copula is derived from multivariate Gaussian distributions. It is symmetric and exhibits no tail dependence. For all u and $v \in [0, 1]$, the bivariate Normal copula can be expressed as

$$C(u,v) = \int_{-\infty}^{\phi^{-1}(u)} \int_{-\infty}^{\phi^{-1}(v)} \frac{1}{2\pi\sqrt{1-\theta^2}} \exp\left(-\frac{x^2 - 2\theta xy + y^2}{2(1-\theta^2)}\right) dxdy, \tag{6.6}$$

where ϕ is the univariate standard normal distribution and θ is the linear correlation coefficient ($\theta \in (-1, 1)$).

The Student-t copula is based on multivariate Student-t distributions. It allows for symmetric non-zero dependence in the tails, where large joint positive or negative observations have the same probability of occurrence. The bivariate Student-t copula can be expressed as

$$C(u,v) = \int_{-\infty}^{t_\upsilon^{-1}(u)} \int_{-\infty}^{t_\upsilon^{-1}(v)} \frac{1}{2\pi\sqrt{1-\theta^2}} \exp\left(1 + \frac{x^2 + y^2 - 2\theta xy}{\upsilon(1-\theta^2)}\right)^{-(\upsilon+2)/2} dxdy, \tag{6.7}$$

where $t_\upsilon^{-1}(u)$ denotes the inverse of the Student-t cumulative distribution function, with υ degrees of freedom.

The Gumbel copula has upper but no lower tail dependence. It can be expressed as

$$C(u,v) = \exp\left\{-[(-\ln u)^{\theta} + (-\ln v)^{\theta}]^{1/\theta}\right\},\ \theta \in [1, +\infty). \tag{6.8}$$

The Clayton copula, on the contrary, has lower but no upper tail dependence. It can be expressed as

$$C(u,v) = \left(u^{-\theta} + v^{-\theta} - 1\right)^{-1/\theta},\ \theta \in [-1, +\infty) / \{0\}. \tag{6.9}$$

The Frank copula is symmetric, with no tail dependence, allowing us to capture the full range of dependence. It can be expressed as

$$C(u,v) = -\frac{1}{\theta}\ln\left(1 + \frac{(\exp(-\theta u) - 1)(\exp(-\theta v) - 1)}{\exp(-\theta) - 1}\right),\ \theta \in (-\infty, +\infty)/\{0\}. \tag{6.10}$$

Estimating and testing the copulas

We apply the pseudo-maximum likelihood method to the filtered series and estimate the copula parameters. We then estimate the marginals F_X and F_Y in a non-parametric way, using their empirical cumulative distribution functions (ECDFs) $\hat{F}_X$ and $\hat{F}_Y$; that is,

$$\hat{F}_X(x) = \frac{1}{n}\sum\nolimits_{i=1}^{n} 1\{X_i < x\} \text{ and } \hat{G}_Y(y) = \frac{1}{n}\sum\nolimits_{i=1}^{n} 1\{Y_i < y\}. \tag{6.11}$$

Here, Xi and Yi are the standardized residuals, obtained through the estimation of Equation (6.5). In the inference of the margin estimations, we apply the rescaled versions of $\hat{F}_X$ and $\hat{F}_Y$, such as $\frac{1}{1+n}\sum\nolimits_{i=1}^{n} 1\{X_i < x\}$ and $\frac{1}{1+n}\sum\nolimits_{i=1}^{n} 1\{Y_i < y\}$, to avoid problems arising from the potential unboundedness when plugging the results into the likelihood function and taking logarithms.[5] We transform the standardized residuals (derived from each EGARCH model) into uniform variables, with the above ECDF of each marginal distribution. Then, we estimate the unknown parameter θ of the copula models as follows:

$$\hat{\theta} = \arg\max_{\theta} \sum\nolimits_{i=1}^{n} \ln c(\hat{F}_X(x_i), \hat{G}_Y(y_i), \theta), \tag{6.12}$$

where $c(\cdot)$ denotes the density of each of the five copulas expressed in Equations (6.6)–(6.10).

To investigate which copula exhibits the best fit, we apply the goodness-of-fit test proposed by Genest et al. (2009). This test is based on the distance between the empirical and the estimated copula:

$$\mathbf{C}_n = \sqrt{n}(C_n - C_{\theta_n}), \tag{6.13}$$

where C_n is the empirical copula of the data, defined by

$$C_n(u) = \frac{1}{n}\sum_{i=1}^{n} 1(\hat{U}_i \leq u) \ , \ u \in [0,1]^d, \tag{6.14}$$

and C_0 is an estimation of copula C, which is derived from the assumption that C belongs to parametric copula family C_0. The test statistic is the Cramer–von Mises distance, given as

$$S_n = \int_{[0,1]^d} \mathbb{C}_n(u)^2 dC_n(u). \tag{6.15}$$

To find the p-values for the test statistic, we employ Kojadinovie and Yan's (2011) multiplier method, which is computationally faster than the parametric bootstrap method. The highest p-value means the smallest distance between the estimated and the empirical copula, implying that the copula under investigation is the best fit for the data.

6.3 Data

We employ daily data on the five-year CDS indices for the U.S., EU, and U.K. insurance sectors. Insurance sector CDS indices are constructed from an average mid-spread calculation of a portfolio of single-name CDSs for several insurance companies. We chose five-year CDS indices because they are the most frequently traded in the indices market, with maturities ranging from one to 10 years. Our sample period is from January 2, 2004, to June 30, 2013. The beginning of the period is restricted by the availability of CDS index data, at the sector level, in Thomson Reuters Datastream.

Table 6.1 reports the descriptive statistics for our dataset. Volatility, as indicated by the standard deviation value, is the highest in the United States, the origin of the 2007 global financial crisis. All three indices are positively skewed, suggesting that the distributions have longer right-hand tails and that therefore, a few

Table 6.1 Summary statistics

Variable	*Mean (b.p.)*	*Maximum (b.p.)*	*Minimum (b.p.)*	*SD*	*Skewness*	*Kurtosis*	*Jarque–Bera*
U.S.	337.1	3182.4	17.2	370.0	1.8	9.1	5295.4***
EU	102.2	333.2	7.8	77.6	0.5	2.2	182.9***
U.K.	121.1	1010.6	8.1	143.4	3.1	14.4	17383.7***

Notes: Statistics on the level data for the daily CDS indices are reported. The sample covers the period between January 2, 2004, and June 30, 2013, for 2,477 daily observations. The abbreviation b.p. means basis points.

*** denotes statistical significance at the 1% level.

high values tend to occur. The high kurtosis levels in the U.S. and U.K. indices indicate that their distributions are more leptokurtic. The Jarque–Bera tests reject the null hypothesis of a normal distribution at the 1 percent significance level, which is consistent with the statistics for skewness and kurtosis. Hence, the CDS indices are not normally distributed. We also carry out augmented Dickey–Fuller unit root tests, with intercepts and intercepts plus trends, for all three indices, and find that they are I(1) variables.[6] Thus, in our analysis, we use first-differenced data,[7] following several related CDS index studies.

6.4 Empirical results

Estimation of the marginal distributions

As noted in Section 2, we model the marginal distributions (by using univariate AR-EGARCH models) and the dependence structure of the variables (by using various copula models) separately. The first step is to fit the univariate models to each data series and select the best AR(k)-EGARCH(p,q) model.

Table 6.2 presents the coefficient estimates for each selected AR-EGARCH model for the entire period. We chose the AR(1)-EGARCH(1, 1) models for the U.S. and EU insurance sector CDS indices and the AR(10)-EGARCH(1, 1) model for the U.K. insurance sector CDS index, following the Schwarz–Bayesian information criterion. Note that each model's variance equation exhibits a good fit to the data. The coefficients of the EGARCH (β_1) and asymmetric (γ_1) terms are significant at the 1 percent level for all three indices. In addition, the p-values of the Ljung–Box Q-statistics, $Q(12)$ and $Q^2(12)$, are larger than 0.05, suggesting no autocorrelation up to order 12 for the standardized residuals and their squares. Indeed, the autocorrelation functions indicate that the standardized residuals are independent and identically distributed, and therefore, more suitable for the estimation of copula functions than the raw data series. Overall, these findings support the adequacy of our model specification.

Estimation of the conditional dependence structure

The second step is to transform the vector of the standardized residuals obtained from each EGARCH model into uniform variables, using the ECDFs. Filtered series are used to estimate the copula functions of the insurance sector CDS indices. We first investigate the rank correlations, specifically Kendall's tau and Spearman's rho, which have appealing copula properties. These are non-parametric dependence measures in that they are independent of the marginal distributions and can capture the non-linear relationships between the variables. Thus, the measures are suitable for analyzing the dependence structures of assets related to credit risks, for which normality assumptions rarely hold.

Table 6.3 presents the results of the rank correlation coefficients for the entire period and the following three sub-periods[8]: the pre-crisis period (January 1, 2004, to August 8, 2007), credit crisis period (August 9, 2007, to October 31,

Table 6.2 Parameter estimates for the marginal distribution models

	U.S. *AR(1)-EGARCH(1,1)*		*EU* *AR(1)-EGARCH(1,1)*		*U.K.* *AR(10)-EGARCH(1,1)*	
	Estimate	*SE*	*Estimate*	*SE*	*Estimate*	*SE*
Conditional mean equation						
φ_0	−0.0652***	0.0089	−0.0065	0.0085	0.0027	0.0129
φ_1	0.1477***	0.0100	0.0773***	0.0156	0.0803***	0.0186
φ_2					0.0408**	0.0190
φ_3					0.0128	0.0192
φ_4					−0.0101	0.0187
φ_5					0.0186	0.0187
φ_6					−0.0092	0.0186
φ_7					0.0101	0.0192
φ_8					−0.0232	0.0186
φ_9					0.0146	0.0187
φ_{10}					0.0302	0.0187
Conditional variance equation						
ω	−0.1708***	0.0143	−0.1509***	0.0123	−0.1401***	0.0138
α_1	0.3318***	0.0234	0.2247***	0.0185	0.2106***	0.0218
γ_1	−0.0432***	0.0155	0.1105***	0.0131	0.0844***	0.0129
β_1	0.9901***	0.0015	0.9962***	0.0013	0.9971***	0.0013
$Q(12)$	19.7130		12.0590			
p-value	0.0730		0.4410		15.2510	
$Q^2(12)$	0.0578		0.7483		0.2280	
p-value	1.0000		1.0000		9.2728	

Notes: $Q(12)$ and $Q^2(12)$ are the Ljung–Box statistics up to order 12 in the standardized residuals and standardized residuals squared.

*** and ** indicate statistical significance at the 1% and 5% levels, respectively.

Table 6.3 Correlation estimates of dependence in insurance sector CDS indices

	Panel A: Entire period (2004/1/2–2013/6/30)		*Panel B: Pre-crisis period (2004/1/2–2007/8/8)*		*Panel C: Credit crisis period (2007/8/9–2009/10/31)*		*Panel D: Debt crisis period (2009/11/1–2013/6/30)*	
	Kendall	*Spearman*	*Kendall*	*Spearman*	*Kendall*	*Spearman*	*Kendall*	*Spearman*
U.S.–EU	0.2640	0.3832	0.2591	0.3766	0.3217	0.4667	0.2941	0.4285
EU–U.K.	0.4740	0.6406	0.3031	0.4292	0.5249	0.7064	0.6056	0.7889
U.K.–U.S.	0.2327	0.3390	0.1630	0.2399	0.2498	0.3606	0.2736	0.3975

Notes: The table summarizes the rank correlation estimates over the entire period and the three sub-periods.

2009), and debt crisis period (November 1, 2009, to June 30, 2013). The beginning of the credit crisis period is based on the assumption that BNP Paribas' suspension of its funds, which was affected by U.S. subprime mortgage liabilities on August 9, 2007, stunned the market. The beginning of the debt crisis period is taken as November 1, 2009, under the assumption that market participants' concerns over the Greek sovereign debt crisis increased in early November 2009. Table 6.3 shows that the pairwise correlation measures (Kendall's tau, Spearman's rho) are positive for all periods, indicating a higher probability of concordance than of discordance. In addition, the correlation measures are higher in the EU–U.K. pair than in the other pairs, reflecting the geographical proximity and economic ties between the EU and United Kingdom. More importantly, we detect substantial increases in the correlation measures for all the pairs during the credit and debt crisis periods compared with the pre-crisis period. This finding suggests that the two crises triggered contagion effects on the credit risks of insurance sectors across countries.

Next, we estimate the dependence parameter θ of the five copulas (Normal, Student-t, Gumbel, Clayton, and Frank) for the entire period as well as the three sub-periods. Table 6.4 reports the estimation results. For all the pairs, the dependence parameters for each of the five copula functions are significant at the 1 percent level for the entire period (Panel A), indicating a high degree of interconnectedness among the U.S., EU, and U.K. insurance sector CDS indices. Furthermore, the values of the dependence parameters for all the pairs and copula functions are markedly higher during the credit (Panel C) and debt crisis (Panel D) periods than during the pre-crisis (Panel A) period. This result further supports the hypothesis that insurance sector CDS indices tend to be more correlated during financial crisis periods owing to the cross-border transmission of credit risks in the industry.

To examine which copula best fits the data, we employ Genest et al.'s (2009) goodness-of-fit test. Table 6.5 summarizes the results of the tests, and Table 6.6 presents the tail dependence coefficients for the selected copula. Two main findings are worthy of note. First, during the pre-crisis period, the dependence patterns vary across the pairs. For the U.S.–EU and EU–U.K. pairs, the symmetric copulas (Normal and Student-t copulas, respectively) exhibit the best fit, implying no asymmetric dependence between these pairs. While the U.S.–EU pair shows zero tail dependence, the EU–U.K. pair shows more observations in the tails, suggesting the occasional occurrence of extreme co-movements in the upper and lower tails. By contrast, for the U.K.–U.S. pair, the Gumbel copula gives the best fit. This result demonstrates that the dependence structures of the U.K. and U.S. insurance sector CDS indices exhibit right tail dependence (the tendency for upper extreme co-movement of indices to occur), implying the possibility of a large simultaneous loss across the two countries. Second, interestingly, the Frank copula is found to be the most appropriate for all pairs during the two financial crises. A key feature of the Frank copula is that it is symmetric, with zero tail dependence, and shows smaller tail concentration on both sides compared with the Normal copula. Thus, contrary to our expectations,

Table 6.4 Estimates of the dependence parameters for the different copula models

	Normal	*Student-t*	*Gumbel*	*Clayton*	*Frank*
Panel A: Entire period (2004/1/2–2013/6/30)					
U.S.–EU	0.3870 (0.0150)***	0.3770 (0.0208)***	1.3103 (0.0184)***	0.4931 (0.0266)***	2.5470 (0.1290)***
EU–U.K.	0.6475 (0.0087)***	0.6779 (0.0115)***	1.8232 (0.0283)***	1.2016 (0.0393)***	5.4480 (0.1430)***
U.K.–U.S.	0.3430 (0.0155)***	0.3340 (0.0215)***	1.2680 (0.0173)***	0.4117 (0.0282)***	2.2260 (0.1260)***
Panel B: Pre-crisis period (2004/1/2–2007/8/8)					
U.S.–EU	0.3821 (0.0165)***	0.3702 (0.0228)***	1.3100 (0.0200)***	0.4782 (0.0292)***	2.5000 (0.1400)***
EU–U.K.	0.4623 (0.0219)***	0.4580 (0.0304)***	1.4230 (0.0360)***	0.6534 (0.0502)***	3.0730 (0.2060)***
U.K.–U.S.	0.2601 (0.0279)***	0.2357 (0.0387)***	1.1967 (0.0285)***	0.2394 (0.0436)***	1,5200 (0.2020)***
Panel C: Credit crisis period (2007/8/9–2009/10/31)					
U.S.–EU	0.4673 (0.0286)***	0.4481 (0.0406)***	1.3990 (0.0447)***	0.6495 (0.0576)***	3.2100 (0.2800)***
EU–U.K.	0.7042 (0.0159)***	0.7179 (0.0214)***	1.9412 (0.0669)***	1.4390 (0.0860)***	6.3520 (0,3290)***
U.K.–U.S.	0.3721 (0.0328)***	0.3579 (0.0436)***	1.2934 (0.0385)***	0.4753 (0.0636)***	2.4030 (0.2580)***
Panel D: Debt crisis period (2009/11/1–2013/6/30)					
U.S.–EU	0.4129 (0.0222)***	0.4099 (0.0317)***	1.3358 (0.0281)***	0.5563 (0.0425)***	2.8670 (0.2140)***
EU–U.K.	0.7860 (0.0087)***	0.8020 (0.0121)***	2.2297 (0.0618)***	1.8394 (0.0868)***	8.1770 (0.3020)***
U.K.–U.S.	0.3840 (0.0220)***	0.3897 (0.0323)***	1.3162 (0.0267)***	0.5034 (0.0451)***	2.6560 (0.2070)***

Notes: *** denotes statistical significance at the 1% level. Standard errors are in parenthesis.

Table 6.5 Results of the goodness-of-fit tests

	Normal	*Student-t*	*Gumbel*	*Clayton*	*Frank*
Panel A: Entire period (2004/1/2–2013/6/30)					
U.S.–EU	**0.0225**	0.0015	0.0005	0.0005	0.0025
EU–U.K.	0.0005	**0.0485**	0.0005	0.0005	0.0005
U.K.–U.S.	**0.0105**	0.0005	0.0005	0.0005	0.0005
Panel B: Pre-crisis period (2004/1/2–2007/8/8)					
U.S.–EU	**0.1513**	0.0145	0.0005	0.0005	0.0135
EU–U.K.	0.0365	**0.3002**	0.0005	0.0005	0.0005
U.K.–U.S.	0.0275	0.0045	**0.8576**	0.0005	0.0015
Panel C: Credit crisis period (2007/8/9–2009/10/31)					
U.S.–EU	0.0784	0.0045	0.0005	0.0005	**0.3472**
EU–U.K.	0.0005	0.0275	0.0005	0.0005	**0.0864**
U.K.–U.S.	0.3132	0.0984	0.0095	0.0005	**0.4011**
Panel D: Debt crisis period (2009/11/1–2013/6/30)					
U.S.–EU	0.0255	0.0015	0.0005	0.0005	**0.9226**
EU–U.K.	0.0005	0.0025	0.0005	0.0005	**0.0035**
U.K.–U.S.	0.0115	0.0075	0.0005	0.0005	**0.1224**

Notes: The table presents the *p*-values of the goodness-of-fit test. Highest *p*-values (bold text) indicate the copula that best fits the data.

Table 6.6 Tail dependence coefficients of the best copulas

	Best copula	λ_L *(lower tail dependence)*	λ_U *(upper tail dependence)*
Panel A: Entire period (2004/1/2–2013/6/30)			
U.S.–EU	Normal	0.0000	0.0000
EU–U.K.	Student-t	0.3977	0.3977
U.K.–U.S.	Normal	0.0000	0.0000
Panel B: Pre-crisis period (2004/1/2–2007/8/8)			
U.S.–EU	Normal	0.0000	0.0000
EU–U.K.	Student-t	0.2186	0.2186
U.K.–U.S.	Gumbel	0.0000	0.2153
Panel C: Credit crisis period (2007/8/9–2009/10/31)			
U.S.–EU	Frank	0.0000	0.0000
EU–U.K.	Frank	0.0000	0.0000
U.K.–U.S.	Frank	0.0000	0.0000
Panel D: Debt crisis period (2009/11/1–2013/6/30)			
U.S.–EU	Frank	0.0000	0.0000
EU–U.K.	Frank	0.0000	0.0000
U.K.–U.S.	Frank	0.0000	0.0000

Notes: The table presents the selected best copula and the lower and upper tail dependence coefficients.

we find no asymmetric dependence between the insurance sector CDS indices during periods of market stress, suggesting the absence of systemic risk.

Discussion

Our findings provide some implications for investors and regulators. On the one hand, knowing the dependence structure of the insurance sector CDS indices across countries is relevant for the portfolio allocation and risk management decisions of investors. Our results show substantial increases in rank coefficients during the credit and debt crisis periods, suggesting cross-country contagion effects in the insurance sector. This finding indicates for investors that the benefits of the international diversification of credit assets related to the insurance sector might be lower in times of market stress. In addition, we also find evidence of asymmetric tail dependence between the U.K. and U.S. insurance sector CDS indices during the pre-crisis period, as shown by the fact that the Gumbel copula provides the best fit for the series. This is crucial for the risk management of investors in that they should be aware of the risks of a substantial simultaneous loss due to extreme co-movements in the value-at-risk calculation of their portfolio exposed to credit risks in the insurance industry.

On the other hand, our results on the dependence structure are important for regulators to model the regulatory framework of the insurance sector. In this regard, one of our key findings is that the Frank copula, which is symmetric with zero tail dependence, is the best-fitting copula during the credit and debt crisis periods; therefore, no asymmetric dependence structure is detected. As Poon et al. (2004) contend, tail dependence has the probability of joint occurrence of extreme observations and hence is a legitimate measure of systemic risk in times of financial crisis. Our result of no evidence of asymmetric tail dependence may thus suggest that at least as far as the cross-country transmission of risks among the U.S., EU, and U.K. insurance sectors is concerned, significant systemic risk may not have been a problem during the two crisis periods. This empirical finding is generally in line with that of Harrington (2009), who examines the role of AIG during the global financial crisis and argues that systemic risk is relatively low in the insurance sector. Our findings provide insights into whether international coordination is required for significant regulatory reforms, with a focus on managing the potential systemic risk in the insurance sector.

6.5 Conclusion

This study investigated the dependence structures of the U.S., EU, and U.K. insurance sector CDS indices from January 2, 2004, to June 30, 2013. The copula-GARCH model used allows us to capture the non-linear dependence structure and analyze upper and lower tail dependence behavior. We also examined whether the dependence structure changed during the global credit crisis and European sovereign debt crisis periods.

Our main findings are threefold. First, the rank correlation coefficients (Kendall's tau, Spearman's rho), for all the index pairs, soared during the credit and debt crisis periods, exhibiting a contagion effect in the credit risks of the insurance sector across countries during periods of market stress. Second, the dependence patterns varied across the pairs during the pre-crisis period. That is, while symmetric copulas (the Normal and Student-t copulas) were found to be the best fit for the U.S.–EU and EU–U.K. pairs, the asymmetric copula (Gumbel copula) was the best fit for the U.K.–U.S. pair, indicating the risks of a large simultaneous loss between the United States and the United Kingdom during this period. Finally, a symmetric copula with zero dependence (the Frank copula) was found to be the most appropriate for all the pairs during the two financial crisis periods, implying that systemic risks may be limited among the insurance sector CDS indices, even in times of financial turmoil.

The presented findings have important implications for investors in terms of portfolio risk management. The results are also relevant for regulators who wish to develop appropriate regulatory policies and ameliorate the transmission of risk. However, while this study is the first to shed light on the cross-country dependence structures of insurance sector CDS indices, further work is still needed to identify the concrete mechanisms through which credit risks are transmitted in the industry. This topic is left for future research.

Notes

1 They lay out three types of systemic risks: (i) counterparty risk, (ii) spillover risk, and (iii) fragile capital structure and asset-liability mismatch risk.

2 A CDS is a bilateral credit derivative contract in which a seller sells protection to a buyer against the risk of the default of the reference entity. The insurance sector is usually a seller of CDS contracts. Harrington (2009) mentions that in the case of AIG, the firm mainly sold CDS contracts to EU banks, which could have reduced its capital requirements to hold the underlying securities.

3 Of the various GARCH-type models in the literature, we select the exponential GARCH (EGARCH) model of Nelson (1991) to model marginal behaviors, as explained in detail in Section 6.2. For examples of copula-GARCH-type models, see Aloui et al. (2013) and Yang and Hamori (2014).

4 Lee and Long (2009) and Zolotko and Okhrin (2014) present a copula-based multivariate GARCH model, which enables us to model the conditional correlation and the remaining dependence simultaneously, and thus may provide a more rigorous framework within which to work with the multivariate data series. We leave the use of their methodology to future research.

5 See Genest et al. (1995) for a more detailed explanation of this issue.

6 The results of the unit root tests are available upon request.

7 The units of the CDS indices are expressed in basis points. Therefore, we do not convert them into logarithms.

8 AR-EGARCH models are applied to the three insurance sector CDS indexes for each sub-period. The estimation results of the AR-EGARCH models are not presented to save space, but the results of each are available upon request.

References

Acharya, V. V., Biggs, J., Richardson, M., and Ryan, S. (2009) On the financial regulations of insurance companies, *Working Paper*, August 2009, NYU Stern School of Business.

Aloui, R., Aissa, M. S. B., and Nguyen, D. K. (2013) Conditional dependence structure between oil prices and exchange rates: A copula-GARCH approach, *Journal of International Money and Finance*, **32**, 719–738.

Arouri, M., Hammoudeh, S., Jawadi, F., and Nguyen, D. K. (2014) Financial linkages between US sector credit default swaps markets, *Journal of International Financial Markets, Institutions, and Money*, **33**, 223–243.

Chen, H., Cummins, J. D., Viswanathan, K. S., and Weiss, M. A. (2013) Systemic risk and the interconnectedness between banks and insures: An econometric analysis, *The Journal of Risk and Insurance*, **81**, 623–652.

Chen, L. H., Hammoudeh, S., and Yuan, Y. (2011) Asymmetric convergence in US financial credit default swap sector index markets, *The Quarterly Review of Economics and Finance*, **51**, 408–418.

Genest, C., Ghoudi, K., and Rivest, L.-P. (1995) A semiparametric estimation procedure of dependence parameters in multivariate families of distributions, *Biometrika*, **82**, 543–552.

Genest, C., Remillard, B., and Beaudoin, D. (2009) Goodness-of-fit tests for copulas: A review and a power study, *Insurance: Mathematics and Economics*, **44**, 199–213.

Glosten, L. R., Jagannathan, R., and Runkle, D. E. (1993) On the relation between the expected value and the volatility of the nominal excess return on stocks, *Journal of Finance*, **48**, 1779–1801.

Hammoudeh, S., Bhar, R., and Liu, T. (2013b) Relationships between financial sectors' CDS spreads and other gauges of risk: Did the Great Recession change them? *The Financial Review*, **48**, 151–178.

Hammoudeh, S., Nandha, M., and Yuan, Y. (2013a). Dynamics of CDS spread indexes of US financial sectors, *Applied Economics*, **45**, 213–223.

Hammoudeh, S. and Sari, R. (2011) Financial CDS, stock market and interest rates: Which drives which? *North American Journal of Economics and Finance*, **22**, 257–276.

Harrington, S. E. (2009) The financial crisis, systemic risk, and the future of insurance regulation, *The Journal of Risk and Insurance*, **76**, 785–819.

Kojadinovie, I. and Yan, J. (2011) A goodness-of-fit test for multivariate multiparameter copulas based on multiplier central limit theorems, *Statistics and Computing*, **21**, 17–30.

Lee, T. H. and Long, X. (2009) Copula-based multivariate GARCH model with uncorrelated dependent errors, *Journal of Econometrics*, **150**, 207–218.

Nelson, D. (1991) Conditional heteroskedasticity in asset returns: A new approach, *Econometrica*, **59**, 347–370.

Poon, S., Rockinger, M., and Tawn, J. (2004) Extreme value dependence in financial markets: Diagnostics, models, and financial implications, *Review of Financial Studies*, **17**, 581–610.

Sklar, A. (1959) Fonctions de repartition a n dimensions et leurs marges, vol. 8. *Publicaitons de l'Institut de Statistique de L'Universite de Paris*, **8**, 229–231.

Yang, L. and Hamori, S. (2014) Dependence structure between CEEC-3 and German government securities markets, *Journal of International Financial Markets, Institutions & Money*, **29**, 109–125.

Zakoian, J. M. (1991) Threshold heteroskedastic models, *Unpublished Paper*, Institut National de la Statistique et des Etudes Economiques, Paris.

Zolotko, M. and Okhrin, O. (2014) Modelling the general dependence between commodity forward curves, *Energy Economics*, **43**, 284–296.

7 Time-varying correlation among bank sector CDS indices

7.1 Introduction

Two recent financial crises, namely the global financial crisis and the European sovereign debt crisis, have focused the attention of market participants on credit default swaps (CDS). A CDS is a bilateral contract in which a seller sells protection to a buyer against the default risk of the reference entity. The buyer of a CDS makes a series of periodic payments to the seller of the CDS during the contract period of the swap agreement, and obtains compensation if a default event takes place. The CDS market has indeed grown from a niche market to an actively traded credit derivatives market that traders and policymakers watch closely as a useful means to measure or transfer credit risks. Various CDS indices, which consist of a portfolio of single-name CDSs for several companies or financial institutions, are traded in relatively unregulated over-the-counter CDS markets. Those indices have been blamed for exacerbating the financial turmoil, as some investors allegedly drove up the prices and triggered overreactions in the markets through speculative trading.

The bank sector CDS index is one of the financial sector indices that have recently attracted the attention of scholars in particular. As Hammoudeh et al. (2013) note, the financial sector indices can be regarded as long-term measures of the health of financial institutions. Among the indices, we take notice of the bank sector CDS index because the bank sector is considered to be the most closely associated with the two recent financial crises, and thus, understanding the credit risks of the sector may be critical for market participants. In fact, the bank sector was caught under the spotlight in the global financial crisis, when several banks that had held a large amount of mortgage securities incurred substantial losses. At that time, regulations enabled them to record less regulatory capital if the protection was bought with a CDS for such mortgage securities. Moreover, the bank sector is also thought of as tied with the European sovereign debt crisis, as the deteriorating bank sector forced policymakers to pursue government rescue programs, which resulted in the exacerbation of the fiscal outlook and in sharp increases in government bond yields in several peripheral countries in the Euro area.

There is recent proliferation of the studies that have investigated financial sector CDS indices. For instance, Hammoudeh and Sari (2011) investigate both the short-run and long-run dynamics of the three U.S. financial sector indices (for the bank, insurance, and financial services sectors) and their relationships with the S&P 500 index and the Treasury securities rates. By constructing autoregressive distributed lag models, they find that the long-run cointegrating relationships among these variables became weaker during the global financial crisis period, compared with the entire study period. Furthermore, their generalized variance decomposition and impulse response analyses reveal that in the short run, the own and cross-shock effects are strongest within the three financial sector CDS indices, implying the existence of contagion across the creditworthiness of these sectors.

Chen et al. (2011) study whether the dynamic behaviors of the three U.S. financial sector CDS indices described above are different under favorable and unfavorable market conditions, exhibiting asymmetric adjustments to the long-term equilibrium. Using momentum-threshold autoregression models, they show that asymmetric cointegration exists for all pairs of the sector CDS indices. In addition, they find that the speeds of adjustment to the long-term equilibrium are much faster during widenings, which take place after negative shocks, than narrowings for all pairs. Moreover, their analysis reveal that while all individual sector CDS indices participate in the convergence to the equilibrium in all pairs in the short run, only one of the two sector indices in each pair contributes to the convergence to the long-run equilibrium.

Hammoudeh et al. (2013) examine the interconnectedness between the bank, insurance, and financial services CDS indices in the short and long run. Using vector error correction models, they show that the insurance sector CDS index exhibits the highest adjustment to the long-run equilibrium, while the bank CDS index is not error correcting. By conducting pairwise Granger causality tests, they also find significant bidirectional causality among the three indices in the short run. Furthermore, their generalized impulse response function analysis demonstrates that the strongest impacts stem from shocks in the bank sector CDS index, while the lowest cross-sector impacts come from shocks in the insurance sector CDS index.

Finally, Benbouzid and Mallick (2013) conduct a rare study that sheds light on the bank sector CDS index. Specifically, they analyze key determinants of the bank sector CDS index in the U.K., focusing on the role of the housing sector using the U.K. nationwide house price index. Using Johansen's cointegration tests and dynamic ordinary least squares methods, they find that a significant long-run cointegration relationship exists between the bank sector CDS index and the house price index. In contrast, their short-run structural VAR (vector autoregressive) analysis reveals that the liquidity premium (TED spread) was the only factor that yielded a significant unexpected structural shock.

This study belongs to such a strand of the existing literature on financial sector CDS indices as described above. The objective of this study is to investigate the dynamic relationship among bank sector CDS indices for the European Union (EU), the U.K., and the U.S. Our study offers three primary contributions. First, to the best of our knowledge, this study is among the first to assess the dynamic interdependence of the bank CDS indices across countries at the sector level. Although a few recent studies have examined the dynamic integration of the CDS markets, they have tended to focus their analysis on either sovereign

CDS spreads (Dooley and Hutchison, 2009; Wang and Moore, 2012) or the CDS spreads of an individual bank (Eichengreen et al., 2009). In contrast, we analyze the dynamics of the correlations among bank industry CDS index spreads at the sector level, which few studies have investigated. This is because the bank industry CDS index is regarded as a key measure of credit stress in the financial system, and thus, analyzing them may be useful to regulators who try to control the sector's credit default risks across countries. Moreover, portfolio managers who are exploring diversification opportunities may be more interested in bank CDS index spreads at the sector level than at the individual firm level.

Second, we explore the asymmetric behavior of time-varying correlations among bank CDS spreads, which are more influenced by downward shocks than upward shocks. We pursue this by employing the asymmetric dynamic conditional correlation (DCC) model proposed by Cappiello et al. (2006). The asymmetric DCC model is an extended version of the original DCC model developed by Engle (2002), which was later used by Wang and Moore (2012). The modification by Cappiello et al. (2006) allows for conditional asymmetries in covariance and correlation dynamics. Figure 7.1, which describes the historical time series data in natural logarithms on the EU, U.K., and U.S. bank CDS indices suggests that the correlations tend to differ depending on whether the CDS indices increase or decrease. Therefore, employing the asymmetric DCC model allows us to investigate the existence of asymmetric responses of dynamic correlations to negative news.

Third, we examine the potential impacts of the two recent financial crises on the estimated DCCs among the bank sector CDS indices using the method employed

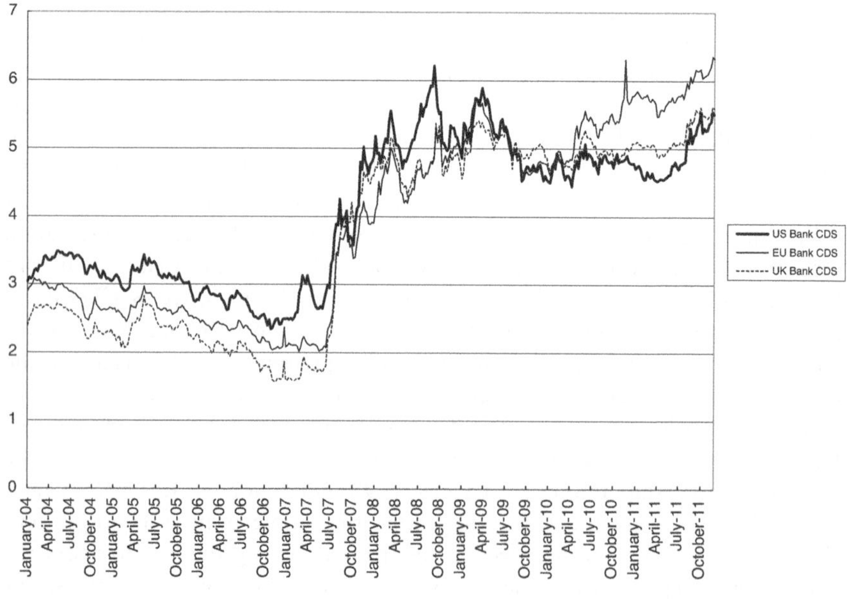

Figure 7.1 Historical data on the bank CDS index spreads (in natural logarithm)

by Yiu et al. (2010). Many previous studies on the promulgation of crises have identified evidence of significant increases in correlations across countries in the case of international stock markets, bond markets, and currency markets.[1] In contrast, Allen and Babus (2009) suggest that contagions triggered by financial crises may weaken the interdependence between financial institutions, and thereby, according to their network theory of contagion, may result in decreased correlations among the asset returns of banks. Given such different perspectives on the impacts of contagions, it is worth empirically assessing how the recent crises have affected the dynamics of correlations among the bank CDS indices, which may reflect the interconnectedness of the bank sectors from the perspective of credit risk.

The remainder of this article proceeds as follows. Section 7.2 presents our empirical methodology, and Section 7.3 explains our dataset. Section 7.4 discusses the empirical results of the causality test, and Section 7.5 concludes the chapter.

7.2 Empirical methodology

We analyze the asymmetric DCCs by taking the following three-step approach. First, we estimate the conditional variances for each bank sector CDS spread change using the univariate autoregressive-exponential generalized autoregressive conditional heteroskedasticity (AR(k)-EGARCH(p,q)) models proposed by Nelson (1991).

If we denote the CDS spread changes by Δr_t, we can represent the conditional mean and variance as follows:

$$\Delta r_t = a_0 + \sum_{i=1}^{k} a_i \Delta r_{t-i} + \varepsilon_t, \quad \varepsilon_t \sim GED(\nu) \tag{7.1}$$

$$\log(\sigma_t^2) = \omega + \sum_{i=1}^{q} (\alpha_i |z_{t-i}| + \gamma_i z_{t-i}) + \sum_{i=1}^{p} \beta_i \log(\sigma_{t-i}^2) \tag{7.2}$$

where $z_t = \varepsilon_t / \sigma_t$ and the optimal lag lengths, k (= 1, 2, . . ., 10), p (= 1, 2) and q (= 1, 2) are selected using the Schwarz Bayesian information criterion (SBIC). For the density function of ε_t, we use the generalized error distribution, which has an additional parameter, ν, to express the thickness of tails, as follows:

$$f(x) = \frac{\nu}{2^{[(\nu+1)/\nu]}\Gamma(1/\nu)\lambda} \exp\left(-\frac{1}{2}\left|\frac{x}{\lambda}\right|^{\nu}\right) \tag{7.3}$$

$$\lambda = \sqrt{\frac{2^{(-2/\nu)}\Gamma(1/\nu)}{\Gamma(3/\nu)}}. \tag{7.4}$$

The logarithm form of the EGARCH model described above ensures the non-negativity of the conditional variance without constraining the coefficients of the model. We can also capture the asymmetric effect of positive and negative innovations by including the term z_{t-i}. Furthermore, the persistence of shocks to the conditional variance is given by $\sum_{i=1}^{p} \beta_i$. Because negative coefficients are not precluded, the EGARCH model allows for the possibility of cyclical behavior in volatility.

Second, with the conditional variance obtained from Equation (7.2), we analyze the conditional correlation by employing the asymmetric DCC model developed by Cappiello et al. (2006). Let us denote the conditional covariance matrix by

$$H_t = E[\varepsilon_t \varepsilon_t'] = D_t P_t D_t \tag{7.5}$$

where the diagonal matrix D_t is the conditional standard deviation derived from Equation (7.2). Now, the asymmetric generalized DCC (AG-DCC) model is given by

$$\begin{aligned} Q_t = {} & (\bar{Q} - A'\bar{Q}A - B'\bar{Q}B - G'\bar{N}G) + A'z_{t-1}z_{t-1}'A \\ & + G'\eta_{t-1}\eta'_{t-1}G + B'Q_{t-1}B \end{aligned} \tag{7.6}$$

where $\bar{Q}$ and $\bar{N}$ are the unconditional correlation matrices of z_t and η_t, respectively. The negative standardized residuals for asymmetric impacts, η_t, are defined by

$$\eta_t = I[z_t < 0] \circ z_t \tag{7.7}$$

where $I[\cdot]$ is an indicator function that takes a value of 1 if the argument is true and 0 otherwise, while "$\circ$" indicates the Hadamard product. The asymmetric DCC (1,1) model is regarded as a special case of the above AG-DCC (1,1) model if the matrices A, B, and G are replaced by scalars (a_1, b_1, and g_1). We can compute the correlation matrix by

$$P_t = Q_t^{*-1} Q_t Q_t^{*-1} \tag{7.8}$$

where Q_t^* is a diagonal matrix with the square root of the ith diagonal element of Q_t on its ith diagonal position.

Third, similar to Yiu et al. (2010), we adopt AR(1) models to model the conditional correlations obtained from the second step. We include three crisis dummy variables ($Crisis_{1t}$, $Crisis_{2t}$, and $Crisis_{3t}$), which represent the pre-Lehman global financial crisis period, post-Lehman global financial crisis period, and sovereign debt crisis period, respectively. This specification enables us to test whether each crisis significantly altered the dynamics of the estimated conditional correlations among the CDS indices studied, that is,

$$\hat{DCC}_t = \delta_0 + \delta_1 \hat{DCC}_{t-1} + \xi_1 Crisis_{1t} + \xi_2 Crisis_{2t} + \xi_3 Crisis_{3t} + v_t. \tag{7.9}$$

7.3 Data

We use weekly data on the five-year CDS index spreads[2] for the EU, U.S., and U.K. bank sectors from January 1, 2004, to November 30, 2011. The beginning of the period is constrained primarily by the availability of the CDS index data at the sector level. All the data are retrieved from Thomson Reuters Datastream. The use of weekly data allows us to avoid the issue of irregular spacing that might occur when employing daily observations because of the variability of trading days in a week. Moreover, weekly data are less prone to noise.[3]

Table 7.1 reports the descriptive statistics for each of the three CDS indices. Jarque–Bera tests reject normality for all the CDS index spreads at the 1 percent significance level.[4] Stationarity is checked by carrying out augmented Dickey–Fuller (ADF) unit root tests for the three CDS index spreads, all expressed in natural logarithmic form. As reported in Table 7.2, the results indicate that all time series are *I*(1) variables. Hence, in subsequent analyses, we model all the index spreads in the first logarithmic difference following several related studies, such as that by Hammoudeh and Sari (2011).

Table 7.1 Summary statistics

Variable	*Mean*	*SD*	*Skewness*	*Kurtosis*	*Jarque–Bera*
Level data					
EU bank sector CDS	3.925	1.373	0.070	1.408	43.937
U.K. bank sector CDS	3.685	1.386	-0.176	1.252	54.696
U.S. bank sector CDS	4.059	1.041	-0.039	1.504	38.594
First-differenced data					
EU bank sector CDS	0.834	11.772	0.615	11.257	1196.467
U.K. bank sector CDS	0.778	10.191	0.912	9.738	836.463
U.S. bank sector CDS	0.601	11.772	0.604	7.453	365.428

Notes: This table provides the statistics for each time series. The sample covers the period between January 2004 and November 2011 for a total of 413 weekly observations. Level data represent the natural logarithm of the time series. First-differenced data represent log-differences of the original series, multiplied by 100.

Table 7.2 Results of the ADF unit root tests

Variable	*ADF test statistics*	
	constant	*constant and trend*
Level data		
EU bank sector CDS	0.128	-1.944
U.K. bank sector CDS	-0.398	-1.573
U.S. bank sector CDS	-0.932	-1.791
First-differenced data		
EU bank sector CDS	-19.727***	-19.774***
U.K. bank sector CDS	-19.568***	-19.560***
U.S. bank sector CDS	-13.009***	-12.999***

Notes: Results of the Augmented Dickey–Fuller (ADF) unit root tests are reported. The unit root hypothesis in which the regression contains a constant and no deterministic components, and a constant, and a trend are tested.

*** denotes statistical significance at the 1% level.

7.4 Empirical results

AR-EGARCH specification

The first step is to fit the best of the univariate AR(k)-EGARCH(p,q) models to each time series. The estimated results of the AR-EGARCH models are reported in Table 7.3. Based on the SBIC, we select AR(1)-EGARCH(1,1) for all index spreads. It is noticeable that the variance equations of each model exhibit a relatively good fit to the data.[5] All parameters are significant at a 5 percent level, with the exception of ω for all index spreads and γ_1 for the U.K. bank sector CDS. In addition, the p-values of the Ljung-Box Q-statistics, $Q(20)$, and $Q^2(20)$, are found to be much larger than 0.05 for the three index spreads, implying no autocorrelation up to order 20 for standardized residuals and standard residuals squared.[6]

Asymmetric DCC models

The second step is to estimate the asymmetric DCC models proposed by Cappiello et al. (2006).[7] Table 7.4 presents the estimated results from the models. The estimates on both the parameter of standardized residuals (a_1) and of innovations in the dynamics of the conditional correlation matrix (b_1) are statistically

Table 7.3 Empirical results of the AR-EGARCH models

	EU bank sector CDS AR(1)-EGARCH(1,1)		*U.K. bank sector CDS AR(1)-EGARCH(1,1)*		*U.S. bank sector CDS AR(1)-EGARCH(1,1)*	
	Estimate	*SE*	*Estimate*	*SE*	*Estimate*	*SE*
Conditional mean equation						
a_0	−0.193	0.246	−0.248	0.292	−0.111	0.367
a_1	0.096**	0.041	0.028	0.045	0.020	0.047
Conditional variance equation						
Ω	0.080	0.066	0.040	0.108	0.006	0.036
α_1	0.122**	0.062	0.269***	0.079	0.107**	0.052
γ_1	0.162***	0.044	0.076	0.050	0.109***	0.033
β_1	0.957***	0.014	0.945***	0.028	0.981***	0.008
GED parameter	1.027***	0.087	1.078***	0.092	1.226***	0.105
$Q(20)$	22.539		17.326		20.192	
p-value	0.312		0.632		0.466	
$Q^2(20)$	17.773		10.837		17.629	
p-value	0.602		0.950		0.612	

Notes: $Q(20)$ and $Q^2(20)$ are the Ljung–Box statistics up to the 20th order in the standardized residuals and standardized residuals squared, respectively.

***, **, and * denote statistical significance at the 1%, 5%, and 10% levels, respectively.

Table 7.4 Dynamic conditional correlation estimates of the CDS indices

	EU bank sector CDS vs. U.K. bank sector CDS		*U.K. bank sector CDS vs. U.S. bank sector CDS*		*U.S. bank sector CDS vs. EU bank sector CDS*	
	Estimate	*SE*	*Estimate*	*SE*	*Estimate*	*SE*
a_1	0.136***	0.046	0.027***	0.006	0.030**	0.015
b_1	0.477**	0.193	0.982***	0.006	0.938***	0.032
g_1	-0.167***	0.047	0.007	0.007	-0.017	0.018

***, **, and * denote statistical significance at the 1%, 5%, and 10% levels, respectively.

significant at the 5 percent significance level for all pairs of CDS indices. The estimates of the parameter of the standardized negative residuals (g_1) are significantly negative at the 1 percent level in the case of a correlation between the EU and U.K. bank sector CDS indices. This is notable because previous studies using the asymmetric DCC models (e.g., Cappiello et al., 2006; Yiu et al., 2010) commonly report that the estimates of g_1 tend to be insignificant. The significance of the coefficient g_1 suggests that, when responding to downward shocks to changes in CDS spreads, the correlations between the EU and U.K. bank sector CDS indices tend to be higher. This observation may reflect the strong interdependence of bank industries between the EU and U.K.

Figure 7.2 provides estimates of the DCCs between each pair of CDS index spreads. The conditional correlations are not stable over the sample period for all pairs, showing that market participants should not rely on simply assuming constant correlations when exploring hedging opportunities among the bank sector CDS index spreads. Nonetheless, it must also be noted that the pair of EU and U.K. bank sector CDS indices exhibit relatively stable trends with high levels of correlations when compared to the other two cases, and this implies sound market integration. Another interesting finding derived from Figure 7.2 is that the DCCs dropped significantly around late 2008 for the pairs of U.S. bank sector CDS and U.K. and E.U. bank sector CDSs. This occurred when the global financial crisis became most intense following the collapse of Lehman Brothers. This result seems consistent with the abovementioned network theory of contagion, which states that the interdependence of banks may be weakened by crises. The identification of some structural breaks for estimated DCCs leads us to assess the impacts of the recent financial crises using dummy variables, which we explain in the next subsection.

AR model for the estimated DCC with dummy variables

The third and last step is to employ AR(1) models with three dummy variables representing financial crisis periods[8] to model the evolution of the estimated DCCs. Table 7.5 indicates the estimation results of the AR(1) models. The coefficients of the AR terms (δ_1) are significant for all three pairs at the 1 percent level, taking values of less than unity. Relatively high values of R^2 also indicate

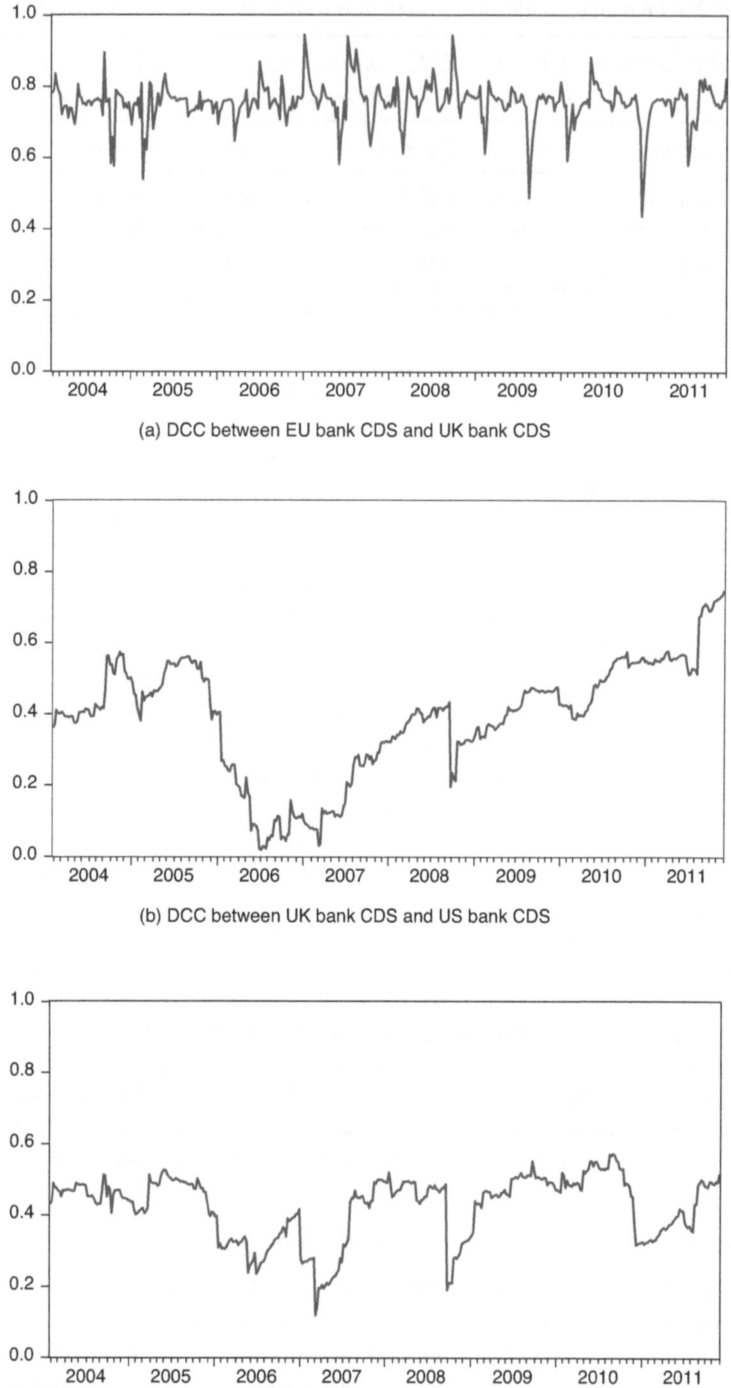

(a) DCC between EU bank CDS and UK bank CDS

(b) DCC between UK bank CDS and US bank CDS

(c) DCC between US bank CDS and EU bank CDS

Figure 7.2 Dynamic correlation between bank sector CDS indices

Table 7.5 Estimation of the AR(1) model for the estimated DCC coefficients

	EU bank sector CDS vs. U.K. bank sector CDS		*U.K. bank sector CDS vs. U.S. bank sector CDS*		*U.S. bank sector CDS vs. EU bank sector CDS*	
	Estimate	*SE*	*Estimate*	*SE*	*Estimate*	*SE*
δ_0	0.287***	0.030	0.004	0.003	0.019***	0.006
δ_1	0.621***	0.039	0.986***	0.009	0.952***	0.015
ξ_1 (Pre-Lehman financial crisis dummy)	0.000	0.007	0.003	0.004	0.004	0.004
ξ_2 (Post-Lehman financial crisis dummy)	–0.001	0.007	0.002	0.004	0.002	0.004
ξ_3 (Sovereign debt crisis dummy)	–0.003	0.005	0.006*	0.004	0.003	0.003
R^2	0.387		0.977		0.917	

***, **, and * denote statistical significance at the 1%, 5%, and 10% levels, respectively.

that the regression models are considered appropriate. Interestingly, the coefficients of the crisis dummies (ξ_1, ξ_2, and ξ_3) are all insignificant at the 10 percent level, with the exception of the sovereign debt crisis dummy for the pair of U.K. and the U.S. bank sector CDS indices. Our finding suggests that the onset of the sovereign debt crisis triggered contagion effects (reflected in the significant increase in the DCCs) between the two bank sector CDS spreads, both of which are outside the EU, the origin of the sovereign debt crisis. This exhibits a sharp contrast to the transitory decreases in the correlations associated with the collapse of Lehman Brothers observed during the global financial crisis period.

7.5 Conclusion

We can summarize the prominent findings from our analysis as follows. (i) The correlations between each pair of EU, U.S., and U.K. bank sector CDS indices fluctuate widely over time, and the DCC estimates of the EU and U.K. bank sector CDSs are relatively stable at high levels, suggesting the existence of solid market integration. (ii) Evidence of asymmetric dynamic correlations is documented between the EU and U.K. bank sector CDS indices, and these correlations tend to be higher, responding to a joint downward movement. (iii) The DCC estimates of the pairs of the U.S. bank sector CDS and the U.K. and the EU bank sector CDS dropped significantly immediately after the collapse of Lehman Brothers, and this result seems to be consistent with the network theory of contagion. (iv) The sovereign debt crisis dummy is significantly positive for the pair of U.K. and U.S. bank sector CDSs, as represented by the increased correlations after the onset of the debt crisis.

Our empirical results are of great relevance for global investors exploring international diversification opportunities in terms of credit risks of the bank sectors across countries. The consistently high DCCs between the U.K. and EU bank sector CDSs indicate little room for diversification; however, the significant decrease in the DCCs between U.S. bank sector CDS and U.K. and EU bank sector CDSs suggests a chance for investors to take advantage of potential diversification opportunities. In addition, our results also may be useful for policymakers seeking regulations to prevent market contagion effects of credit default risks in the bank sectors. They need to be especially mindful about the significant increase in the DCCs between U.S. and U.K. bank sector CDSs, as this suggests that cross-border contagion in the creditworthiness of bank sectors across countries may happen in an unexpected and counterintuitive manner.

Notes

1 Dungey and Martin (2007) provide a list of works in the related empirical financial crisis literature in detail.
2 The bank sector CDS indices incorporate an average mid-spread calculation of a portfolio of single-name CDS for several banks. Among the CDS indices ranging in maturity from one to 10 years, the five-year CDS index is the most actively traded.
3 Wang and Moore (2012), who analyze the sovereign CDS markets with the DCC framework, use weekly observations as well.

4 See Jarque and Bera (1987).
5 In contrast, most parameters in the mean equations are not significant at the 5 percent level. However, we think this is not a major concern because our study primarily focuses on the dynamics of the correlations and hence, is concerned only with the fit of the variance equations.
6 See Ljung and Box (1978).
7 For an application of the asymmetric DCC approach, refer to, for example, Tamakoshi and Hamori (2013, 2014) and Toyoshima et al. (2012).
8 We select August 9, 2007, as the beginning of the global financial crisis, when BNP Paribas suspended its funds badly affected by their exposures to the U.S. subprime mortgage liabilities. We also assume that the post-Lehman global financial crisis begins after September 15, 2008, when Lehman Brothers went bankrupt. Furthermore, November 5, 2009, is chosen as the onset of the sovereign debt crisis because of Greece's disclosure of its fiscal deficit amounting to twice the size announced previously, triggering investors' concerns about solvency issues.

References

Allen, F. and Babus, A. (2009) Networks in finance. *The Network Challenge*, Edited by Paul Kleindorfer and Jerry Wind. Wharton School Publishing, New Jersey, 367–382.

Benbouzid, N. and Mallick, S. (2013) Determinants of bank credit default swap spreads: The role of the housing sector, *The North American Journal of Economics and Finance*, **24**, 243–259.

Cappiello, L., Engle, R. F., and Sheppard, K. (2006) Asymmetric dynamics in the correlations of global equity and bond returns, *Journal of Financial Econometrics*, **4**, 537–572.

Chen, L.-H., Hammoudeh, S., and Yuan, Y. (2011) Asymmetric convergence in US financial credit default swap sector index markets, *The Quarterly Review of Economics and Finance*, **51**, 408–418.

Dooley, M. and Hutchison, M. (2009) Transmission of the U.S. subprime crisis to emerging markets: Evidence on the decoupling-recoupling hypothesis, *Journal of International Money and Finance*, **28**, 1331–1349.

Dungey, M. and Martin, V. L. (2007) Unravelling financial market linkages during crises, *Journal of Applied Econometrics*, **22**, 89–119.

Eichengreen, B., Mody, A., Nedeljkovic, M., and Sarno, L. (2009) How the subprime crisis went global: Evidence from bank credit default swap spreads, *NBER Working Paper No. 14904.*

Engle, R. (2002) Dynamic conditional correlation: A simple class of multivariate generalized autoregressive conditional heteroskedasticity models, *Journal of Business & Economic Statistics*, **20**, 339–350.

Hammoudeh, S., Nandha, M., and Yuan, Y. (2013) Dynamics of CDS spread indexes of US financial sectors, *Applied Economics*, **45**, 213–223.

Hammoudeh, S. and Sari, R. (2011) Financial CDS, stock market and interest rates: Which drives which? *The North American Journal of Economics and Finance*, **22**, 257–276.

Jarque, C. M. and Bera, A. K. (1987) Test for normality of observations and regression residuals, *International Statistical Review*, **55**, 163–172.

Ljung, G. and Box, G. (1978) On a measure of lack of fit in time series models, *Biometrika*, **65**, 297–303.

Nelson, D. B. (1991) Conditional heteroskedasticity in asset returns: A new approach, *Econometrica*, **59**, 347–370.

Tamakoshi, G. and Hamori, S. (2013) An asymmetric dynamic conditional correlation analysis of linkages of European financial institutions during the Greek sovereign debt crisis, *The European Journal of Finance*, **19**, 939–950.

Tamakoshi, G. and Hamori, S. (2014) Co-movements among major European exchange rates: A multivariate time-varying asymmetric approach, *International Review of Economics & Finance*, **31**, 105–113.

Toyoshima, Y., Tamakoshi, G., and Hamori, S. (2012) Asymmetric dynamics in correlations of treasury and swap markets: Evidence from the US market, *Journal of International Financial Markets, Institutions and Money*, **22**, 381–394.

Wang, P. and Moore, T. (2012) The integration of the credit default swap markets during the US subprime crisis: Dynamic correlation analysis, *Journal of International Financial Markets, Institutions and Money*, **22**, 1–15.

Yiu, M. S., Ho, W.-Y. A., and Choi, D. F. (2010) Dynamic correlation analysis of financial contagion in Asian markets in global financial turmoil, *Applied Financial Economics*, **20**, 345–354.

Part III

Firm-level CDS markets

8 Dynamic correlation among banks' CDS spreads

8.1 Introduction

This study examines the co-movement of credit default swap (CDS) spreads of Eurozone banks, employing the dynamic equicorrelation (DECO) model developed by Engle and Kelly (2012). The sample period ranges from January 2004 to June 2013, encompassing the recent European sovereign debt crisis that severely affected the banking sectors in the Eurozone. Our study is motivated primarily by the importance of understanding systemic risks in the banking sector, as we have recently observed that simultaneous collapses of several banks propagated financial turmoil, triggering serious concerns for regulators. As Allen et al. (2010) argued, systemic risks are created when multiple banks collapse owing to a common shock or contagion. Recently, CDS spreads of individual banks, which represent insurance premiums for default risks, have increasingly gained attention as measures of credit risks. Because such CDS spreads reflect the perceptions of market participants about the creditworthiness of entities, policymakers can use CDS spreads to extract warning signals with respect to the banking system. Thus, analysis of the time-varying linkages between banks' CDS spreads may help regulators monitor the sector's systemic risks and take appropriate actions to prevent system-wide failures.

To our knowledge, only a small number of empirical studies have analyzed the CDS spreads of financial institutions, presumably because of restrictions regarding data availability. Using a seemingly unrelated regression analysis, Düllmann and Sosinska (2007) analyzed risk factors that drove the CDS premiums of German banks over 2001 to 2005. They found that the German stock market index (a proxy for the systematic risk factor) and the bid–ask spread of CDS quotes (a proxy for liquidity risk) had a relatively high explanatory power for the movement of the CDS premiums. In contrast, Annaert et al. (2013) employed panel estimation methods to investigate determinants of CDS spreads of 32 listed Eurozone banks from 2004 to 2010. They detected that traditional credit risk drivers, such as financial leverage, asset volatility, and risk-free interest rate, were indeed key drivers for changes in CDS spreads; however, liquidity as well as market-wide and business-cycle variables also explained a substantial portion of the spread changes. In addition, their analysis concluded that the main factors explaining the CDS spread changes varied substantially over time.

However, these studies focused on identifying the key *determinants* of bank CDS spreads, not their *co-movement*. A seminal work on time-varying linkages of individual bank CDS spreads is that of Eichengreen et al. (2012). They applied principal components analysis to CDS quotes of 45 global banks during 2002 to 2008 and discovered that the common factors underlying changes in the bank CDS spreads existed even in normal times. Furthermore, they found that the common factors played a progressively important role during the global credit crisis in particular, and became increasingly associated with a proxy for the credit risk premium of the banking sector.

This study extends the work of Eichengreen et al. (2012) and makes two primary contributions to the literature. First, we examine the co-movement of bank CDS spreads for the first time, focusing on Eurozone banks. The European debt crisis has led policymakers to beware of the substantial exposure of banks to debt in peripheral nations, which may increase the probability of coincidental losses being triggered by the downgrading of those government securities held by the banks. Against this background, it is worthwhile to investigate the time variation of interrelationships between credit risk measures of the banks and to assess whether contagion occurred across them, especially during periods of market turbulence. Moreover, our regression analysis identifies potential economic drivers for the time-varying correlations among the CDS spread changes.

Second, our use of the latest DECO approach enables us to efficiently analyze correlation dynamics among the whole set of banks. This method, which assumes the same correlation across all variables contemporaneously, avoids the difficulty of interpreting pair-wise correlations derived from the conventional dynamic conditional correlation (DCC) model of Engle (2002). This is especially true when there are a large number of variables (n), as the DCC model would require us to face computational burdens for $n(n-1)/2$ pairs of dynamic correlations. A limited number of recent empirical studies have applied the DECO model to examine time-varying relationships, for instance, between stocks comprising the S&P 500 index (e.g., Engle and Kelly, 2012); between returns of equities, bonds, foreign exchange, and commodities (e.g., Aboura and Chevallier, 2013); between volatility of equities, bonds, foreign exchange, and commodities (e.g., Aboura and Chevallier, 2014); and between trading volumes and volatilities for non-financial firms' stock returns (e.g., Carroll and Kearney, 2012). To the best of our knowledge, this is the first study to use this novel approach to investigate the co-movement of burgeoning CDS markets for financial institutions.

Our empirical results reveal the existence of a high level of estimated equicorrelation among the banks' CDS spreads even prior to the two recent crises. This implies that all the banks were subject to common risks. In addition, the results indicate evidence of contagion, with sharp increases in equicorrelation coinciding with some crisis events linked to not only the global financial crisis but also the European debt crisis, at a time when it is possible that perceived common risks increased. Furthermore, our findings suggest that the VSTOXX index, as a proxy for implied volatility, is an economic factor that significantly drove the co-movement of the banks' CDS spreads, indicating that increased fears of market participants over systemic failure in the financial system (rather than bank-specific risks) may have triggered coincidental increases in the CDS spreads. The implications of these findings for policymakers are discussed.

The rest of this paper is organized as follows. Section 8.2 explains the econometric methods, and Section 8.3 describes the data. Section 8.4 presents our empirical results and discussion. Section 8.5 concludes.

8.2 Empirical methodology

We briefly describe our modeling approach, which consists of the following three steps. First, we use the exponential general autoregressive conditional heteroskedasticity (EGARCH) model[1] with a generalized error distribution (GED) to specify a return equation and a variance equation:

$$r_{i,t} = \mu + \varepsilon_{i,t}, \tag{8.1}$$

$$\log(\sigma_{i,t}^2) = \omega + (\alpha_1 |z_{i,t-1}| + \gamma_1 z_{i,t-1}) + \beta_1 \log(\sigma_{i,t-1}^2), \tag{8.2}$$

where $r_{i,t}$ is the first-differenced CDS spread for each bank, μ is the mean, $\varepsilon_{i,t}$ is the effect of innovations, $\sigma_{i,t}^2$ represents the conditional variances, and $z_{i,t} = \varepsilon_{i,t}/\sigma_{i,t}$ denotes the standardized residuals.

Second, we employ the DECO model of Engle and Kelly (2012) to estimate the conditional correlations. An unconditional correlation matrix (R_t) is represented as follows:

$$R_t = (1-\rho_t)I_n + \rho_t J_n, \tag{8.3}$$

where I_n is an n-dimensional identity matrix, J_n is an $n \times n$ matrix of ones, and ρ_t is the equicorrelation, expressed as

$$\rho_t = \frac{2}{n(n-1)} \sum_{i \neq j} \frac{q_{ij,t}}{\sqrt{q_{ii,t} q_{jj,t}}}. \tag{8.4}$$

Here, $q_{ij,t}$ represents the i-j^{th} element of Q_t (the covariance matrix of the standardized residuals). Hence, it is notable that ρ_t is calculated as the average of the $n(n-1)/2$ correlations. In the DECO model's scalar version, the evolution of Q_t is provided by

$$Q_t = (1-a-b)\overline{Q} + a z_{t-1} z_{t-1}' + b Q_{t-1}, \tag{8.5}$$

where $\overline{Q}$ is the unconditional covariance matrix of the standardized residuals.

Third, we apply the autoregressive (AR) model to the estimated equicorrelation ($\hat{\rho}_t$) to identify factors driving the co-movement of the CDS spreads. As explanatory variables, we include lagged equicorrelation ($\hat{\rho}_{t-1}$) and four economic variables: (i) the Eurozone stock index return to represent economic prospects of market participants (STK_t), (ii) the rate of change in implied volatility to represent investors' risk aversion[2] (VOL_t), (iii) the rate of change in the AAA–BBB corporate bond spread to represent corporate default risks (BDS_t), and (iv) the rate of change in the London Interbank Offered Rates (LIBOR)–Overnight Index Swap (OIS) spread to represent credit risks perceived in the interbank market (LOS_t). These economic factors are used typically in the previous literature on the determinants of CDS spreads. Thus, our AR(1) model is expressed as

$$\hat{\rho}_t = k_0 + k_{rho}\hat{\rho}_{t-1} + k_{STK}STK_{t-1} + k_{VOL}VOL_{t-1} + \kappa_{BDS}BDS_{t-1} + \kappa_{LOS}LOS_{t-1} + e_t. \quad (8.6)$$

8.3 Data

Our data consist of the weekly five-year CDS quotes for 15 Eurozone banks[3] from January 1, 2004, to June 30, 2013. The beginning of the sample is set, given that sufficient CDS data from Bloomberg, our data source, are not available before that date. Similar to Eichengreen et al. (2012), we use the five-year CDS rates because this maturity is the most actively traded. In addition, we employ a weekly (Wednesday-to-Wednesday) series to remove irregularities of daily CDS movements, resulting in 495 observations for each bank. Our selection criterion for banks is the availability of valid CDS data throughout the sample period.

With regard to economic variables used for the AR model of dynamic equicorrelation, we employ the MSCI's Eurozone stock market index for STK_t, the VSTOXX index[4] for VOL_t, the five-year AAA–BBB corporate bond spreads for BDS_t, and the spread between the three-month Euro LIBOR and the three-month Euro OIS rate for LOS_t. All the data are extracted from Datastream.

Table 8.1 presents summary statistics of the CDS spreads for 15 banks. Notably, the substantial difference between the maximum and minimum values implies that the spreads fluctuate widely over time. Volatility is highest for Banco Comercial Português and lowest for Deutsche Bank. A high level of kurtosis for many of the banks indicates leptokurtic distributions, which have heavier tails and acute peaks. The Jarque–Bera statistics suggest that the null hypothesis of normal distribution is rejected for the entire series. By employing the Augmented Dickey–Fuller (ADF) and Phillips–Perron (PP) tests, we find that the CDS series are I(1) variables, as reported in Table 8.2. Hence, we take the first difference[5] of the CDS rates to induce stationarity.

Table 8.1 Summary statistics

Bank	*Country*	*Mean*	*Max*	*Min*	*SD*	*Skewness*	*Kurtosis*	*Jarque–Bera*
HVB Group	Germany	94.45	394.05	6.37	90.22	1.24	3.63	134.47***
Commerzbank	Germany	92.46	347.36	7.85	82.00	0.97	3.04	77.27***
Deutsche Bank	Germany	76.87	287.12	9.55	59.70	0.57	2.51	32.05***
BNP Paribas	France	76.15	354.33	5.47	77.33	1.22	3.79	135.95***
Crédit Lyonnais	France	93.42	386.28	6.00	90.69	1.00	3.32	83.94***
Société Générale	France	97.81	424.18	5.96	99.80	1.19	3.75	129.36***
Banca Monte dei Paschi	Italy	170.39	883.31	6.17	211.87	1.37	3.59	162.23***
Mediobanca	Italy	116.07	555.90	7.19	129.06	1.41	4.15	190.45***
UniCredito Italiano	Italy	135.58	625.57	7.62	152.07	1.34	3.88	163.24***
Banco Santander	Spain	121.41	475.70	7.67	123.27	0.92	2.71	72.12***
BBVA	Spain	127.14	500.12	7.83	131.38	0.91	2.65	70.61***
Banco Comercial Português	Portugal	305.23	1701.08	8.25	427.44	1.60	4.63	265.51***
Banco Espirito Santo	Portugal	268.47	1210.99	8.83	331.79	1.18	3.06	114.56***
ING Bank	Netherlands	78.96	269.76	4.47	69.43	0.62	2.37	39.96***
Fortis NL	Netherlands	82.78	316.75	7.50	68.05	0.80	2.82	52.85***

Notes: Reported statistics are for level data.

*** denotes statistical significance at the 1% level.

Table 8.2 Results of the ADF and PP unit root tests

Variable	*ADF test statistics*	*PP test statistics*
	constant	*constant*
Level data		
HVB Group	-1.154	-1.199
Commerzbank	-1.473	-1.639
Deutsche Bank	-1.962	-1.915
BNP Paribas	-1.434	-1.799
Crédit Lyonnais	-1.586	-1.539
Société Générale	-1.128	-1.555
Banca Monte dei Paschi	-0.412	-0.214
Mediobanca	-1.468	-1.379
UniCredito Italiano	-1.264	-1.266
Banco Santander	-1.128	-1.123
BBVA	-1.117	-1.132
Banco Comercial Português	-1.324	-1.259
Banco Espirito Santo	-1.343	-1.201
ING Bank	-1.655	-1.755
Fortis NL	-1.890	-2.067
First-differenced data		
HVB Group	-21.561***	-21.561***
Commerzbank	-27.762***	-27.494***
Deutsche Bank	-26.791***	-27.827***
BNP Paribas	-27.751***	-27.808***
Crédit Lyonnais	-25.892***	-26.346***
Société Générale	-26.184***	-26.886***
Banca Monte dei Paschi	-24.359***	-24.383***
Mediobanca	-9.831***	-24.458***
UniCredito Italiano	-22.762***	-22.757***
Banco Santander	-26.184***	-26.366***
BBVA	-25.553***	-25.694***
Banco Comercial Português	-9.957***	-19.551***
Banco Espirito Santo	-8.232***	-18.785***
ING Bank	-23.356***	-23.348***
Fortis NL	-16.156***	-27.557***

Notes: Results of the Augmented Dickey–Fuller (ADF) and Phillips–Perron (PP) unit root tests are reported. The unit root hypothesis in which the regression contains a constant and no deterministic components are tested.

*** denotes statistical significance at the 1% level.

8.4 Empirical results

We first apply the univariate EGARCH(1,1) model to each bank's CDS series, after which we employ the DECO model to capture the conditional equicorrelation. The estimation results are shown in Table 8.3. All the parameters in each variance equation (ω, α_1, γ_1, β_1, and GED parameter) are found to be significant at the 5 percent level.[6] Furthermore, the estimates of the equicorrelation parameters (0.0528 for a and 0.9289 for b) are significant at the 1 percent level and lie within the reasonable range of the DECO model estimation. The value of $a + b$ is close to unity, suggesting a high level of persistency of the estimated dynamic equicorrelation. These results lead us to conclude that our model specification is adequate.

Figure 8.1 plots the path of the estimated equicorrelation over time. We detect that even before mid-2007, that is, before the outbreak of the global financial crisis, the bank CDS spreads exhibit substantial co-movement, with the equicorrelation value lying in the range of 0.4 to 0.7. This may mean that even during calm periods, market participants perceive the risks of several Eurozone banks' defaults to be common risks that affected the region's banking sector as a whole. These results are generally consistent with the study of Eichengreen et al. (2012) on 45 global banks in the U.S., U.K., and some European countries, although the method which they used (i.e., principal component analysis) differs from ours.

In addition, we find that the estimated equicorrelation shows large jumps, particularly in the middle of 2007, late 2008, and late 2009, coinciding mostly with the outbreaks of the global financial crisis, the bankruptcy of Lehman Brothers, and the European sovereign debt crisis, respectively. Indeed, sharp increases in the co-movement of bank CDS spreads are closely associated with the recent crisis episodes. This means that in the wake of the crisis events, market participants perceived that the banks, as a group, were subject to higher common risks, thus recognizing the existence of systemic risks in the sector. Specifically, it is worthwhile to mention that the co-movement increased even at the inception of the European debt crisis, triggered by problems in Greek government bond markets. Our results may thus partially support the view that the banking crisis, first triggered in the U.S. subprime loan markets, severely affected the Eurozone banking sector, transforming itself into the sovereign debt crisis. The combination of massive capital injections for bank rescues and easing of the recession may have led some peripheral companies to doubt their creditworthiness owing to their heavy burden of debt (e.g., Arnold, 2012; Grammatikos and Vermeulen, 2012).

Table 8.4 reexamines the estimated time-varying equicorrelation, which is assumed to be equal across all banks' CDS spreads at any point of time. The table summarizes key statistics in the entire period (Panel A), the pre-crisis period (Panel B; January 1, 2004, to August 8, 2007), the credit crisis period (Panel C; August 9, 2007, to October 31, 2009), and the debt crisis period (Panel D; November 1, 2009, to June 30, 2013). Here, we regard August 9, 2007, as

Table 8.3 Results of the EGARCH and DECO models

	HVB Group		*Commerzbank*		*Deutsche Bank*	
	Estimate	*SE*	*Estimate*	*SE*	*Estimate*	*SE*
First step: GARCH model estimation						
ω	−0.1466***	0.0320	−0.2844***	0.0493	−0.2153***	0.0491
α_1	0.2597***	0.0499	0.4525***	0.0705	0.3364***	0.0701
γ_1	0.1817***	0.0302	0.1821***	0.0486	0.1760***	0.0436
β_1	0.9908***	0.0036	0.9889***	0.0056	0.9894***	0.0040
GED parameter	0.8642***	0.0505	0.9865***	0.0650	1.1218***	0.0660
	BNP Paribas		*Crédit Lyonnais*		*Société Générale*	
	Estimate	*SE*	*Estimate*	*SE*	*Estimate*	*SE*
ω	−0.2963***	0.0401	−0.2765***	0.0479	−0.2380***	0.0374
α_1	0.4598***	0.0669	0.4439***	0.0845	0.3775***	0.0625
γ_1	0.1549***	0.0482	0.1575**	0.0646	0.1536***	0.0460
β_1	0.9920***	0.0041	0.9975***	0.0042	0.9944***	0.0032
GED parameter	0.9435***	0.0577	0.7499***	0.0462	0.8690***	0.0558
	Banca Monte dei Paschi		*Mediobanca*		*UniCredito Italiano*	
	Estimate	*SE*	*Estimate*	*SE*	*Estimate*	*SE*
ω	−0.2206***	0.0340	−0.3269***	0.0507	−0.2797***	0.0500
α_1	0.3545***	0.0569	0.5142***	0.0837	0.4366***	0.0747
γ_1	0.1440***	0.0434	0.1534**	0.0607	0.1256***	0.0432
β_1	0.9942***	0.0035	0.9907***	0.0053	0.9930***	0.0041
GED parameter	0.9442***	0.0646	0.9334***	0.0659	1.0551***	0.0684
	Banco Santander		*BBVA*		*Banco Commercial Português*	
	Estimate	*SE*	*Estimate*	*SE*	*Estimate*	*SE*
ω	−0.0942***	0.0287	−0.0977***	0.0262	−0.1678***	0.0306
α_1	0.1316***	0.0445	0.1285***	0.0419	0.2693***	0.0482
γ_1	0.2568***	0.0407	0.2699***	0.0389	0.1540***	0.0312
β_1	0.9960***	0.0013	0.9971***	0.0013	0.9969***	0.0020
GED parameter	1.1383***	0.0725	1.0587***	0.0698	0.9273***	0.0585
	Banco Espirito Santo		*ING Bank*		*Fortis NL*	
	Estimate	*SE*	*Estimate*	*SE*	*Estimate*	*SE*
ω	−0.1925***	0.0395	−0.1642***	0.0341	−0.0766***	0.0240
α_1	0.3024***	0.0613	0.2629***	0.0511	0.1353***	0.0401
γ_1	0.1640***	0.0396	0.1866***	0.0327	0.2637***	0.0373
β_1	0.9963***	0.0024	0.9930***	0.0026	0.9883***	0.0030
GED parameter	0.9233***	0.0566	0.9023***	0.0636	0.8946***	0.0582
Second step: DECO model estimation						
A	0.0528***	0.0058				
B	0.9289***	0.0076				

***, **, and * denote statistical significance at the 1%, 5%, and 10% levels, respectively.

Figure 8.1 Estimated dynamic equicorrelation derived by the DECO model

Table 8.4 Summary of the estimated dynamic equicorrelation

	Panel A: Entire period	*Panel B: Pre-crisis period*	*Panel C: Credit crisis period*	*Panel D: Debt crisis period*
Mean	0.6609	0.5572	0.7767	0.6916
Max	0.9175	0.7303	0.9175	0.7620
Min	0.4220	0.4220	0.6994	0.5973
Std. Dev.	0.1017	0.0642	0.0544	0.0357

Notes: This table summarizes the statistics of time-varying equicorrelation, which is derived from the DECO–GARCH model, for the entire period and each sub-period.

the onset of the credit crisis because on that date, BNP Paribas acknowledged the severe exposure of its funds to the crisis and closed the funds. November 1, 2009, is viewed as the beginning of the debt crisis, given that in early November 2009, Greece disclosed that its fiscal deficit would be much larger than announced previously. Table 8.4 indicates that the average level of estimated equicorrelation during both crises is much higher than in the pre-crisis period. This reinforces the view that contagion may have occurred between the bank CDS spreads during periods of market turbulence.

Our third step is to estimate the AR models, namely, Equation (8.6), in order to identify key drivers of the co-movement of bank CDS spreads. Table 8.5 reports the estimated results. The high values of the adjusted R^2 indicate the good fit of our model. Throughout the periods, the coefficients of the AR(1)

Table 8.5 Estimation of the AR model for dynamic equicorrelation

	Panel A: Entire period		*Panel B: Pre-crisis period*		*Panel C: Credit crisis period*		*Panel D: Debt crisis period*	
	Estimate	*SE*	*Estimate*	*SE*	*Estimate*	*SE*	*Estimate*	*SE*
k_0	0.0097*	0.0054	0.0305**	0.0141	0.0384	0.0237	0.0553***	0.0199
k_{RHO}	0.9854***	0.0081	0.9455***	0.0251	0.9505***	0.0305	0.9200***	0.0287
k_{STK}	0.0267	0.0461	–0.0213	0.1568	–0.0059	0.0695	0.0885	0.0561
k_{VOL}	0.0257**	0.0109	0.0243	0.0269	0.0309	0.0199	0.0255*	0.0131
k_{BDS}	–0.0087	0.0096	0.0077	0.0309	–0.0143	0.0140	–0.0080	0.0117
k_{LOS}	0.0066	0.0158	–0.1061	0.1378	0.0126	0.0173	–0.0065	0.0291
Adjusted R^2	0.9686		0.8847		0.9002		0.8443	

***, **, and * denote statistical significance at the 1%, 5%, and 10% levels, respectively.

term are significant at the 1 percent level, with values close to unity, implying strongly persistent equicorrelation. Intriguingly, the results reveal that the lagged value of implied volatility is the only economic variable that significantly affects the equicorrelation, and its coefficients are significant for the entire and debt crisis periods. The positive values of these coefficients indicate that the larger the volatility measure, the higher the linkage between bank CDS spreads. The increases in VSTOXX may reflect investors' higher risk aversion, which is typically reflected in their sell-off of financial assets in periods of financial turbulence. A possible explanation is that investors became more risk averse, especially in the wake of the debt crisis, and thus, became more concerned with common risks associated with banks' portfolios rather than with bank-specific risks, realizing that all major Eurozone banks were more or less highly exposed to debt in peripheral nations. Such general concerns may have caused the increased association between the co-movement of bank CDS spreads and the risk aversion measure.

8.5 Conclusion

Using the DECO–GARCH framework developed by Engle and Kelly (2012), we investigate the time-varying interrelationship among CDS spreads of 15 Eurozone banks during 2004 to 2013. Our approach assumes that the conditional correlation is equal across all assets at any given point of time, which enables us to interpret estimation results more easily than in the conventional DCC method, which often provides too many pair-wise conditional correlations. In addition, we adopt the AR model to identify key economic factors explaining the movement of the estimated equicorrelation.

Our results yield the following main findings. (i) The banks' CDS spreads displayed a high level of co-movement even before the financial crises, inferring the existence of common risks perceived with regard to the Eurozone banking sector as a whole. (ii) The level of estimated equicorrelation was higher during the two crises than during the pre-crisis period, implying the occurrence of contagion. Spikes of the time-varying equicorrelation coincided with several crisis events, including even the onset of the European debt crisis. (iii) The implied volatility measure was a key factor that significantly drove the co-movement of the CDS spreads in the entire and debt crisis periods. This may suggest that increased risk aversion, spurred by the occurrence of the debt crisis in particular, caused investors to worry about the systemic risks for all banks whose exposure to the debt of peripheral nations was high, rather than bank-specific risks.

Our findings have key implications for policymakers. First, the high degree of the co-movement among the banks' CDS spreads indicates that the authorities in the Eurozone should focus their policy responses toward attenuating the common risks that might affect all banks concerned, taking into account the possibility that the failure of one particular bank may trigger chain reactions. Second, the significant association between the co-movement of banks' CDS spreads and the implied volatility measure underscores the importance of monitoring market-wide indicators, such as the VSTOXX, to prevent contagion and systemic failure in the banking system. Policymakers should not only pay attention to credit risks of individual banks but should also attempt to capture signs of deterioration in market conditions that might adversely affect a group of banks as a whole.

Notes

1 See Nelson (1991) for details. We select the EGARCH model to reflect the asymmetric behavior of volatility driven by past shocks.
2 According to Pan and Singleton (2008), decreases in volatility measure can reflect the growing risk appetite of investors.
3 The word "bank" is used for simplicity, although some of the studied firms have business lines other than banking.
4 VSTOXX measures the market expectations of volatility for the real-time option prices of the Euro Stoxx 50, a stock index consisting of 50 Eurozone firms.
5 Note that we do not have to take log differences in order to express percentage points because the bank CDS spreads are already expressed in basis points.
6 In addition, by checking the *p*-values of the Ljung–Box statistics for standardized residuals and standardized residuals squared, we confirm that there is no serial correlation issue.

References

Aboura, S. and Chevallier, J. (2013) An equicorrelation measure for equity, bond, foreign exchange and commodity returns, *Applied Economics Letters*, **20**, 1618–1624.

Aboura, S. and Chevallier, J. (2014) Volatility equicorrelation: A cross-market perspective, *Economics Letters*, **122**, 289–295.

Allen, F., Babus, A., and Carletti, E. (2010) Financial connections and systemic risk, *NBER Working Paper No. 16177.*

Annaert, J., Ceuster, M. D., Roy, P. V., and Vespro, C. (2013) What determines Euro area bank CDS spreads? *Journal of International Money and Finance*, **32**, 444–461.

Arnold, I. J. M. (2012) Sovereign debt exposures and banking risks in the current EU financial crisis, *Journal of Policy Modeling*, **34**, 906–920.

Carroll, R. and Kearney, C. (2012) Do trading volumes explain the persistence of GARCH effects? *Applied Financial Economics*, **22**, 1993–2008.

Düllmann, K. and Sosinska, A. (2007) Credit default swap prices as risk indicators of listed German banks, *Financial Markets and Portfolio Management*, **21**, 269–292.

Eichengreen, B., Mody, A., Nedeljkovic, M., and Sarno, L. (2012) How the subprime crisis went global: Evidence from bank credit default swap spreads, *Journal of International Money and Finance*, **31**, 1299–1318.

Engle, R. (2002) Dynamic conditional correlation: A simple class of multivariate generalized autoregressive conditional heteroskedasticity models, *Journal of Business & Economic Statistics*, **20**, 339–350.

Engle, R. and Kelly, B. (2012) Dynamic equicorrelation, *Journal of Business & Economic Statistics*, **30**, 212–228.

Grammatikos, T. and Vermeulen, R. (2012) Transmission of the financial and sovereign debt crises to the EMU: Stock prices, CDS spreads and exchange rates, *Journal of International Money and Finance*, **31**, 517–533.

Nelson, D. B. (1991) Conditional heteroskedasticity in asset returns: A new approach, *Econometrica*, **59**, 347–370.

Pan, J. and Singleton, K. J. (2008) Default and recovery implicit in the term structure of sovereign CDS spreads, *Journal of Finance*, **63**, 2345–2384.

9 Dependence structures among corporate CDS indices

9.1 Introduction

The growing need for trading and hedging corporate credit risks on the investors' end has facilitated the market development of corporate credit default swaps (CDS) indices. A corporate CDS index is an instrument that is formed by a portfolio of single-name CDS spreads. The outbreak of the recent financial crises has indeed attracted attention to corporate CDS indices, as the default risks of corporations across the globe were keenly realized during market turbulences. As Alexander and Kaeck (2008) note, an increasing number of traders has found corporate CDS indices to be preferred proxies for corporate default risk premium, rather than baskets of single-name CDS spreads owing to the liquidity of the indices, and thus, used as more convenient trading and hedging tools of corporate credit risks.

This study deals with the three most popular investment grade corporate CDS indices: iTraxx.Japan (IJPN), iTraxx.Europe (IEUR), and CDX.NA.IG (NAIG). IJPN, IEUR, and NAIG comprise a portfolio of equally weighted single-name CDS spreads for 50, 125, and 125 investment-grade reference entities in Japan, Europe, and the United States, respectively. New series are created for these three indices on a six-month basis, and the most recent "on-the-run" series has attracted particular attention because they are the most liquid. The reference entities are typically the most liquid investment grade corporations, and thus, each corporate CDS index is expected to serve as a useful measure of the liquid market prices of credit risks for each country's corporate sector. From this standpoint, analyzing the interconnectedness between the corporate CDS indices would be relevant for investors who attempt to seek diversification of corporate credit risks across countries. Moreover, we believe that the investigation of the co-movement provides important implications for policymakers interested in understanding how corporate default risk premiums are possibly linked across different countries to maintain the stability of the corporate sector in the concerned country.

Although the previous literature on corporate CDS indices remains scarce, compared to that on sovereign CDS indices or single-name CDS spreads, we identify the following three categories of literature. First, some scholars have focused on investigating the key determinants of corporate CDS indices. For example, using a Markov switching model, Alexander and Kaeck (2008) show that the main determinants of the iTraxx Europe indices are time dependent, that is, the indices are primarily influenced by stock returns in an ordinary market environment, but significantly more affected by stock volatility during CDS market turbulences. Fabozzi et al. (2009), using an ordinary least squares regression model to identify the main determinants of the North America CDS indices and its tranches, find that they are more responsive to financial market factors than macroeconomic ones. Naifar (2011a) applies a two-state Markov switching model to iTraxx Japan CDS indices and shows that the indices are more sensitive to stock volatility and the industrial production index during crisis periods than during non-crisis periods, thus providing evidence of the regime-dependent behaviors of the CDS indices.

Second, other scholars have investigated the relationships between corporate CDS indices and the stocks of their reference entities. Adopting a copula approach, Naifar (2011b) examines the dependence structures among the iTraxx Australia CDS indices, portfolio of stocks of their reference entities, and jump risk represented by the kurtosis of the stocks and offers evidence of extreme co-movement between the CDS indices and stock market conditions. Naifar (2012) also applies various copulas to analyze the dependence structure among corporate CDS indices, volatility of equity returns of their reference entities, and jump risk in the Japanese and Australian markets. He finds the existence of extreme co-movement between the CDS indices and their stock return volatility and jump risk during the global financial crisis. Applying several copula to more recent data on the iTraxx Australia CDS indices and equities of their reference entities, Fenech et al. (2014) also provide evidence an asymmetric co-movement during the post-global financial crisis periods.

Third, another strand of research investigates the interconnectedness between corporate CDS indices. A rare example of this strand is Madhavan (2013), who uses the Brock et al. (1987) (hereinafter BDS) test[1] and a close-return test to study the relationships between the North America CDS and iTraxx Europe indices. Both tests reveal evidence of a non-chaotic, non-linear relationship between the two investment-grade CDS indices. Indeed, our study belongs to the third category.

Given the scarcity of research on the interrelationships among the growing corporate CDS indices, in this study, we investigate the conditional dependence structure of the three CDS indices in Japan (IJPN), Europe (IEUR), and the United States (NAIG). We use recent data spanning from January 3, 2005, to December 31, 2015. The study makes two main contributions to the previous literature on corporate CDS indices. First, we believe this study is unique because it uncovers the interconnectedness between the corporate CDS indices across countries. In particular, we attempt to investigate the possibility of extreme co-movement events among the corporate CDS indices across Japan, Europe, and the United States before and after the recent financial crises, which is yet to be extensively explored in the literature. Second, we apply the three Archimedean copula (Gumbel, Clayton, and Frank) to thoroughly examine the non-linear aspects of the dependence structures. Identifying the copula that would best fit the data would help clarify whether the tail distribution of each bivariate combination of the three CDS indices is asymmetric. In particular, the fit to the Gumbel copula indicates the possibility of systemic risks that may arise because of the joint increases in the corporate CDS indices in times of financial turmoil.

The remainder of this study is organized as follows. Section 9.2 presents our empirical methodology in copula estimation. Section 9.3 describes our dataset. Section 9.4 reports the empirical results and facilitates related discussions. Section 9.5 concludes.

9.2 Empirical methodology

A copula is a joint distribution function of marginal distributions, each of which is uniformly distributed. Sklar's (1959) theorem indicates that the joint distribution (H(x,y)) of two random variables X and Y with margins $F_x(x)$ and $F_y(y)$ can be specified by a copula C such that for all x and y in R,

$$H(u,v) = C(F_x(x), F_y(y)). \tag{9.1}$$

An advantage of a copula function is that we can model the univariate marginal distributions first and then, separately select a copula to represent the dependence structure. Another positive feature is that it can be used to measure the probability that the two random variables are in the lower or upper joint tails of bivariate distributions by analyzing the coefficients of the lower (λ_L) and upper tail dependence (λ_U), represented as follows:

$$\lambda_L = \lim_{u \to 0} \Pr[X \le F_X^{-1}(u) | Y \le F_Y^{-1}(u)], \tag{9.2}$$

$$\lambda_U = \lim_{u \to 1} \Pr[X > F_X^{-1}(u) | Y > F_Y^{-1}(u)], \tag{9.3}$$

where F_X^{-1} and F_Y^{-1} are marginal quantile functions. If $\lambda_L = \lambda_U$, we cannot reject the existence of symmetric tail dependence; otherwise, we conclude that asymmetric tail dependence exists.

Among the numerous copulas that have been applied to the finance literature, this study employs the class of Archimedean copulas (specifically, Gumbel, Clayton, and Frank). While the Gaussian copula and Student-*t* copula do not allow for tail and asymmetric tail dependence, these Archimedean copulas allow us to analyze dependence in the upper and lower tails. This property fits the objectives of our study because we are particularly interested in analyzing the probability of the joint occurrence of extreme values for the corporate CDS indices in view of the recent financial crises, to which major corporations in Japan, Europe, and the United States have been exposed.

Here, we employ the following three Archimedean copula models to capture the various patterns of dependence structures. First, the Gumbel copula has upper but no lower tail dependence. For all u and $v \in [0, 1]$, it is represented by

$$C(u, v) = e^{-\left[(-\ln u)^{\theta} + (-\ln v)^{\theta}\right]^{1/\theta}}, \theta \in [1, +\infty). \tag{9.4}$$

Second, the Clayton copula, in contrast, has lower but no upper tail dependence, which is denoted by

$$C(u, v) = \left(u^{-\theta} + v^{-\theta} - 1\right)^{-1/\theta}, \theta \in [-1, +\infty) / \{0\}. \tag{9.5}$$

Third, the Frank copula is symmetric with no tail dependence, allowing for the capturing of the full range of dependence:

$$C(u, v) = -\frac{1}{\theta}\ln\left(1 + \frac{\left(e^{-\theta u} - 1\right)\left(e^{-\theta v} - 1\right)}{e^{-\theta} - 1}\right), \theta \in (-\infty, +\infty) / \{0\}. \tag{9.6}$$

In our estimation procedure, we adopt two-step estimation approaches, considering that financial asset data such as the CDS indices used in this study tend to have the ARCH effects. Indeed, our first step is to filter the first-differenced CDS indices data to obtain approximate *i.i.d.* data by employing AR-EGARCH models.[2] The use of the EGARCH models[3] allows for the incorporation of the asymmetric movement in the volatility caused by past shocks. Then, the second step is to transform the filtered standardized residuals into uniform variables so that we can use them for the estimation of the copula parameters. Here, we estimate margins $F_x(x)$ and $F_y(y)$ using their empirical cumulative distribution functions (ECDFs) $\widehat{F_X}(x)$ and $\widehat{F_Y}(y)$, which are expressed by

$$\widehat{F_X}(x) = \frac{1}{n}\sum_{i=1}^{n} 1\{X_i < x\} \text{ and } \widehat{G_X}(y) = \frac{1}{n}\sum_{i=1}^{n} 1\{Y_i < y\}, \tag{9.7}$$

where X and Y are the standardized residuals filtered through the EGARCH models. With these estimated ECDFs, we derive the unknown parameter θ of the copula models using

$$\hat{\theta} = argmax_{\theta} \sum_{i=1}^{n} \ln c\left(\widehat{F_X}(x), \widehat{G_X}(y), \theta\right), \tag{9.8}$$

where $c(\cdot)$ denotes the density of each of the three Archimedean copulas.

After estimating the three copulas for each bivariate set of the corporate CDS indices, we perform Genest et al.'s (2009) goodness-of-fit test to identify the copula that exhibits the best fit. In this method, the highest p-value[4] for the test statistic, known as the Cramer–von Mises distance, represents the smallest distance between the estimated and empirical copula, suggesting that the copula under investigation best fits the dataset.

9.3 Data

Our dataset contains daily closing quotes data on the three five-year corporate CDS indices, namely IJPN, IEUR, and NAIG. These three CDS indices are traded on spreads and expressed in basis points. We account for the mid-points of the daily closing bid and ask spreads of the CDS indices. The data employed in this study are sourced from Bloomberg, and owing to the availability of CDS indices data, the sample covers the period from January 3, 2005, to December 31, 2015. We investigate the dependence structures between the three CDS indices for not only the entire period (Panel A) but also the four sub-periods: the pre-credit crisis (Panel B, January 3, 2005, to August 8, 2007), credit crisis (Panel C, August 9, 2007, to October 31, 2009), debt crisis (Panel D, November 1, 2009, to December 31, 2013), and post-debt crisis (Panel E, January 1, 2014, to December 31, 2015) period. As the start date of the credit crisis, we consider August 9, 2007, when the first global credit crunch panic was immediately recognized after BNP Paribas froze its three funds. The debt crisis period is considered to have begun on November 1, 2009, when investors began to perceive substantial default risks of Greek sovereign debt, and ceased at the end of 2013, when the Eurozone gradually regained financial health and Ireland and Spain ended their bailout program.

The historical paths of the three corporate CDS indices are shown in Figure 9.1. Although the three indices share a similar pattern of movement with several peaks occurring simultaneously, IJPN particularly exhibits larger swings

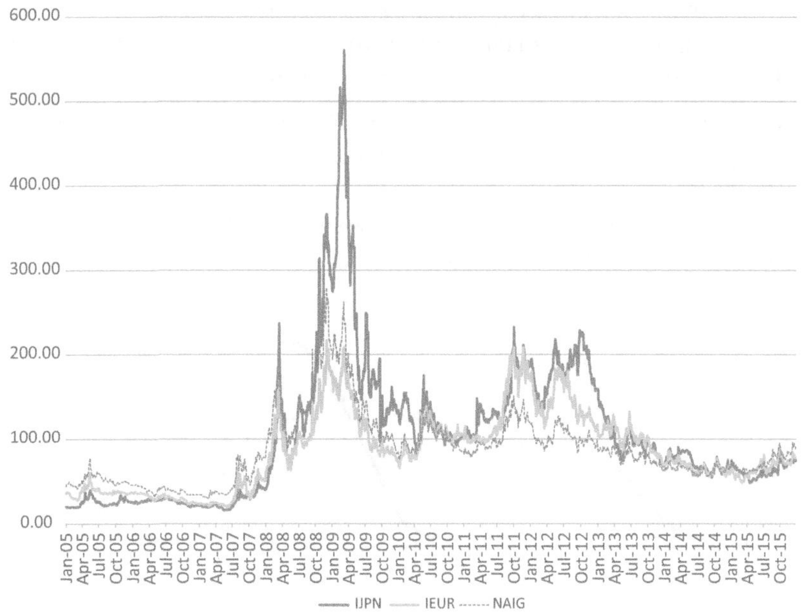

Figure 9.1 Historical plot of the iTraxx and CDX CDS indices

and spikes at different timings, such as mid-2011 and late 2012. Table 9.1 presents the descriptive statistics for both level and first-differenced data. As expected, IJPN has the highest volatility represented by the standard deviation. All three indices have positive skewness, implying that large negative values are more likely to occur. The high kurtosis levels observed in IJPN and NAIG suggest that they are more leptokurtically distributed. Consistent with these findings on skewness and kurtosis, the Jarque–Bera test shows that the null hypothesis of a normal distribution is rejected at the 1 percent significance level. Figure 9.2 presents the normal QQ-plots of the three CDS indices and the shapes of these plots additionally support the three indices being normally distributed. The augmented Dickey–Fuller unit root tests with an intercept, as reported in Table 9.1, imply that all three indices are I(1) variables, and hence, we employ first-differenced data[5] in our subsequent analysis. In the final analysis, the Lagrange multiplier

Table 9.1 Summary statistics

Variable	*Mean (b.p.)*	*Max. (b.p.)*	*Min. (b.p.)*	*SD*	*Skewness*	*Kurtosis*	*ADF*	*JB*
Level data:								
IJPN	103.92	560.11	15.98	81.53	1.85	8.28	-2.42	4800.15***
IEUR	86.10	216.87	20.16	44.91	0.53	2.57	-2.18	149.48***
NAIG	87.26	279.31	29.03	42.01	1.42	5.77	-2.34	1822.47***
First-differenced data:								
IJPN	0.02	59.38	-94.15	6.33	-2.15	49.29	-46.38***	12.86***
IEUR	0.01	24.43	-30.00	3.61	-0.20	11.51	-32.75***	46.26***
NAIG	0.02	43.34	-31.07	3.43	0.39	27.96	-32.34***	34.55***

Notes: Statistics on the level and first-differenced data for the daily CDS indices are reported.

ADF is the augmented Dickey–Fuller test for unit root (with intercept) and JB is the Jarque–Bera test for normality.

ARCH(12) is the Lagrange multiplier test for autogregressive conditional heteroskedasticity.

*** denotes statistical significance at the 1% level.

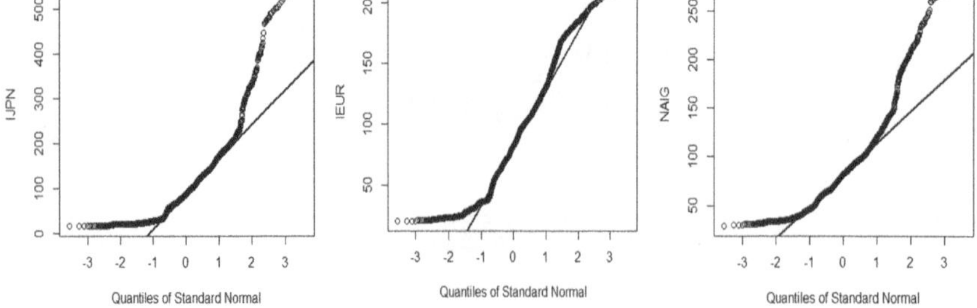

Figure 9.2 Normal QQ-plots of the iTraxx and CDX CDS indices

test for autoregressive conditional heteroscedasticity shows the presence of the ARCH effects in the first-differenced data. Therefore, we believe that using the standardized residuals data filtered through our EGARCH models is more desirable than the raw data on the CDS indices themselves.

9.4 Empirical results

First, we estimate univariate AR-EGARCH models for each of the three corporate CDS indices to model the marginal distributions. Table 9.2 reports the parameter estimates for the marginal distribution models in the entire period. The AR(1)-EGARCH(1, 1) models are selected for IJPN and IEUR, while the selected model specification is AR(6)-EGARCH(1, 1) for NAIG based on the Schwarz–Bayesian information criteria. The coefficients in the conditional variance equation are significant at the 1 percent level for all three indices, indicating that our specification exhibits a good fit to the data. The Ljung–Box *Q*-statistics, $Q(12)$ and $Q^2(12)$, also suggest no autocorrelation up to order 12 for the standardized residuals and their squares. Moreover, by performing the

Table 9.2 Parameter estimates for the marginal distribution models

	IJPN *AR(1)-EGARCH(1,1)*		*IEUR* *AR(1)-EGARCH(1,1)*		*NAIG* *AR(6)-EGARCH(1,1)*	
	Estimate	*SE*	*Estimate*	*SE*	*Estimate*	*SE*
Conditional mean equation						
φ_0	-0.00001	0.0054	-0.0360**	0.0085	-0.0396***	0.0144
φ_1	0.0862***	0.0113	0.1172***	0.0156	0.1131***	0.0172
φ_2					-0.0227	0.0172
φ_3					0.0162	0.0169
φ_4					-0.0188	0.0167
φ_5					0.0178	0.0168
φ_6					-0.0631***	0.0163
Conditional variance equation						
ω	-0.1760***	0.0136	-0.1744***	0.0165	-0.1802***	0.0150
α_1	0.2845***	0.0230	0.2461***	0.0232	0.2666***	0.0210
γ_1	0.0806***	0.0146	0.0986***	0.0151	0.0811***	0.0153
β_1	0.9923***	0.0016	0.9921***	0.0018	0.9893***	0.0024
GED parameter	0.7629***		1.2556***	0.0296	1.1061***	0.0272
$Q(12)$	18.7850**		9.2338***		10.8070***	
$Q^2(12)$	6.1605***		2.4620***		4.2188***	

Notes: $Q(12)$ and $Q^2(12)$ are the Ljung–Box statistics up to the 12th order in standardized residuals and their squares.

*** and ** indicate statistical significance at the 1% and 5% levels.

Lagrange multiplier test for autoregressive conditional heteroscedasticity on the estimated standardized residuals, we find no evidence of the ARCH effects.[6] These results provide support for our notion that using the standardized residuals data filtered through the AR-EGARCH models are more desirable than the (first-differenced) corporate CDS indices data.

Second, we transform the standardized residuals into uniform variables. Here, to explore the nature of dependence between them, we compute two rank correlation measures, namely, Kendall's tau and Spearman's rho, both of which are useful in capturing the non-linear relationships between the variables. The estimated rank correlation coefficients for each period are reported in Table 9.3. From the table, we find substantial increases in the correlation measures during the credit and debt crises for the IJPN–IEUR and NAIG–IJPN pairs. This implies that both crises generated the transmission of credit risks even in the relationships involving Japanese companies. More interestingly, the rank correlation coefficients for the IEUR–NAIG pair remained high even during the post-debt crisis, suggesting that the European debt crisis, which originated in the Greek sovereign bond markets, may have triggered a higher degree of cross-country transmission of corporate credit risks between the European and U.S. firms.

Then, employing the pseudo-maximum likelihood method, we estimate the unknown dependence parameter θ of the three copulas (Gumbel, Clayton, and Frank) in Equations (9.4)–(9.6) for each period. The results of the estimation are presented in Table 9.4. The dependence parameters are found to be significant at the 1 percent level for all pairs across the periods. In view of this, we are interested in which of the three copula best fits the data. Table 9.5 presents the results of the goodness-of-fit test and tail dependence. The best-fitting copulas are denoted by bold letters. We derive the following two main findings from the table.

Table 9.3 Rank correlation estimates for dependence

Pair		*IJPN-IEUR*	*IEUR-NAIG*	*NAIG-IJPN*
Panel A: Entire period	Kendall	0.1860	0.4429	0.1135
	Spearman	0.2740	0.6150	0.1687
Panel B: Pre-credit crisis	Kendall	0.1251	0.3576	0.0756
	Spearman	0.1846	0.5007	0.1125
Panel C: Credit crisis	Kendall	0.2571	0.4352	0.2020
	Spearman	0.3790	0.6083	0.2998
Panel D: Debt crisis	Kendall	0.1891	0.4807	0.0992
	Spearman	0.2794	0.6621	0.1483
Panel E: Post-debt crisis	Kendall	0.1585	0.4742	0.0877
	Spearman	0.2325	0.6533	0.1304

Notes: The table describes rank correlation estimates over the entire period and four sub-periods.

Table 9.4 Estimates of the dependence parameters for the different copula models

Copula type	*Gumbel*	*Clayton*	*Frank*
Panel A: Entire period			
IJPN–IEUR	1.2071 (0.0160)***	0.3164 (0.0269)***	1.7323 (0.1186)***
IEUR–NAIG	1.7116 (0.0252)***	1.0222 (0.0316)***	4.8209 (0.1455)***
NAIG–IJPN	1.1163 (0.0148)***	0.1673 (0.0241)***	1.0366 (0.1155)***
Panel B: Pre-credit crisis			
IJPN–IEUR	1.1481 (0.0301)***	0.2084 (0.0641)***	1.4193 (0.2642)***
IEUR–NAIG	1.5597 (0.0536)***	0.8114 (0.0591)***	4.2320 (0.2670)***
NAIG–IJPN	1.0487 (0.0272)***	0.1168 (0.0538)***	0.7889 (0.2667)***
Panel C: Credit crisis			
IJPN–IEUR	1.2846 (0.0378)***	0.3969 (0.0531)***	2.3306 (0.2652)***
IEUR–NAIG	1.6333 (0.0604)***	0.8722 (0.0786)***	4.3635 (0.3240)***
NAIG–IJPN	1.2150 (0.0404)***	0.2137 (0.0442)***	1.7796 (0.2564)***
Panel D: Debt crisis			
IJPN–IEUR	1.2022 (0.0258)***	0.3266 (0.0423)***	1.6591 (0.1870)***
IEUR–NAIG	1.7927 (0.0470)***	1.1609 (0.0656)***	5.1937 (0.2495)***
NAIG–IJPN	1.0975 (0.0234)***	0.1565 (0.0393)***	0.8586 (0.1807)***
Panel E: Post-debt crisis			
IJPN–IEUR	1.2009 (0.0427)***	0.3198 (0.0689)***	1.5093 (0.2762)***
IEUR–NAIG	1.8487 (0.0769)***	1.1931 (0.0904)***	5.3737 (0.3693)***
NAIG–IJPN	1.1217 (0.0385)***	0.1980 (0.0657)***	0.8082 (0.2665)***

Notes: *** denotes statistical significance at the 1% level. Standard errors are reported in parentheses.

First, the dependence pattern of the NAIG–IJPN pair is highlighted from portfolio managers' perspectives. Prior to the two crises, the Frank copula,[7] which is a symmetric copula with zero tail dependence, exhibits the best fit. In contrast, during both the credit and debt crises, the best-fitting copula is the Gumbel copula, which is asymmetric with right tail dependence, implying that the two CDS indices tend to exhibit a more upward extreme co-movement[8] than a downward one. Such asymmetric dependence in times of the financial crises implies the existence of systemic risks across the two indices. The key implication of the findings is that portfolio managers should pay attention to the potential risks of a substantial simultaneous loss resulting from the exposure of their portfolio to credit risks reflected in NAIG and IJPN. While prior studies such as Naifar (2011b) point out asymmetric dependence between a corporate CDS index (i.e., iTraxx Australia) and a portfolio of stocks of the reference entities, this study may be the first to provide insight into the existence of asymmetric co-movement between the major investment-grade corporate CDS indices.

Table 9.5 Goodness-of-fit tests and tail dependence

Pair	*Gumbel*			*Clayton*			*Frank*		
	Sn	λL	λU	*Sn*	λL	λU	*Sn*	λL	λU
Panel A: Entire period									
IJPN–IEUR	0.0531	0.0000	0.2242	0.3208	0.1118	0.0000	0.0506	0.0000	0.0000
	[0.0055]			[0.0005]			[0.0015]		
IEUR–NAIG	0.1640	0.0000	0.5007	1.2575	0.5076	0.0000	0.1327	0.0000	0.0000
	[0.0005]			[0.0005]			[0.0005]		
NAIG–IJPN	**0.0253**	0.0000	0.1393	0.1516	0.0159	0.0000	0.0325	0.0000	0.0000
	[0.2213]			[0.0005]			[0.0225]		
Panel B: Pre-credit crisis									
IJPN–IEUR	**0.0261**	0.0000	0.1711	0.0967	0.0359	0.0000	0.0422	0.0000	0.0000
	[0.1943]			[0.0005]			[0.0085]		
IEUR–NAIG	0.0590	0.0000	0.4404	0.1847	0.4256	0.0000	0.0434	0.0000	0.0000
	[0.0005]			[0.0005]			[0.0065]		
NAIG–IJPN	0.0291	0.0000	0.0634	0.0212	0.0026	0.0000	**0.0104**	0.0000	0.0000
	[0.1364]			[0.4171]			**[0.9486]**		
Panel C: Credit crisis									
IJPN–IEUR	0.0673	0.0000	0.2847	0.1679	0.1736	0.0000	**0.0163**	0.0000	0.0000
	[0.0015]			[0.0005]			**[0.5540]**		
IEUR–NAIG	0.0484	0.0000	0.4714	0.2814	0.4517	0.0000	**0.0301**	0.0000	0.0000
	[0.0005]			[0.0005]			**[0.0445]**		
NAIG–IJPN	**0.0226**	0.0000	0.2309	0.1657	0.0391	0.0000	0.0243	0.0000	0.0000
	[0.3062]			[0.0005]			[0.1474]		

Panel D: Debt crisis									
IJPN–IEUR	0.0400	0.0000	0.2201	0.0924	0.1198	0.0000	**0.0175**	0.0000	0.0000
	[0.0205]			[0.0005]			**[0.4730]**		
IEUR–NAIG	0.0633	0.0000	0.5280	0.6322	0.5504	0.0000	0.0531		
	[0.0015]			[0.0005]			[0.0015]		
NAIG–IJPN	**0.0193**	0.0000	0.1194	0.0522	0.0119	0.0000	0.0206	0.0000	0.0000
	[0.5280]			[0.0095]			[0.2852]		
Panel E: Post-debt crisis									
IJPN–IEUR	**0.0211**	0.0000	0.2190	0.0507	0.1145	0.0000	0.0332	0.0000	0.0000
	[0.4061]			[0.0115]			[0.0345]		
IEUR–NAIG	**0.0290**	0.0000	0.5451	0.2688	0.5594	0.0000	0.0389	0.0000	0.0000
	[0.0984]			[0.0005]			[0.0064]		
NAIG–IJPN	**0.0266**	0.0000	0.1449	0.2688	0.0302	0.0000	0.0304	0.0000	0.0000
	[0.2842]			[0.0005]			[0.0664]		

Notes: The table presents the statistics (Sn) and *p*-values (in brackets) of the goodness-of-fit test.

Bold letters indicate that the copula exhibits the best fit to the data and the null hypothesis that the estimated copula belongs to the empirical copula family is not rejected at the 1% significance level.

It also shows the upper and lower tail dependence coefficients (λU and λL) for each copula.

Second, from the regulators' perspectives, it is noteworthy that the Gumbel copula is the best-fitted copula for all pairs during the post-debt crisis period. This holds true even for the IJPN–IEUR and IEUR–NAIG pairs, in which the Frank copula appears to be a better-fitted copula during the two financial crisis periods. It is indeed counter-intuitive to observe such asymmetric dependence after the periods of market stress. However, as we can see from Figure 9.1, the three CDS indices seem to show more upward extreme than downward co-movement, especially after April 2015. Despite the growing importance of the corporate CDS indices compared to single-name CDSs, little attention has been paid to modeling a solid regulatory platform on the corporate CDS indices market.[9] This may be partly because the CDX and iTraxx CDS indices, owned and managed by the private financial service provider, Markit Group Ltd., have not been relatively visible in contrast to the sovereign CDS markets, where the European debt crisis took place. Our results on the recent pairwise dependence structures among the three corporate CDS indices may warrant, on the regulators' end, greater awareness of the potential systemic risks in the corporate CDS indices, which have not been widely recognized during the financial turmoil.

9.5 Conclusion

In this chapter, the dependence structures between the three corporate CDS indices were examined from January 3, 2005, to December 31, 2015. We employ two-step estimation approaches consisting of extracting and transforming the estimated standardized residuals through AR-EGARCH models into uniform variables and then, applying three Archimedean copula (Gumbel, Clayton, and Frank) to assess the dependence structures, including upper and lower dependence.

Our estimation results lead us to derive two main findings. First, the NAIG–IJPN pair showed an interesting pattern of dependence structures across the periods. While the Frank copula (symmetric copula with zero tail dependence) was the best fit during the pre-crisis period, the Gumbel copula (asymmetric with upper tail dependence) fit best during the global credit crisis and European debt crisis. This implies that the exposure to the two corporate CDS indices and the credit risks related to their reference entities may possibly result in a substantial simultaneous loss. Second, contrary to our initial expectations, the Gumbel copula exhibited the best fit to the data during the post-debt crisis period (2014–2015) for all pairwise combinations of the three CDS indices (IJPN–IEUR, IEUR–NAIG, and NAIG–IJPN). This suggests that even after the sovereign default risks were mitigated, systemic risks surrounding the investment-grade corporate CDS indices and thus, the corporate credit risks across Japan, Europe, and the United States have recently become more evident.

Our results provide an important implication for investors, that is, when considering diversification strategies, they should pay attention to the cross-country transmission of corporate credit risks between Japan and the United

States in particular, as reflected in the asymmetric dependence structure of their corporate CDS indices. In addition, our findings suggest that regulators should be more aware of the sign of potential systemic risks among the corporate CDS indices, which have recently emerged despite the European sovereign debt crisis being ameliorated. This study focused on identifying the pairwise dependence structures of the three representative corporate CDS indices. However, it did not fully investigate how multivariate dependence structures among the various classes of corporate CDS indices, which may deserve investors' attention in the diversification of credit risks, have changed over time. We leave the topic for future research.

Notes

1 See Brock et al. (1987) for details on the BDS test.
2 To model marginal distribution behaviors, we select the best of AR(k)-EGARCH(p,q) on the basis of the Schwarz–Bayesian information criteria. See Nelson (1991) for details on EGARCH models.
3 Moreover, unlike the standard GARCH models, the EGARCH models with a logarithmic form are not constrained by the signs of the coefficients, ensuring the non-negativity of conditional variance.
4 To identify the p-values, we apply Kojadinovie and Yan's (2011) multiplier method, which is faster than the parametric bootstrap method in terms of computation speed.
5 Converting the first-differenced data into logarithms is not necessary because the units of the CDS indices are in basis points (i.e., 100 basis points equal 1 percent).
6 The results of the Lagrange multiplier test are not reported but can be made available upon request.
7 The Frank copula has a smaller tail concentration in both the lower and upper tails than the Normal copula, which is also symmetric with zero tail dependence.
8 Note that the increases in the CDS indices indicate the simultaneous rise in their credit risks.
9 A rare example of the regulatory move is that in July 2013, the European Commission raised competition concerns that Markit and the ISDA breached the European Union's antitrust rules by refusing to license the CDX and iTraxx CDS indices for exchange trading.

References

Alexander, C. and Kaeck, A. (2008) Regime dependent determinants of credit default swap spreads, *Journal of Banking and Finance*, **32**, 1008–1021.

Brock, W. A., Dechert, W. D., and Scheinkman, J. A. (1987) A test for independence based on the correlation dimension. Department of Economics, *University of Wisconsin Madison Working Paper No. 8702.*

Fabozzi, F. J., Wang, Y. C., Yeh, S. K., and Chen, R. R. (2009) An empirical analysis of the CDX index and its tranches, *Applied Economics Letters*, **16**, 1425–1431.

Fenech, J., Vosgha, H., and Shafik, S. (2014) Modelling the dependence structures of Australian iTraxx CDS index, *Applied Economics*, **46**, 420–431.

Genest, C., Remillard, B., and Beaudoin, D. (2009) Goodness-of-fit tests for copulas: A review and a power study, *Insurance: Mathematics and Economics*, **44**, 199–213.

Kojadinovie, I. and Yan, J. (2011) A goodness-of-fit test for multivariate multiparameter copulas based on multiplier central limit theorems, *Statistics and Computing*, **21**, 17–30.

Madhavan, V. (2013) Nonlinearity in investment grade credit default swap (CDS) indices of US and Europe: Evidence from BDS and close-return tests, *Global Finance Journal*, **24**, 266–279.

Naifar, N. (2011a) What explains default risk premium during the financial crisis? Evidence from Japan, *Journal of Economics and Business*, **63**, 412–430.

Naifar, N. (2011b) Modelling dependence structure with Archimedean copulas and applications to the iTraxx CDS index, *Journal of Computational and Applied Mathematics*, **235**, 2459–2466.

Naifar, N. (2012) Modeling the dependence structure between default risk premium, equity return volatility and the jump risk: Evidence from a financial crisis, *Economic Modelling*, **29**, 119–131.

Nelson, D. (1991) Conditional heteroskedasticity in asset returns: A new approach, *Econometrica*, **59**, 347–370.

Sklar, A. (1959) Fonctions de repartition a n dimensions et leurs marges, *Publicaitons de l'Institut de Statistique de L'Universite de Paris*, **8**, 229–231.

10 Interdependence between corporate CDS indices

Application of continuous wavelet transform

10.1 Introduction

The wavelet transform was developed by Morlet et al. (1982a, 1982b) as a method for analyzing signal characteristics. It has wide ranging applications, including voice processing and image processing. A wavelet transform can derive the structure of data that includes waves of various frequencies by applying scaling and shifting to the given data. It is characterized by its ability to grasp a signal in the domains of time and frequency. Furthermore, wavelet transforms are suited for the analyses of irregular and non-stationary variables; hence, they are expected to be applicable to time series analyses of financial data.[1]

In general, the movement of an economic variable is a localized cyclical fluctuation. Many of these variables change their frequency over time. For example, an economic variable may continue to move at a constant frequency for a time before changing to a different frequency. Determining the localized cyclical fluctuation over time (i.e., $x(t)$ in terms of time and frequency) is known as a time–frequency analysis. Such analysis enables the movement of a variable to be expressed geometrically on a time–frequency plane. The wavelet transform is the method used to conduct a time–frequency analysis of a variable, $x(t)$.

Following Chapter 9, we use the three most popular investment grade corporate CDS indices: iTraxx.Japan (IJPN), iTraxx.Europe (IEUR), and CDX.NA.IG (NAIG). IJPN, IEUR, and NAIG comprise a portfolio of equally weighted single-name CDS spreads for 50, 125, and 125 investment-grade reference entities in Japan, Europe, and the United States, respectively. Then, we analyze the interdependence between the corporate CDS indices of Japan, Europe, and the United States using wavelet transform.

Modeling the interdependency between the corporate CDS indices is an important problem in portfolio risk management, because it is necessary to appropriately rebalance portfolios in response to fluctuations in the indices. However, there is a lack of research on important problems such as risk management in different cycles and the interdependency between corporate CDS indices. In this study, we use continuous wavelet transforms to analyze the dynamic interdependency of CDS indices in different cycles.

The remainder of the paper is structured as follows. Section 10.2 provides a simple outline of the analysis methods that use continuous wavelet transforms, Section 10.3 describes the basic characteristics of the data, and Section 10.4 presents the test results. Finally, Section 10.5 concludes the paper.

10.2 Methodology

Wavelet transform and power spectrum

Consider a variable $x(t)$ that is dependent on time t, which we will refer to as the signal. Assume that the amplitude and frequency of the signal change over time. To determine the local appearance of each signal, we substitute the variable t of wavelet $\psi(t)$ with $(t-b)/a$. We can now make $\psi((t-b)/a)$ correspond to the local changes in the signal by selecting the real number values for a and b. Here, a is called the scaling parameter and b is called the shifting parameter.

In general, wavelet transforms are of two kinds, continuous wavelet transform (CWT) and discrete wavelet transform (DWT). CWT corresponds to cases where a and b are continuous, while DWT corresponds to cases where a and b are discrete.

The original wavelet $\psi(t)$ is called the mother wavelet. The wavelet $\psi((t-b)/a)$ is the mother wavelet $\psi(t)$ shifted by the value of b and scaled by the value of a.

Shifting refers to the lateral movement of the center position of the mother wavelet along the time axis. Transforming the mother wavelet $\psi(t)\rightarrow\psi(t-b)$ shifts the center position by the value of b. This operation enables the extraction of a similar waveform for any desired time.

Scaling refers to extending or compressing the mother wavelet in a lateral direction, thus changing the cycle (frequency). Transforming the mother wavelet $\psi(t)\rightarrow\psi(t/a)$ scales the width of the wavelet $\psi(t)$ by a factor of a. A larger value for a produces a wider wavelet. Wavelets with a high a value and a large width indicate components that change slowly over a long period (i.e., long cycle, low frequency). On the other hand, wavelets with a low a value and narrow width indicate components that change rapidly within a short period (i.e., short cycle, high frequency) (see Figure 10.1).

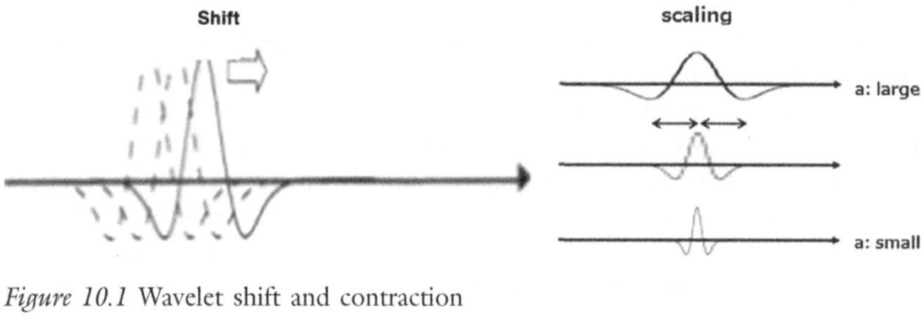

Figure 10.1 Wavelet shift and contraction

Each signal section extracted by wavelets indicates the respective position along the time axis and its local frequency. These can be conceived on a two-dimensional plane, with the horizontal axis representing time and the vertical axis representing the frequency. Thus, the plane is called a time–frequency plane. By plotting each component on this plane, we can determine the distribution of the frequencies for each part of the signal. Here, we consider the following wavelet function:

$$\psi_{a,b}(t) = \frac{1}{\sqrt{a}}\psi\left(\frac{t-b}{a}\right). \tag{10.1}$$

The CWT of the variable $x(t)$ $x(t)$ is defined as follows:

$$W_x(a,b) = \int_{-\infty}^{\infty} x(t)\psi_{a.b}^{*}(t)dt. \tag{10.2}$$

Here, ψ^* represents a complex conjugate. In Expression (10.2), $W_x(a,b)$ is called the wavelet coefficient. In a wavelet transform, the original time series is expressed as a function of a and b to provide information about both the time and the frequency domains simultaneously. When a is small, $W_x(a,b)$ corresponds to a high-frequency component, and when a is large, $W_x(a,b)$ corresponds to a low frequency component. The value of the shifting coefficient b enables us to use different shift amounts for each frequency component.

Conversely, the original time series $x(t)$ can be recovered from the wavelet transform depicted in Expression (10.2). When the wavelet function satisfies the following admissibility condition,

$$C_\psi = \int_{-\infty}^{\infty} \frac{|\hat{\psi}(\omega)|}{|\omega|} d\omega < \infty, \tag{10.3}$$

a reverse wavelet transform exists, which can be obtained as follows:

$$x(t) = \frac{1}{C_\psi}\int_0^{\infty}\int_{-\infty}^{\infty} W_x(a,b)\psi_{a,b}(t)db\frac{da}{a^2}, \quad a > 0. \tag{10.4}$$

Here, $\hat{\psi}$ is the Fourier transform of ψ, and the value of C_ψ is the admissible constant. Moreover, in place of the general admissibility condition expressed in (10.4), the following conditional expression is often used:

$$\int_{-\infty}^{\infty} \psi(x)dx = 0. \tag{10.5}$$

Expression (10.5) means that $\psi(x)$ is oscillatory.

The wavelet power spectrum (WPS) is defined as follows, and it indicates the local variation of the variable $x(t)$:

$$(WPS)_x(a,b) = |W_x(a,b)|^2. \tag{10.6}$$

The WPS in Expression (10.6) is depicted as a two-dimensional graph comprising of a time axis as the horizontal axis and frequency (or cycle) on the vertical axis, with the strength of each frequency expressed by the intensity of the color. This graph is called a scaleogram.

Cross wavelet

A cross wavelet power spectrum is used to evaluate the variation of a single data series. However, most applied research requires a measure to evaluate the interrelationship between two data series. There are three basic methods for analyzing the interdependence of the time and frequency domains between two time series: cross wavelet transform (XWT), wavelet coherency, and wavelet phase difference.

Following Hudgins et al. (1993), the XWT of two signals $x(t)$ and $y(t)$ is defined as follows:

$$W_{xy}(a,b) = W_x(a,b)W_y^*(a,b). \tag{10.7}$$

Here, $W_x(a,b)$ and $W_y(a,b)$ are the wavelet transforms of $x(t)$ and $y(t)$, respectively.

Furthermore, the cross-wavelet power (XWP) is defined as follows:

$$(XWP)_{xy}(a,b) = |W_{xy}(a,b)|. \tag{10.8}$$

If $x = y$ in Expression (10.8), then we can determine the XWP spectrum given by Expression (10.6). In contrast, the power spectrum indicates the local variance for each time and frequency, while the cross-wavelet power indicates the local covariance.

An effective indicator for the evaluation of the relationship between two variables is wavelet coherence (R_{xy}).[2] As explained by Torrence and Compo (1998) and Aguiar-Conraria et al. (2008), this can be expressed as follows:

$$R_{xy} = \frac{|S(W_{xy}(a,b))|}{[S(|W_x(a,b)|^2)S(|W_y(a,b)|^2)]^{1/2}}. \tag{10.9}$$

In addition, the squared wavelet coherence (R_{xy}^2) of (10.9) is defined as follows:

$$R_{xy}^2 = \frac{|S(W_{xy}(a,b))|^2}{S(|W_x(a,b)|^2)S(|W_y(a,b)|^2)}. \tag{10.10}$$

Here, S is a smoothing operator and R_{xy}^2 takes values between 0 and 1 ($0 \leq R_{xy}^2 \leq 1$). When the correlation is weak, R_{xy}^2 takes a value closer to 0, and when it is strong, it takes a value closer to 1.

Furthermore, using the phase-difference allows us to understand more about the relationship between two variables (whether the relationship is positive or negative or whether there is a lead or lag relationship). As a wavelet transform is a complex number, it can be divided into a real part and an imaginary part. The phase difference is defined as follows:

$$\phi_{xy} = \arctan\left(\frac{\mathrm{Im}\{S(W_{xy}(a,b))\}}{\mathrm{Re}\{S(W_{xy}(a,b))\}}\right), \quad \phi_{xy} \in [-\pi, \pi]. \tag{10.11}$$

Phase information is indicated by the direction and angle of the arrow. When the phase difference is zero ($\phi_{xy} = 0$), it indicates that the two variables are moving in the same cycle, implying that they are "in phase." When the phase difference is π (or $-\pi$), it indicates that the two variables are in cycles shifted by 180°, thus implying that they are "out of phase" (or antiphase). If the phase difference is between 0 and $\pi/2$, ($\phi_{xy} \in \left(0, \frac{\pi}{2}\right)$), then the two variables are moving in phase, but variable X is leading variable Y (X leads Y). If the phase difference is between $-\pi/2$ and 0, ($\phi_{xy} \in \left(-\frac{\pi}{2}, 0\right)$), then the two variables are moving in phase, but variable Y is leading variable X (Y leads X). If the phase difference is between $\pi/2$ and π ($\phi_{xy} \in \left(\frac{\pi}{2}, \pi\right)$), the two variables are out of phase, and variable Y is leading variable X (Y leads X). If the phase difference is between $-\pi$ and $-\pi/2$ ($\phi_{xy} \in \left(-\pi, -\frac{\pi}{2}\right)$), then the two variables are out of phase and variable X is leading variable Y (X leads Y). Here, "in phase" implies a positive correlation and "out of phase" implies a negative correlation. The relationships are summarized in Table 10.1.

Table 10.1 Relationship between two variables in each domain

$\left(0, \frac{\pi}{2}\right)$	$\left(-\frac{\pi}{2}, 0\right)$	$\left(\frac{\pi}{2}, \pi\right)$	$\left(-\pi, -\frac{\pi}{2}\right)$
In phase (same direction) X leads Y	In phase (same direction) Y leads X	Out of phase (opposite direction) Y leads X	Out of phase (opposite direction) X leads Y

10.3 Data

Following Chapter 9, we use the three most popular investment grade corporate CDS indices: iTraxx.Japan (IJPN), iTraxx.Europe (IEUR), and CDX.NA.IG (NAIG). IJPN, IEUR, and NAIG comprise a portfolio of equally weighted single-name CDS spreads for 50, 125, and 125 investment-grade reference entities in Japan, Europe, and the United States, respectively. Our data set contains daily closing quote data on the three five-year corporate CDS indices, namely Japan (IJPN), Europe (IEUR), and the United States (NAIG). These three CDS indices are traded on spreads and expressed in basis points. We account for the mid-points of the daily closing bid and ask spreads of the CDS indices. The data employed in this study are sourced from Bloomberg and based on the availability of data; the sample covers the period from January 3, 2005, to December 31, 2013. Note that the actual analysis uses the difference between each CDS index.

Table 10.2 presents the summary statistics for each variable. The result of the Jarque–Bera (JB) test indicates that we reject the null hypothesis (at the 1 percent significance level) of the economies' earnings ratios following a normal distribution. Table 10.3 presents the mutual correlations (Pearson correlations) between each variable, indicating a statistically significant positive correlation between the variables. This table also indicates a relatively large positive correlation between the United States and the EU.

Table 10.2 Summary statistics

	Mean	*Median*	*Max*	*Min*	*SD*	*Skewness*	*Kurtosis*	*Jarque–Bera*
US	0.0078	-0.040	43.3360	-31.0740	3.7215	0.4122	25.0224	4.6017E04***
EU	0.0151	-0.0480	32.8460	-29.9960	3.8973	-0.0832	12.3766	8.3332E03***
JP	0.0208	0.000	59.3810	-94.1500	6.8643	-2.0889	42.1794	1.4710E05***

Notes: SD denotes standard deviation; Jarque–Bera corresponds to the Jarque–Bera test statistics.
*** Significance at 1% level.

Table 10.3 Pearson correlation matrix

	US	*EU*	*JP*
US	1.0000		
EU	0.6938 (0.000)	1.0000	
JP	0.3409 (0.000)	0.4004 (0.000)	1.0000

Notes: Numbers in brackets indicate the *p*-value of the *t*-test; the null hypothesis is that there is no correlation between the variables.

10.4 Empirical results

Power spectrum

Figure 10.2 depicts a series of scaleograms based on wavelet power spectrums for the CDS indices of the United States (Figure 10.2(a)), the EU (Figure 10.2(b)), and Japan (Figure 10.2(c)). Each scaleogram depicts the cycle along the vertical axis, with the cycle growing longer (i.e., the frequency becoming lower) as the value on the vertical axis grows larger. In other words, moving from top to bottom, the cycle becomes longer, changing from a short to a long cycle (i.e., the frequency changing from high to low). Areas of the chart where the power spectrum level is high indicate a large change and areas where the power spectrum level is low indicate a small change. Thus, as the power spectrum level decreases, the degree of change becomes smaller. The areas enclosed with bold black lines represent areas of statistically significant changes.

First, from Figure 10.2(a) we can see that the U.S. CDS index indicates a strong spectrum around the time of the 2008 global financial crisis. However, the figure depicts a relatively smaller increase in the power spectrum associated with the subsequent European debt crisis. Figure 10.2(b) indicates that the EU also has a strong spectrum around the time of the 2008 global financial crisis,

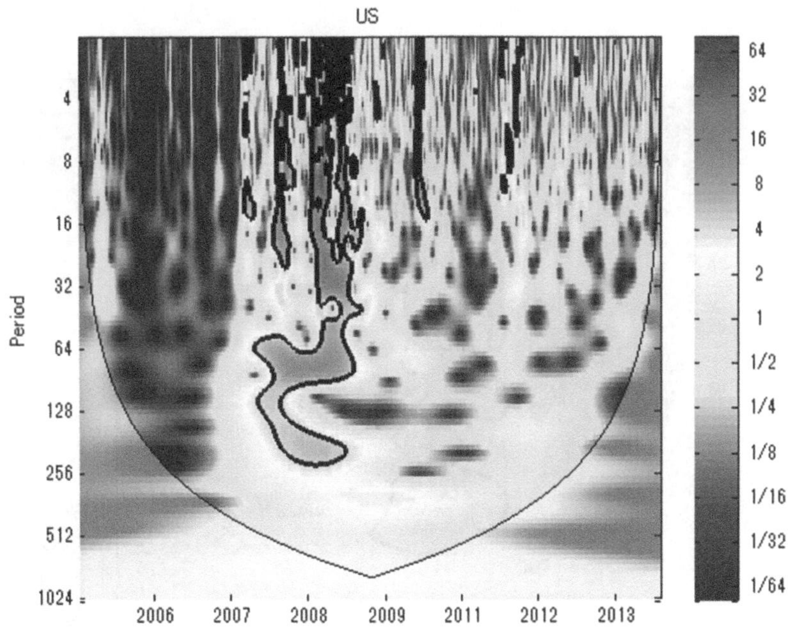

Figure 10.2(a) Continuous wavelet power spectrum: U.S.

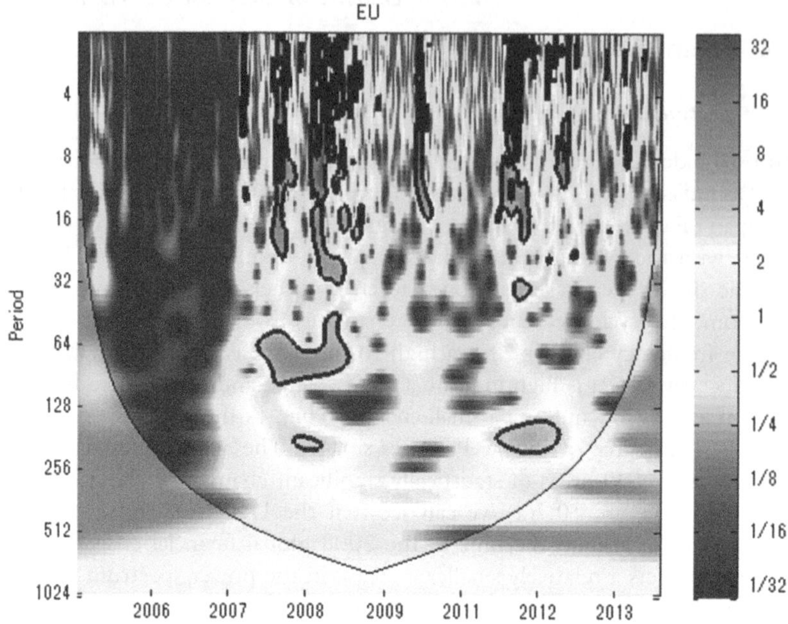

Figure 10.2(b) Continuous wavelet power spectrum: EU

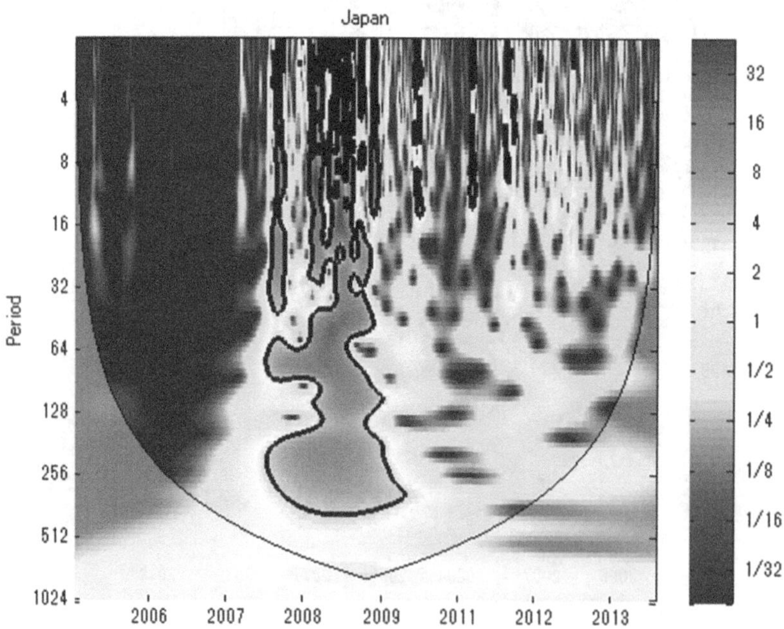

Figure 10.2(c) Continuous wavelet power spectrum: Japan

as in the U.S. case. However, in this case, there is a strong spectrum during the European debt crisis, as well as in the subsequent period. Figure 10.2(c) depicts a similar trend in Japan to that of the United States, with a strong power spectrum around the time of the 2008 global financial crisis. Moreover, as in the U.S. case, the Japanese chart does not indicate a significant rise in the power spectrum during the European debt crisis.

Cross wavelet and coherence

Figures 10.3(a), 10.3(b), and 10.3(c) depict the XWP spectrums for the United States and the EU, the United States and Japan, and the EU and Japan, respectively. Each scaleogram depicts the cycle along the vertical axis, with the cycle growing longer (i.e., the frequency becoming lower) as the value on the vertical axis grows larger. In other words, moving from top to bottom, the cycle becomes longer, changing from a short to a long cycle (i.e., the frequency changing from high to low). Areas of the chart where the cross power spectrum level is large indicate a large covariance and areas where the power spectrum level is small indicate a small covariance. Thus, as the power spectrum values decrease, the amount of covariance becomes smaller. The area enclosed with bold black lines represents the area of statistically significant change.

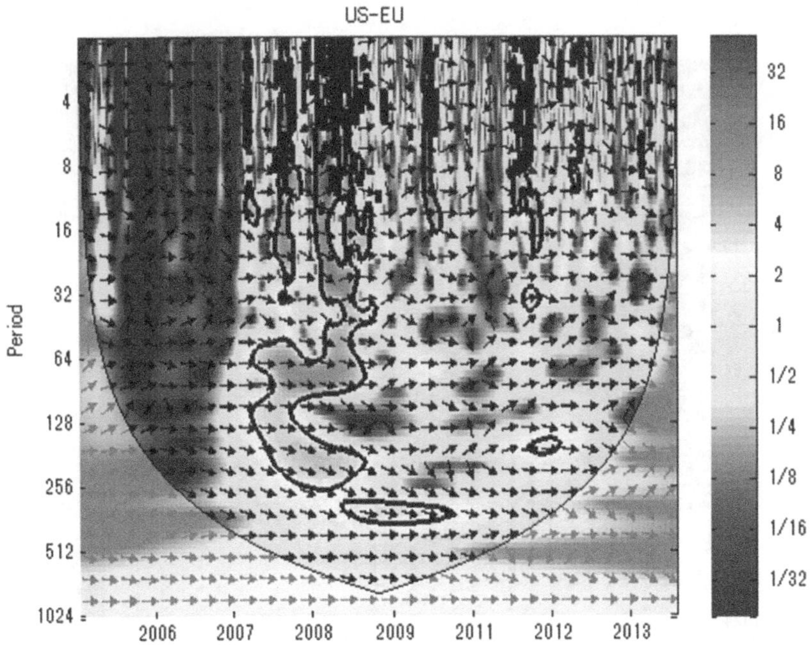

Figure 10.3(a) Cross wavelet power: U.S.–EU

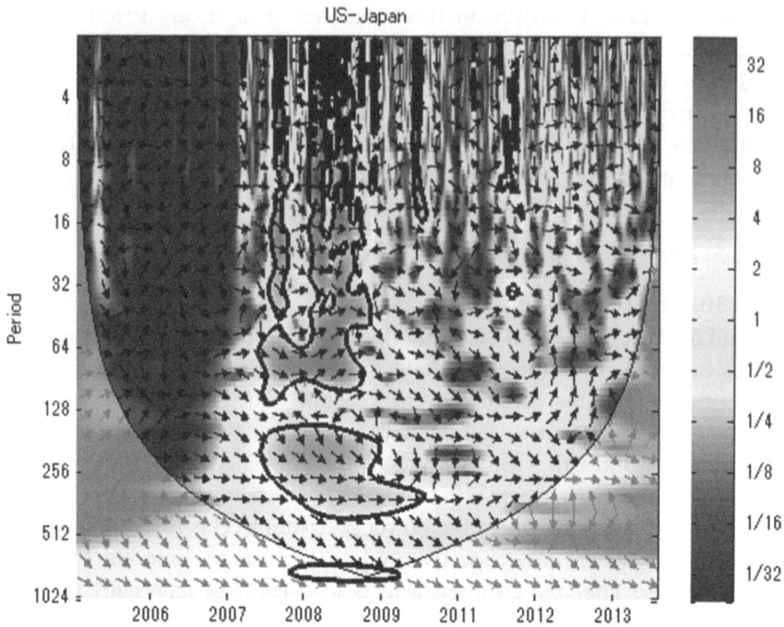

Figure 10.3(b) Cross wavelet power: U.S.–Japan

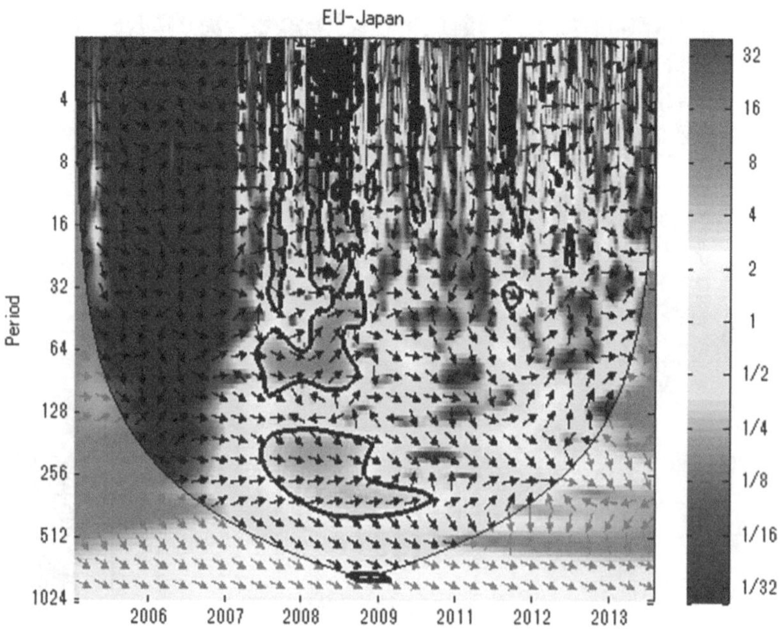

Figure 10.3(c) Cross wavelet power: EU–Japan

Considering the relationship between the United States and the EU in Figure 10.3(a), a strong cross power spectrum is observed during the global financial crisis and the European crises. This trend is particularly prominent in the relatively long cycles of 64–256 days. Figures 10.3(b) and 10.3(c) clearly depict the same trend with respect to the relationships between the United States and Japan and the EU and Japan.

Next, we use coherence to analyze the relationship between the variables. Figure 10.4 depicts the phase difference. The domain on the right half of the circle represents the in-phase pairs, and the domain on the left half represents the out-of-phase pairs. The in-phase domain indicates that the two variables are moving in the same direction (positive relationship), while the out-of-phase domain indicates that the two variables are moving in opposite directions (negative relationship). Furthermore, the arrows pointing upward to the right or downward to the left indicate that X leads Y, while arrows pointing upward to the left or downward to the right indicate that Y leads X.

Figures 10.5(a), 10.5(b), and 10.5(c) depict the coherence of the CDS indices of the United States, the EU, and Japan. Figure 10.5(a) depicts the relationship between the United States and the EU, Figure 10.5(b) depicts the relationship between the United States and Japan, and Figure 10.5(c) depicts the relationship between the EU and Japan. In Figure 10.5, the vertical axis

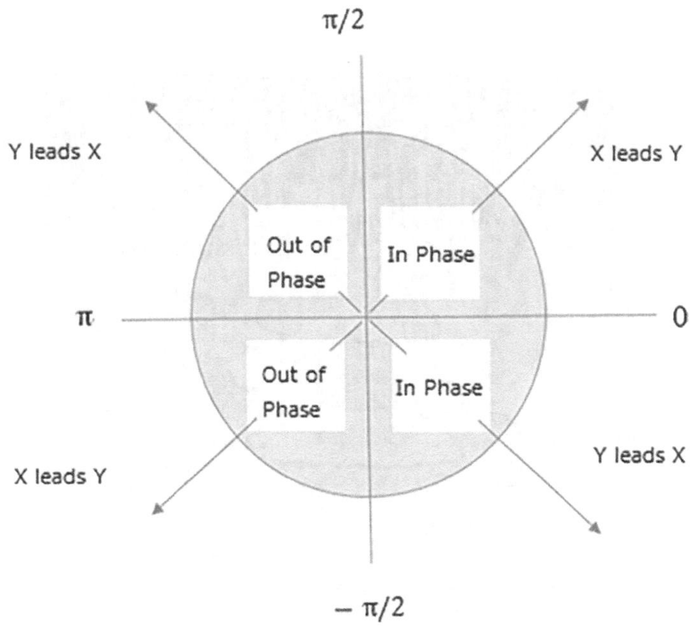

Figure 10.4 Phase difference

Sources: Aguiar-Conraria and Soares (2014); Figure 10.3 (Partial modification by the author)

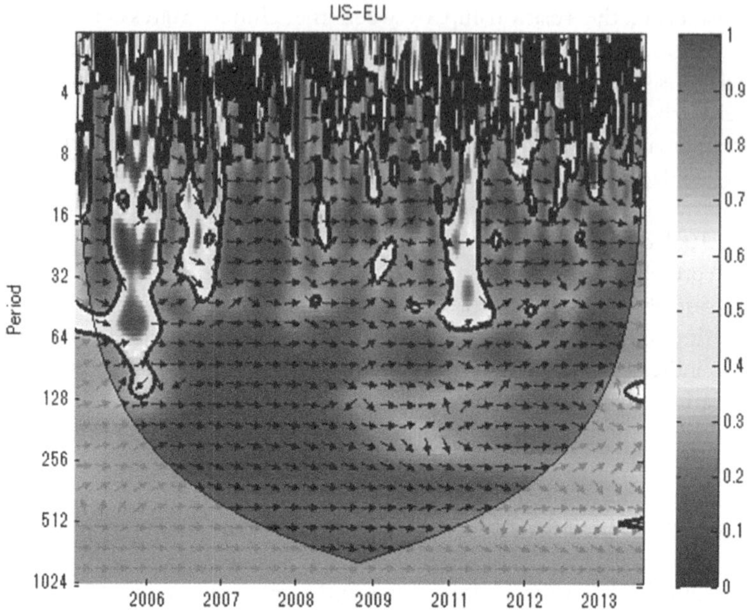

Figure 10.5(a) Wavelet coherence plot: U.S.–EU

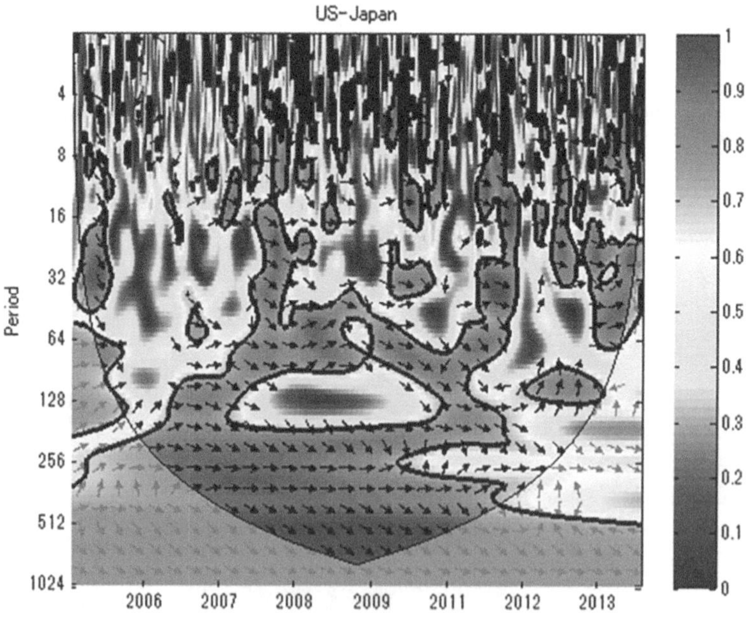

Figure 10.5(b) Wavelet coherence plot: U.S.–Japan

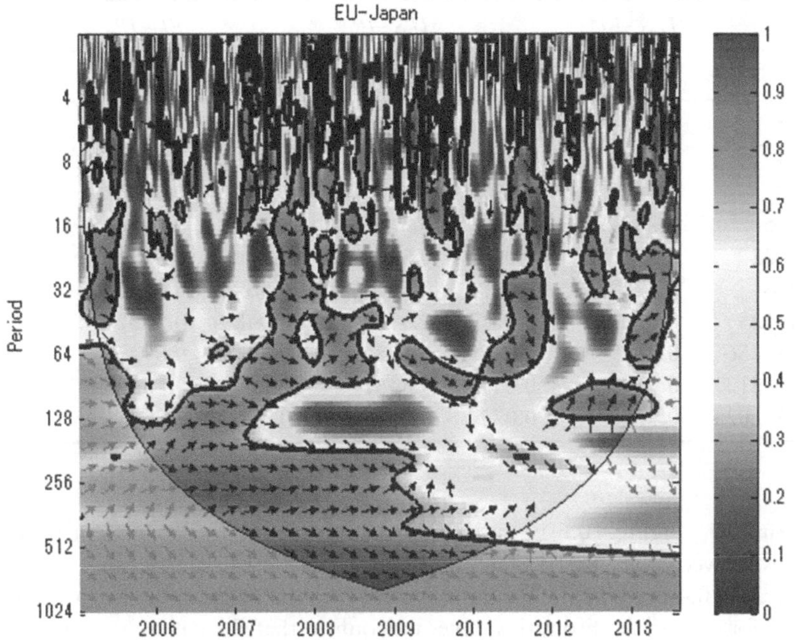

Figure 10.5(c) Wavelet coherence plot: EU–Japan

on the left-hand side of each chart indicates the cycle, while the horizontal axis indicates time. In the coherence chart, an additional axis on the right-hand side is limited between zero and one. As the coherence level moves from one to zero, the coherence value diminishes, indicating a weaker relationship between the two variables. In other words, in areas where the coherence value approaches one, the relationship between the variables is strong, while in areas where it approaches zero, the relationship between the variables is weak.

As regards the relationship between the United States and the EU in Figure 10.5(a), a strong coherence between the two is not apparent in the short-cycle (high-frequency) domain, but it is observed in the long-cycle (low-frequency) domain. In other words, the relationship between the earnings ratios in both markets has no relevance with regard to short-term variations, but the two are closely related with regard to long-term variations. Furthermore, as the arrows are pointing to the right, the chart indicates that both economies are in phase in the long run, with the United States and the EU indicating the similar variations. Here, strong coherence between the variables in the short cycles (high frequency) can be interpreted as contagion between the stock markets, while strong coherence between the variables in the long cycles (low frequency) can be interpreted as interdependence between them.[3]

Table 10.4 Coherency and phase difference

Days Cycle	*U.S.–EU*		*U.S.–JP*		*EU–JP*	
	Coherency	*Phase*	*Coherency*	*Phase*	*Coherency*	*Phase*
1–2	0.5120	0.2290	0.4243	0.5299	0.4324	0.3554
2–4	0.6605	0.1423	0.4487	0.4253	0.4728	0.3814
4–8	0.7407	0.0927	0.4933	0.4242	0.5004	0.3193
8–16	0.7834	0.0599	0.5068	0.1742	0.4956	0.1744
16–32	0.7983	-0.0900	0.5480	0.3086	0.5171	0.3582
32–64	0.8747	-0.0296	0.6218	0.0672	0.6085	0.1900
64–128	0.8969	0.0377	0.5986	-0.0489	0.5632	-0.1341
128–256	0.9199	0.0489	0.7321	0.1914	0.6925	0.1792
256–512	0.9195	0.0419	0.8481	0.3703	0.7316	0.5362
512–1024	0.9618	0.0724	0.9685	0.4582	0.9834	0.3858

Similarly, Figure 10.5(b) and Figure 10.5(c) depict the dependent relationships between the United States and Japan and the EU and Japan.

Table 10.4 presents the relationships between the phase difference and coherence for each cycle. From this table, we confirm that the coherence value tends to increase as the cycle grows longer.

10.5 Conclusion

The main objective of this study is to analyze corporate CDS index variations in the United States, the EU, and Japan from short-cycle (high frequency) to long-cycle (low frequency) waves to clarify the interdependency between the CDS indices markets. Here, the interdependency of short-cycle waves implies contagion, while the interdependency of long-cycle waves indicates interdependence based on fundamentals. Clearly distinguishing between short-term and long-term variations enables investors to conduct rational asset distribution strategies and select optimal portfolio compositions. It also enables policymakers to promote reliable policy responses to crises.

The results indicate several points of interest:

- The power spectrum analysis reveals that the CDS indices had a large power spectrum value during the 2008 global financial crisis. It also reveals that during the subsequent European debt crisis, the power spectrum of the EU CDS index rose, but its impact on the United States and Japan was relatively weak.
- The result of the coherence test for interdependency between the CDS indices of the three economies indicates that coherence is stronger for variations with a long-term cycle vis-à-vis a short-term cycle. In addition,

the relationship between the markets is in phase, indicating that they move in the same direction.

The market participants range from those who trade with a relatively short-term view to those who trade with a long-term view. Conducting a wavelet analysis enables participants to conduct analyses from the perspectives of both the time and the frequency domains. This allows for detailed analyses of the variations in the earnings ratios of the CDS indices and provides market participants with important information.

Notes

1 For further information about wavelet transforms, refer to Gençay et al. (2001) and Percival and Walden (2000).
2 For information regarding wavelet coherence analysis, refer to Aloui and Hkiri (2014), Uddina et al. (2013), and Aguiar-Conraria and Soares (2014), among others.
3 For more information on interdependence and contagion analyses based on different cycles, see Bodart and Candelon (2009) and Orlov (2009).

References

Aguiar-Conraria, L., Azevedo, N., and Soares, M. J. (2008) Using wavelets to decompose the time-frequency effects of monetary policy, *Physical A*, **387**, 2863–2878.

Aguiar-Conraria, L. and Soares, M. J. (2014) The continuous wavelet transform: Moving beyond uni-and bivariate analysis, *Journal of Economic Surveys*, **28**, 344–375.

Aloui, C. and Hkiri, B. (2014) Co-movements of GCC emerging stock markets: New evidence from wavelet coherence analysis, *Economic Modelling*, **36**, 421–431.

Bodart, V. and Candelon, B. (2009) Evidences of interdependence and contagion using a frequency domain framework, *Emerging Markets Review*, **10**, 140–150.

Gençay, R., Selçuk, F., and Whitcher, B. (2001) *An Introduction to Wavelets and Other Filtering Methods in Finance and Economics*. Academic Press, San Diego.

Hudgins, L., Friehe, C., and Mayer, M. (1993) Wavelet transforms and atmospheric turbulence, *Physical Review Letters*, **71**, 3279–3282.

Morlet, J., Arens, G., Fourgeau, E., and Giard, D. (1982a) Wave propagation and sampling theory–Part I: Complex signal and scattering in multilayered media, *Geophysics*, **47**, 203–221.

Morlet, J., Arens, G., Fourgeau, E., and Giard, D. (1982b) Wave propagation and sampling theory–Part II: Sampling theory and complex waves, *Geophysics*, **47**, 222–236.

Orlov, A. G. (2009) A cospectral analysis of exchange rate comovements during Asian financial crisis, *Journal of International Financial Markets, Institutions and Money*, **19**, 742–758.

Percival, D. B. and Walden, A. T. (2000) *Wavelet Methods for Time Series Analysis*. Cambridge University Press, London.

Torrence, C. and Compo, G. P. (1998) A practical guide to wavelet analysis, *Bulletin of the American Meteorological Society*, **79**, 61–78.

Uddina, G. S., Tiwari, A. K., Arouri, M., and Teulon, F. (2013). On the relationship between oil price and exchange rates: A wavelet analysis, *Economic Modelling*, **35**, 502–507.

Concluding chapter

1. Purpose

In the preceding chapters, we investigated the dynamics of the sovereign (Part I), sector-level (Part II), and firm-level (Part III) CDS markets, with a particular focus on exploring the interconnectedness (e.g., causality, co-movements, and cointegrating relationships) among several CDS markets in these segments, or between CDS and other financial markets. We repeatedly discussed that CDS, which acts as an insurance contract against default, can provide market participants with liquid, market-based measures about the credit conditions of the underlying entity. Thus, in several chapters, we implied that investors who pursue risk management of portfolios exposed to credit risks may find CDS a useful hedging tool on a real-time basis. Accordingly, we also argued that policymakers may be able to use CDS as an important signal to monitor deteriorating credit risk conditions of a particular sector or country in order to take timely and appropriate regulatory actions. Moreover, as some financial economists argue, CDS can essentially increase the welfare of the economy through the optimal allocation of credit risks (e.g., Jarrow, 2011). Indeed, CDS contracts can enable a buyer to easily short the underlying debt instrument, thereby providing a simple way to trade credit risks.

Despite having such significant benefits, the global CDS market size has exhibited a sharp decline after the inception of the global financial crisis. According to the semiannual survey conducted by the BIS (Bank for International Settlements; www.bis.org/statistics/derstats.htm), the notional outstanding amounts of the global CDS market had increased from USD 6.4 trillion in the second half of 2004[1] to its peak at USD 58.2 trillion in the second half of 2007. After the peak, the CDS market faced challenges as some commentators viewed CDS as a potential cause for the global financial crisis and the European sovereign debt crisis. In fact, the CDS market size decreased to USD 9.9 trillion in the second half of 2016. This decline is partly because of the trade compression after Lehman Brothers' fall, which led to meaningful reductions in the gross notional amounts outstanding for CDS contracts. That is, the peak CDS market size in 2007 is considered to have been inflated due to an inability to compress trades to their true market positions. Another reason behind the considerable decline in the global CDS market is the collapse of the synthetic collateralized debt obligations (CDO)[2] market whose growth had been largely supported by the flexibility of tailoring CDS contracts during the period 2001–2007 (See, for instance, Morgan, 2012).

Given the remarkable rise and fall of the CDS market, it is intriguing to examine what the future prospects of the CDS market development would be. The remainder of this chapter is structured as follows. We first review the key characteristics of the CDS market concisely in Section 2. Then, in Section 3, we identify the key growth drivers of the future market development and discuss the potential impact of each driver on the market. Finally, we conclude the paper in Section 4.

2. Key characteristics of the CDS market

We highlight the following three characteristics that help us better understand the current situation of the CDS markets in order to provide future prediction: (i) trading in over-the-counter (OTC) markets, (ii) concentration of players, and (iii) development of CDS indices. First, CDS is traded in OTC markets, and not in organized exchanges. Thus, CDS contracts are usually bilateral, that is, a buyer and a seller can determine the units, the contractual terms, and the underlying asset(s) of products, although guidance on model agreement is provided by the International Swaps and Derivatives Association (ISDA) to ensure a certain level of standardization of contracts. Such a flexible feature of CDS is highly appreciated by proponents. Nonetheless, Bolton and Oehmke (2013) contend the CDS' nature as OTC market transactions indicate that little transparency is offered in terms of information disclosure about pricing and transaction terms for CDS contracts. Furthermore, as O'Connor (2015) describes, the ease of customizing CDS contracts implies that any form of standardized regulation may not necessarily be applicable to the CDS markets because there are several CDSs with different contract terms. One method to address this inability to exert uniform regulation would be to trade CDSs on regulated exchanges, and not in OTC markets. This idea was strongly argued by Barney Frank, a former member of the U.S. House of Representatives, but did not gain solid support from concerned parties in the industry.

Second, CDS markets are concentrated by a limited number of large investment banks who act as market makers, or dealers. Atkeson et al. (2013) document that large financial institutions such as Bank of America, Citigroup, JP Morgan Chase, Goldman Sachs, and Morgan Stanley account for a substantially large share of the gross notional amounts in the CDS markets, and that these global dealer banks tend to play intermediary roles rather than hedging activities, offsetting long and short contracts. In contrast, small- to mid-sized banks tend to be customers in the CDS markets and are likely to use CDSs to hedge or change their exposures to credit risks. One implication of such a concentrated market is that combined with the nature of CDS contracts as OTC transactions, it is easier for the abovementioned investment banks to earn profits by tailoring the bilateral contracts between protection buyers and sellers in a way that buyers cannot easily compare prices. Another implication of the concentration is the possibility of systemic risks arising when the fall of one dealer may result in triggering contagion effects, and thereby impairing the functioning of the entire CDS market.

Third, CDS markets are also characterized by the development of CDS indices. As thoroughly discussed in Parts II and III of this book, a CDS index, either at the sector or corporate level, is a portfolio of actively traded single-name CDSs used to hedge the credit risks of a basket of credit entities. The semiannual statistics by BIS indicate that the gross notional amount outstanding of the CDS indices (or multiname CDS) was USD 4.3 trillion in the second half of 2016, constituting 43 percent of the entire CDS market.[3] As Augustin et al. (2014) point out, the main benefits of CDS indices lie in their standardized product features as well as their liquidity, both of which may help the aggregation of information and price discovery on credit risks. One of the key factors that drove the market development of CDS indices was their central clearing, which was required by the Dodd–Frank Wall Street Reform and Consumer Protection Act (known as Dodd–Frank) passed in 2010 in the U.S.[4] CDS indices need to clear through clearing houses (centralized counterparty or CCP) that can act as intermediaries between parties by collecting money from members and paying the outstanding debt when a CDS protection seller is unable to pay. Augustin et al. (2016) argue that because single-name CDS is not yet subject to central clearing, market participants are likely to use CDS indices instead of single-name CDS in order to hedge their credit risk exposures.

3. Future prospects of CDS markets

In this section, we highlight the key growth drivers that could have substantial impacts on the future prospects of CDS markets. In our framework, we focus on potential growth drivers in the two relevant dimensions, that is, regulatory change and technology innovation, which have been relevant when the global CDS market faced structural changes in the past.

First, the enhancement of regulatory oversight over CDS, especially after the recent financial crises, has caused material influences on the current CDS market structure,[5] and any future regulatory change in this aspect will continue to do so. A natural direction of an expected future change in line with Dodd–Frank is the requirement for central clearing of single-name CDS. Currently, investors are motivated to use CDS indices with central clearing for hedging purposes, although the hedging can only provide indirect insurance coverage over a large portfolio of credit risks (hence, imperfect hedge), compared to purchasing specific single-name CDS protection. If single-name CDS is centrally cleared, spurring its trading activities is expected, resulting in the growth of the entire CDS market. In fact, BlackRock Inc., a major global asset management firm, is reportedly leading an industry-led effort to revise single-name CDS markets, aiming to push it toward central clearing (e.g., Ahmed and Natarajan, 2015). Another direction of future regulatory change that could accelerate CDS market growth is the improvement in the post-trade transparency that requires disclosure of price and volume information on CDS transactions. A final report by the Board of the International Organization of Securities Commissions (IOSCO) reveals that the post-trade transparency may facilitate more efficient price discovery of the CDS markets, encouraging CDS trading activities of more market participants (See IOSCO, 2015). The implementation status of the post-trade transparency regulatory system differs among countries,[6] but its coherent introduction across the globe might also contribute to future growth of the CDS markets whose lack of price comparison may be deterring the market entry of potential protection buyers to some degree.

Second, technology innovation is another important factor potentially driving the future growth of CDS markets. We observed that prior to 2007, the advent of synthetic CDO had spurred the trading of CDS, which provided buyers of CDO with protection over credit risks. Unfortunately, there is little sign of new product innovation that could occur related to the CDS markets. Credit default swap exchange-trading funds (ETF) were first released by ProShares in 2014, with an expectation that investor bases of CDS markets might be expanded from purely institutional to retail investors; however, it has not yet gained visible support. Perhaps a more important technological innovation, which may improve transparency and standardization of CDS transactions, could thus accelerate CDS trading is blockchain. Blockchain technology refers to a type of distributed ledger to record transactions in reliable manners in a permissioned, peer-to-peer network. Four global financial institutions, the Depository Trust & Clearing Corporation (DTCC), Markit Group, and a distributed ledger software firm, Axoni, successfully completed the test of blockchain technology to manage complex events for single-name CDS in April 2016. Further, the DTCC has released a plan to initiate its blockchain-based platform for CDS reporting in 2018. There are at least two ways in which blockchain technology may enhance transparency of CDS markets. Blockchain's smart contracts automatically trigger payment based on a CDS contract agreement in the case of a default, which may reduce the widely concerned uncertainty issue regarding the CDS insurance payout. In addition, blockchain technology provides an efficient platform for improved bookkeeping and records verification, enabling regulators to efficiently monitor the activities in the CDS markets and ensure compliance. If implemented effectively, blockchain technology has the potential to drive the future growth of CDS markets, generating better collaboration between regulators and the industry.

4. Concluding remarks

Apparently, global CDS markets have experienced a significant rise and fall, with the peak of the gross notional amount outstanding in late 2007. CDS is traded in OTC markets where contractual terms are determined bilaterally and the market information tends to be limited to a few large investment banks occupying oligopolistic positions as market makers or dealers. With such characteristics, CDS markets were often considered to lack transparency, and the markets were blamed for having triggered the global financial crisis and the European debt crisis, resulting in the market decline after the crises, partly due to trade contraction.

Despite the criticism, CDS has various benefits and could increase the welfare, if used appropriately. It can serve as liquid, market-based measures about the credit risks of a reference entity. Traders can utilize CDS as a real-time hedging and credit risk management tool, while policymakers can use it as a tool to ensure macro prudence. In fact, after the recent financial turmoil, enormous efforts have been made to improve regulatory oversight over the CDS markets for improving transparency. Moreover, index products have extensively been developed at a sector and corporate level through product standardization. The global CDS market size is still worth multi-trillion dollars, demonstrating resilience.

In terms of future market development, we foresee that there is much room for the global CDS markets to revive in the near future. In fact, some signs of tangible growth drivers are already observed in the markets. From the viewpoints of regulatory changes, the central clearing of single-name CDS as well as the post-trade transparency regulatory system will improve the credibility and transparency of the CDS markets, and hence enhance trading activities if implemented. Moreover, from the perspectives of technology innovation, blockchain technology is expected to reduce the uncertainty and transaction/monitoring costs of CDS contracts, contributing to the growth of the markets. We believe that one should not underestimate the importance of global CDS markets just because the gross notional amount appears to have exhibited decreasing trends.

Notes

1 Although CDS was first developed by a U.S. investment bank, JP Morgan, in 1994, the semiannual survey by the BIS is only available since the second half of 2004.
2 Synthetic CDO is a form of collateralized debt obligation that invests in single-name CDS.
3 In the second half of 2004, CDS indices accounted for only 20 percent of the gross notional amount outstanding of the global CDS market.
4 See O'Connor (2015), for instance, for detailed explanations of Dodd–Frank.
5 See Augustin et al. (2016) for a detailed review of regulatory measures and their impacts on CDS, which have been implemented globally after the recent financial turmoil.
6 IOSCO (2015) asserts that as of July 2015, only the U.S. Commodity Futures Trading Commission (CFTC) has executed such a system for CDS indices, and the U.S. Securities and Exchange Commission (SEC) has rules for single-name CDS but has no compliance schedule.

References

Ahmed, N. and Natarajan, S. (2015) BlackRock's on a mission to save the credit-default swaps market, *Bloomberg*, May 5.

Atkeson, A., Eisfeldt, A., and Weill, P.-O. (2013) The market for OTC derivatives, *Federal Reserve Bank of Minneapolis Research Department Staff Report*, **479**, 1–69.

Augustin, P., Subrahmanyam, M., Tang, D., and Wang, S. (2014) Credit default swaps: A survey, *Foundations and Trends in Finance*, **9**, 1–196.

Augustin, P., Subrahmanyam, M., Tang, D., and Wang, S. (2016) Credit default swaps: Past, present, and future, *Annual Review of Financial Economics*, **8**, 175–196.

Bolton, P. and Oehmke, M. (2013) Strategic conduct in credit derivative markets, *International Journal of Industrial Organization*, **31**, 652–658.

IOSCO (2015) *Post-trade Transparency in the Credit Default Swaps Market: Final Report*, www.iosco.org/library/pubdocs/pdf/IOSCOPD499.pdf.

Jarrow, R. A. (2011) The economics of credit default swaps, *Annual Review of Financial Economics*, **3**, Annual Reviews.

Morgan, G. (2012) Reforming OTC markets: The politics and economics of technical fixes, *European Business Organization Law Review*, **13**, 391–412.

O'Connor, B. (2015) Taming the wild west of Wall Street: Regulating credit default swaps after Dodd–Frank, 48J, *The John Marshall Law Review*, **48**, 564–604.

First publication of each chapter

Introduction

Unpublished article.

Chapter 1 Relationship between sovereign CDS and banking sector CDS

Tamakoshi, G. and Hamori, S. (2013) Volatility and mean spillovers between sovereign and banking sector CDS markets: A note on the European sovereign debt crisis, *Applied Economics Letters*, **20**, 262–266.

Chapter 2 Key determinants of sovereign CDS spreads

Unpublished article.

Chapter 3 Dynamic spillover among sovereign CDS spreads

Unpublished article.

Chapter 4 Causality among financial sector CDS indices

Tamakoshi, G. and Hamori, S. (2014) Spillovers among CDS indexes in the US financial sector, *North American Journal of Economics and Finance*, **27**, 104–113.

Chapter 5 Co-movement and spillovers among financial sector CDS indices

Tamakoshi, G. and Hamori, S. (2016) Time-varying co-movements and volatility spillovers among financial sector CDS indexes in the UK, *Research in International Business and Finance*, **36**, 288–296.

Chapter 6 Dependence structure of insurance sector CDS indices

Tamakoshi, G. and Hamori, S. (2014) The conditional dependence structure of insurance sector credit default swap indices, *North American Journal of Economics and Finance*, **30**, 122–132.

Chapter 7 Time-varying correlation among bank sector CDS indices

Tamakoshi, G. and Hamori, S. (2013) An asymmetric DCC analysis of correlations among bank CDS indices, *Applied Financial Economics*, **23**, 475–481.

Chapter 8 Dynamic correlation among banks' CDS spreads

Unpublished article.

Chapter 9 Dependence structures among corporate CDS indices

Unpublished article.

Chapter 10 Interdependence between corporate CDS indices

Unpublished article.

Concluding chapter

Unpublished article.

Index